Stirring the Pot of Haitian History

Stirring the Pot of Haitian History

Ti difé boulé sou istoua Ayiti
(Brooklyn: Kolèksion Lakansièl, 1977)

By **Michel-Rolph Trouillot** (1949–2012)

Introduced by **Lyonel Antoine Trouillot**

Edited and translated by
Mariana Past and **Benjamin Hebblethwaite**
Afterword by **Jean Jonassaint**

Liverpool University Press

First published 2021 by
Liverpool University Press
4 Cambridge Street
Liverpool
L69 7ZU

Copyright © 2021 Liverpool University Press

The right of Mariana Past and Benjamin Hebblethwaite to be identified as the editors of this book has been asserted by them in accordance with the Copyright, Designs and Patents Act 1988.

The maps in this volume were created courtesy of Joe Aufmuth, Geospatial Consultant at the University of Florida's George A. Smathers Libraries.

All rights reserved. No part of this book may be reproduced, stored in a retrieval system, or transmitted, in any form or by any means, electronic, mechanical, photocopying, recording, or otherwise, without the prior written permission of the publisher.

British Library Cataloguing-in-Publication data
A British Library CIP record is available

ISBN 978-1-800-85967-8 cased

Typeset by Carnegie Book Production, Lancaster
Printed and bound by CPI Group (UK) Ltd, Croydon CR0 4YY

Contents

Preface by Lyonel Antoine Trouillot	ix
English Translation of the Preface by Mariana Past and Benjamin Hebblethwaite	xvii
Translators' Note by Mariana Past and Benjamin Hebblethwaite	xxv
Acknowledgments	xxxv

Stirring the Pot of Haitian History

1. **I'm holding a gathering** — 5
   Lamèsi's gathering—Grinn Prominnin begins the conversation—1820–1825.

2. **A *Kòd Noua* [Black Code/Cord] to tie up little pigs** — 9
   Saint-Domingue long ago, in colonial times—Conflicts in society—The function of the Kòd Noua.

3. **Keep reading and you'll understand** — 21
   Saint-Domingue's primary industry—Hidden conflicts— Primary conflicts.

4. **Fire in the house** — 39
   The various coalitions of classes in power: the white colonist coalition, the freedmen and white coalition—How those various coalitions split.

   The native culture of Ayiti Toma: land, Creole, Vodou—The rallying cry of Freedom.

5. Open the gate   **61**

> *The Second Civil Commission—The political apparatus and political situation in Saint-Domingue—Entangled social powers—Galbaud Affair—Freedom for All.*

6. The little orange tree grew   **75**

     6.1   Mister I gave it to you... Thank you, father!   77

> *The rebel slaves' weak spots—Political agenda and strategies of Louverture's organization—The organization's deal-making with French commissioners.*

     6.2   **Come and pout**   85

> *The Vilatte Affair—Conflicts between leaders of* nouveaux libres *and leaders of* anciens libres.

     6.3   **Iron cuts iron**   91

> *The Third Civil Commission—The position of Toussaint's organization—Sonthonax's arrival—The dominance of the camp of nouveaux libres—The position of Hédouville, Rigaud and Louverture—The specific role of the Americans and English in the Rigaud/Toussaint war—The role of color prejudice—The war. Overthrow of the Spanish.*

7. Cousin that's not what you told me   **119**

> *1802—Where did the bound kòd break?—Social origins and rebel slave leaders' particular social mobility.*

*

> *The position of Toussaint's organization and Toussaint's government on issues of Dependence, Commodity crops, and Plantations.*

*

> *Louverture's State—The repressive agrarian system.*

*

> *The Moïse Affair—Conflicts between government and organization—Infighting—The meaning of the Moïse Affair.*

*

The masquerade of Louverture's Ideology—'Family', 'elite', 'religion', 'work', and 'property' within that ideology—Indigenist roots of Louverture's Ideology—Freedom for All as cornerstone of Louverture's Ideology—Grinn Prominnin takes a break ...

Bibliography of the Original (1977) Text   171

For the Trouillots: An Afterword to the English Translation of *Ti difé boulé sou istoua Ayiti*   175
   Jean Jonassaint

Appendix   191

   'ki mò ki touyé lanpérè'   192
   ('What bad spirit killed the emperor')
   by L. Raymond, pseudonym of M-R. Trouillot
   (*Lakansièl* 3, 1975, pp. 37–39)

   'lindépandans dévan-dèyè: dapiyanp sou révolision'   196
   ('Independence Upside-Down: Seizing Revolution')
   by L. Raymond (*Lakansièl*, Spécial nouvelle année, 1976, pp. 46–50)

Bibliography for English Translation, Translators' Note, and Afterword   201

Index   207

Preface

by Lyonel Antoine Trouillot

Le pire qu'on ait pu dire de Michel-Rolph Trouillot, en croyant lui adresser un compliment, c'est qu'il était un brillant universitaire. Il l'a été, si l'on considère l'influence de ses travaux et le respect qu'ils inspirent à ses collègues et aux étudiants des diverses disciplines des sciences humaines. Mais ces émules et admirateurs, fervents de références et de citations, auront raté l'essentiel. Si L'Université n'a pas été pour lui une couverture,—il vivait aux Etats-Unis—comme elle a pu l'être pour d'autres vivant en Haïti dans les années Duvalier, (quand des militants clandestins luttant contre la dictature jouaient le jour aux bons étudiants ou aux bons profs pour ne vivre vraiment que la nuit dans le risque des tracts à distribuer, des cellules à diriger, et la quête d'une « pensée » ou d'une « théorie révolutionnaire »,) elle n'était pas le lieu d'élaboration de sa pensée, ni le lieu d'affirmation de sa conception du travail de l'intellectuel. Il avait certes développé une passion pour la discipline qu'il enseignait, l'anthropologie, mais sa passion première était autre : la production d'une pensée partant du réel et susceptible de contribuer à sa transformation ; le regard critique sur l'Histoire et sur les discours sur l'Histoire pour leur opposer un contre-discours, une perturbation, un savoir subversif. Celui qu'on appelait respectueusement « doctor Trouillot », avait quelque chose du « trickster ». Dans le sens de celui qui cache son jeu. L'Université lui offrait le cadre et les arguments d'autorité, et le confort relatif pour habiter en même temps cet ailleurs d'où il venait : la production du neuf à partir d'une nécessité extérieure à lui-même, d'un élément du réel, en y incluant le langage sur cet élément. Avant son accident cérébral, suite aux discussions avec les membres de la revue *Les Cahiers du vendredi* qui deviendra *Lire Haïti*, il était, comme eux, arrivé à la conclusion que le jean-claudisme avait quelque chose de spécifique et de transformateur dans l'histoire d'Haïti, et qu'il était urgent de l'analyser pour pouvoir mieux agir. En contre. Il avait ainsi écrit le premier chapitre d'un projet « d'anthropologie du jean-claudisme ». *Lakansièl, Les Cahiers du vendredi, Lire Haïti*, revues dont il était membre fondateur et actif, étaient pour lui un lieu privilégié d'échanges avec des jeunes devenus des vieux compagnons de partage intellectuel, des frères et sœurs de pensée et de lutte. Il ne s'est jamais éloigné de cette vision de la production intellectuelle comme inscrite dans un projet de transformation de la société. De Chicago, il prenait souvent l'avion vers Port-au-Prince pour participer aux discussions de préparation des numéros de *Les Cahiers du vendredi* et de *Lire Haïti*. L'Université de Chicago d'un côté, *Lire Haïti* de l'autre, le prof et l'intellectuel (il y a tant de profs aujourd'hui qui n'apportent pas grand-chose à l'intellectualité), c'est quelque vingt ans après la publication de *Ti difé boulé sou istoua Ayiti*, mais c'était dans le même esprit.

J'ai préféré commencer par l'après, les années succès du grand prof, pour remonter au commencement. Pour une raison personnelle. Parler des années *Tanbou Libète/Lakansièl/ Ti difé boulé* éveille en moi une émotion que je ne peux que retarder faute de pouvoir la cacher. Aussi pour une raison de méthode et de vérité humaine. La fortune intellectuelle de Michel-Rolph Trouillot est immense, il est facile pour ceux qui ont rencontré son travail, son œuvre, son aura à partir de ces années succès de la couper en deux temps, faisant ainsi quelque chose qui lui aurait profondément déplu intellectuellement et sur le plan éthique : ignorer, voire nier, le processus d'élaboration des discours, des pratiques, dans leur capacité de rompre avec la pensée dominante ou de s'intégrer dans la reproduction des structures.

Au début des années soixante-dix du siècle dernier, lorsque François Duvalier désigne son fils Jean-Claude comme son successeur, des centaines de jeunes Haïtiens, originaires des classes moyennes, se retrouvent en Amérique du Nord. La vie les a comme jetés là, pour des causes complexes et pas toujours connexes : les difficultés économiques ; la peur de la dictature qui pouvait frapper n'importe qui au hasard ; les incertitudes du quotidien et de l'avenir ; les boursiers qui étaient partis faire des études en Europe et qui, face aux difficultés, avaient choisi d'émigrer pour les Etats-Unis. A cette époque, sauf exception, la vague de départ était une décision parentale. Je n'oublierai pas ce matin de soixante-huit quand Anne-Marie m'a dit : « Réveille-toi, va saluer Rolph ». Ce n'était pas son anniversaire. Je ne comprenais pas. J'ai appris en lui disant au revoir qu'il partait pour New York ce jour-là. Ce que lui-même n'avait dû apprendre que quelques heures avant moi. Trois ans plus tard, ce serait notre tour à Evelyne et à moi.

New York. « Mini Jazz », « factories », taxis réguliers et taxis « gypsies ». Le sentiment général d'un pays perdu. Des politiciens de droite habitant le mythe du retour, chefs de prétendus partis dont ils étaient parfois les seuls membres, réunissant leurs quelques fidèles chez des coiffeurs ou dans leurs appartements. Le conservatisme traditionnel de la petite bourgeoisie haïtienne : la reproduction des préjugés sociaux, linguistiques ; le choix de l'assimilation chez un grand nombre. Le choix des études universitaires chez des jeunes. Mais un peu timidement. Surtout parce qu'on est bien obligé de faire quelque chose, de choisir un métier ou d'avoir un diplôme. C'est dans ce flou, avec l'idée d'un pays qu'on ne reverrait pas de si tôt que naît ce vaste ensemble, hétéroclite, qu'on appellera plus tard l'Action patriotique. Pour des jeunes armés d'une conscience sociale, il faut faire quelque chose, se donner du mouvement, une activité ou une action. Rolph écrit et compose des chansons. Avec Jean-Baptiste Obas, Jean-Edouard Morisset, Frantz Saint-Hubert et Ernst Bruny, il crée un groupe, *les Ménestrels*. Un peu mini jazz, comme c'était la mode. Mais ils ne peuvent pas faire comme les autres. Accepter ce vide des mots. Un peu comme les fondateurs de la troupe *Kouidor*, quasiment au même moment, ne peuvent habiter à l'ancienne leur passion du théâtre. Il faut faire autre chose. D'autant que, se réclamant du maoïsme ou du léninisme, se mettent en place des groupes, plus souvent des groupuscules, qui chantent l'hymne de la révolution. Au début, ils sont les seuls à se prendre au sérieux. D'aucuns s'entraînent dans les sous-sols ; d'aucuns parlent de soutenir le « front intérieur ». Mais liant l'impasse existentielle (un dictateur qui a vingt ans, est en bonne santé, protégé par une armée régulière et une armée de tontons macoutes, tant qu'il sera là, on risque de ne pas revoir le pays) à la critique du capitalisme, cette Action patriotique qui souffre de toutes les maladies infantiles s'inscrit résolument à gauche. Voilà d'anciens brillants d'écoles, des fils de notables devenus ouvriers dans la construction immobilière, chauffeurs de taxis clandestins, ouvriers, anonymes, et donnant leur temps libre à s'improviser chefs de cellules ou militants de base, dans un milieu hostile, une grande partie de la diaspora haïtienne de l'époque ayant fait une croix sur Haïti. Rolph est l'un des rédacteurs de « le patriote haïtien », organe du MHAP, mouvement haïtien d'action patriotique. Il est aussi (fini les mini jazz) avec les mêmes Jean-Baptiste Obas et Jean-Jean Morisset, et Kettly, Edwidge et Guy-Gérald Ménard, l'un des membres fondateurs de *Tanbou Libète*, en 1971 ; un groupe musical, pionnier dans la chanson

Preface

patriotique. Il écrit en créole la moitié du répertoire du groupe. (Plus tard, dans la même veine, viendront *Solèy leve, Atis endepandan* ...) Ces expériences sont fondamentales dans ses choix et son parcours. Il parlera très peu de sa rupture obligée avec le MHAP et le journal, quelque chose qu'il a dû vivre douloureusement. Sur le fond, en plus de petites luttes de pouvoir au sein du groupuscule, l'obscurantisme d'un dogmatisme et le rejet du principe pourtant marxiste de la conjonction entre réalisation personnelle et réalisation collective. Une structure étouffante, vouée à la sclérose. Pour Rolph, être à gauche, c'était pouvoir penser. L'expérience de Tanbou Libète était autrement formatrice. Lorsque Evelyne et moi rejoignons le groupe, il a déjà produit un disque et s'est déjà produit en public de nombreuses fois. Là encore, les relents de stalinisme s'affirment comme une menace. On reproche au groupe trop d'autonomie par rapport aux groupes proprement « politiques » auxquels il devrait être « rattaché ». On lui reproche aussi de ne pas faire des choses toujours « accessibles », trop modernes, trop élaborées. Pour affirmer cette autonomie dont il est fier, le groupe se transforme en « *òganizasyon revolisyonè Tanbou Libète* », ajoute à sa pratique la recherche théorique de manière globale, plus particulièrement sur les questions d'idéologie, de production de formes et de sens. Cette dénomination un peu prétentieuse, organisation révolutionnaire, pour un groupe qui ne fait que du culturel, renvoie à deux principes connexes : la production d'une pensée collective et l'institutionnalisation de cette démarche, et le choix du champ culturel comme terrain de lutte au même titre que le politique. Ce moment *Tanbou Libète* a été pour nous la plus belle université libre que l'on puisse imaginer : lectures, discussions, confrontations, création collective, de jour, de nuit pour les plus robustes. Je me rappelle que, travaillant sur un article pour *Lakansièl*, nous avions passé deux jours, deux nuits à rédiger, nous engueuler, discuter, rerédiger. Nous avions eu une longue conversation au téléphone avec l'anthropologue Jean Coulanges qui vivait lors à Montréal. Nous n'étions pas satisfaits de nos hypothèses. Dans l'après-midi nous avons reçu un autre appel de Jean, nous demandant de venir le chercher à la gare, sans nous en avertir il avait pris un train pour New York pour prolonger la discussion. Il est reparti le lendemain. Nous n'étions toujours pas satisfaits. Rolph possédait lors une coccinelle en fort mauvais état, sans plaques d'immatriculation. Nous avons vissé des plaques « empruntées » au véhicule, emprunté vingt dollars de notre ami Cauvin Paul, membre de *Tanbou Libète* et de la revue, et nous sommes partis dans la nuit pour Montréal où nous sommes arrivés ... en pleine tempête de neige. C'était ça vivre. La création de *Lakansièl* (1975) répondait à un besoin de fixer par une trace écrite notre quête collective et nos quêtes individuelles, mais c'était aussi un ensemble de principes : la rupture avec la vieille dichotomie entre forme et contenu, la production de sens impliquait de penser la question du langage de cette production ; la modestie d'admettre que nous connaissions mal l'Histoire, les structures et les pratiques sociales d'Haïti et qu'il fallait partir du réel et non de slogans ; la discussion libre comme forme d'apprentissage et la disponibilité de chacun pour les zones d'intérêt des autres. A l'intérieur du groupe, Rolph privilégiait l'Histoire (comme il l'a lui-même raconté, les soirées ou les après-midi à écouter le père, Ernst, et l'oncle, Hénock, convoquer les figures et les événements du passé, avaient nourri l'enfant qu'il avait été), les logiques de groupe, les effets structurants des contradictions entre les groupes et leurs modes d'expression. Fortement marqué à l'époque par Gramsci et Poulantzas, et un peu Althusser, mais aussi par tant d'autres—cet homme avait la force d'une machine à lire et développait au quotidien un impressionnant arsenal théorique—il était persuadé qu'il fallait chercher dans les conditions de la naissance de l'Etat haïtien pour comprendre les contradictions et le processus de structuration de la société haïtienne, et les rapports entre Etat et société. *Ti difé boulé*, le livre, est né d'un article publié dans la revue *Lakansièl*. La revue donnait une grande place à la langue créole et sortait ainsi de la logique « coin du créole » qui dominait dans les productions « progressistes ». Le créole n'était pas considéré véritablement comme un outil de travail au service de la réflexion, on lui donnait un coin souvent constitué de mauvais poèmes (accumulation de proverbes, imitation de la perception qu'on avait du langage « populaire »). Deux livres-événements venaient de sortir et annonçaient une rupture et une évolution, *Dézafi* de Frankétienne et *Konbèlann* de Georges Castera, un roman et une somme poétique accompagnée d'un texte théorique. Le travail dans, sur, avec la langue avançait. En littérature. L'article de Rolph dans *Lakansièl* (sous le pseudonyme de L. Raymond ; c'était le temps des pseudonymes pour la majorité des membres de la rédaction et peu savaient qui se cachait derrière L. Raymond, Michel Amer, Jules Laventure, Henriette Saint-Victor …) était l'une des premières tentatives d'une réflexion approfondie dans le domaine des sciences humaines. Un article, c'était bien. Et pourquoi pas un livre ? Avec son incroyable force de travail il s'y est mis, abattant un énorme travail de recherche, nous appelant sans cesse à la discussion, obsédé par la question du langage, non comme un ornement mais comme élément constitutif de la démarche théorique : aller chercher dans l'imaginaire populaire, la philosophie orale, la rythmique et la symbolique populaire la matière dont on s'approprie en la transformant pour produire du texte, à la fois une

Preface xiii

pensée et une écriture. Ce qui fait que ce livre n'est pas qu'un répertoire de trouvailles—ce qu'il est aussi—mais encore et surtout une restitution de la dynamique du langage populaire dans sa fusion avec la production d'une pensée critique. L'audience, le conte, le chœur, la charge allusive, le mythe, les figures (synecdoque, paronomase, métaphore réveillée …), tout y est convoqué, non comme un déjà là mais comme élément intrinsèquement lié au sérieux des hypothèses. On pourrait dire, mais ce serait singer l'œuvre et d'une trop grande facilité, que c'est une démarche « marasa ».

A l'époque, nous jouions aux imprimeurs, Rolph à la composition et moi (et quelquefois Evelyne) à « rentrer » les textes. Il n'y avait pas d'édition à proprement parler qu'un pareil texte pouvait intéresser. La quasi-totalité des livres publiés dans la diaspora étaient à compte d'auteur, à l'exception de quelques titres parus en France et au Canada. Les mille exemplaires se sont vite écoulés. Je n'ai pas souvenir d'articles de presse dans les journaux de la diaspora, mais le livre bénéficiait d'un bouche à oreille qui lui assurait un énorme succès de prestige. Nous avions, à partir de 1976, renoué contact avec le pays, ayant compris qu'on ne renverserait pas le régime de Duvalier à partir des « basements » des appartements new yorkais, et les échos de la publication du livre attirèrent l'attention de quelques maîtres du secondaire qui l'utilisèrent, à leurs risques et périls, comme livre de référence ou même comme manuel. A la chute de Jean-Claude Duvalier en 1986, *Ti difé boulé* devenait enfin une référence qu'on pouvait nommer librement. Les reproductions artisanales, photocopies, furent nombreuses. Et Rolph était devenu monsieur *Ti difé boulé*. En 2014, les éditions de l'université Caraïbe dirigées par notre sœur Jocelyne, ont eu la bonne idée de le rééditer. Les demandes sont nombreuses, et je reçois souvent des appels d'individus ou de collectifs désireux de se le procurer.

Tanbou Libète et surtout *Lakansièl*, impossible de penser la production de *Ti difé boulé* sans la lier à ces aventures collectives au sein desquelles Rolph faisait un peu figure de leader naturel. Quelque chose qui se perd aujourd'hui dans les milieux intellectuels et « progressistes », la conversation thématique faite d'échanges à bâtons rompus sur une proposition, un texte ou un projet de texte, avait enrichi la démarche de Rolph. La bande à l'époque avait ses présences constantes, Evelyne, Cauvin Paul, Jean Coulanges, moi-même, d'autres sporadiques ou éphémères, Karl Toulanmanche, Guy-Gérald Ménard présent dès le début dans Tanbou Libète mais absent de *Lakansièl*, Julien Jumelle et quelques autres. Plus tard, quand les portes d'Haïti se rouvrirent pour nous, les rencontres avec Pierre Buteau et Michel Acacia seront essentielles dans la vie de Rolph et les leurs. C'est d'abord par *Ti difé boulé* qu'ils l'ont connu, c'était comme son passeport pour Haïti, on pouvait faire confiance à l'homme qui avait réalisé ce travail. Buteau et Acacia, tous deux membres de la rédaction de *Les Cahiers du vendredi*, puis de *Lire Haïti*, devinrent des compagnons privilégiés de discussion avec Rolph, et j'ai vécu comme une blessure le fait que des « doctorants » organisant un colloque sur le travail de Rolph avaient décliné de les inviter.

Mais la mémoire est infidèle. J'oublie sans doute des noms, des rencontres et m'en excuse auprès de ceux que je n'ai pas mentionnés ici. Je terminerai cette trop longue introduction en soulignant deux éléments importants pour comprendre (l'une des expressions favorites de Rolph) « les conditions de production » de *Ti difé boulé*. Sans un rapport direct avec le livre, mais permettant de le situer dans un mouvement et une mouvance, toute la démarche de création, de production de formes et de sens, dans les chansons de *Tanbou Libète* avec Guy-Gérald et un temps les sœurs Kettly et Edwidge Ménard, avec le guitariste, lui aussi auteur compositeur, Jean-Edouard Morisset ; dans les écritures collectives de spectacles de théâtre, en particulier *Si kacho pran pale*, tout cela a été le lieu d'un travail sur la langue qui a aidé Rolph à enrichir sa démarche personnelle. De ce point de vue, ce livre c'est une contemporanéité, comme l'apogée d'un moment. Le deuxième point, sans doute le plus important, et je reviens à ce que je disais au début de cette présentation, c'est chez ce large groupe et chez Rolph en particulier un anti ou plutôt un contre académisme, avec une grande connaissance de la littérature « académique » sur les domaines explorés, insistant beaucoup sur l'originalité du savoir à produire, sur la nécessité de défaire (la mode n'était pas encore au verbe déconstruire) pour faire autrement, pour s'opposer à l'interdiction de savoir que portent les lieux « officiels » de production et de distribution des savoirs. Il y a dans *Ti difé boulé* une critique virulente par ses propositions d'un ensemble de propositions de l'historiographie traditionnelle. « Trickster » donc l'universitaire dont la démarche et les travaux postérieurs ont continué, parfois sans le dire, ce travail de désacralisation des discours et de production d'un discours qui entend subvertir un ordre qui produit du mal vivre et de l'injustice. *Ti difé boulé* est né d'une intention politique : avec quels groupes, quels sujets collectifs transformer le réel haïtien ? Pour cela il fallait produire un savoir remontant à la constitution de ces groupes pour suivre leur évolution.

Je crois que toute sa vie, Rolph est resté ce politique et cet écrivain-écrivant ... Il avait d'ailleurs dans la tête un roman en créole : *anba pla pye lanmè*. Ses chansons, ses réflexions, son travail d'universitaire, son activisme, les revues, cela faisait un tout dont *Ti difé boulé* constitue un moment fort et fonde son entrée dans l'histoire de la pensée haïtienne, plus exactement dans l'histoire de la pensée révolutionnaire d'Haïti.

Merci frère,

à toujours

Lyonel Antoine Trouillot

English Translation of the Preface

by Mariana Past and Benjamin Hebblethwaite

The worst thing one could say about Michel Rolph Trouillot, believing it was a compliment, is that he was a brilliant academic. He was, if one considers the influence of his works and the respect they inspired in his colleagues and students across the various social science disciplines. But those imitators and admirers, keen on references and citations, will have missed the point. If for him the University was not a cover—he lived in the United States—like it was for others who lived in Haiti during the Duvalier years (when underground militants opposing the dictatorship played the part of good students or professors by day, only to truly live by night to hazard distributing leaflets, directing cells, and seeking out a 'set of ideas' or 'revolutionary theory'), it was neither the place where his ideas developed or his approach to intellectual labor was affirmed. He certainly developed a passion for anthropology, the discipline he taught, but his primary passion was something distinct: generating a set of ideas based on reality and capable of contributing to its transformation; a critical view on History and discourses on History in order to oppose them with a counter-discourse, a disturbance, a subversive knowledge. The one who everyone respectfully called 'Doctor Trouillot' was akin to the 'trickster' in the sense of one who keeps his cards close. The University provided him with the framework, the authoritative arguments, and the relative comfort to jointly inhabit that elsewhere from which he hailed: producing a new approach out of a necessity external to himself, out of an element of reality, including language about said element. Before his brain injury, from discussions with the members of the journal *Les Cahiers du vendredi* which would become *Lire Haïti*, he had reached the conclusion, as had they, that Jean-Claudism harbored something specific and transformative in Haiti's history that was urgent to analyze so that people could more effectively take action. Against it. That's what he said in the first chapter of a project called 'The Anthropology of Jean-Claudism'.

Lakansièl, *Les Cahiers du vendredi*, and *Lire Haïti*, journals for which he was a founding and active member, were a privileged space for him to exchange with young people who became old companions of intellectual solicitude, brothers and sisters in thought and in struggle. He never strayed from this vision of intellectual development inscribed within a socially transformative project. From Chicago, he often flew to Port-au-Prince to take part in planning discussions for issues of *Les Cahiers du vendredi* and *Lire Haïti*. The University of Chicago on the one hand, and *Lire Haïti* on the other, the professor and the intellectual (there are so many professors today who bring little to intellectuality); this was some twenty years after *Ti difé boulé sou istoua Ayiti* was published, but it was in the same spirit.

I opted to start with the later years, the prime years of the eminent professor, and go back to the beginning. For personal reasons. Speaking of the *Tanbou Libète/Lakansièl/Ti difé boulé* era arouses an emotion in me that I can merely hold back, as I can't hide it. For reasons of method and human truth as well. Michel-Rolph Trouillot's intellectual legacy is immense, and it is easy for those who have encountered his work, his œuvre, and his aura during these prime years to split the period into two parts, thus doing what would have thoroughly displeased him both intellectually and ethically: ignoring or even denying the process of developing arguments and practices, and their ability to break with prevailing thought or conform to the reproduction of structures.

At the start of the 1970s, when François Duvalier named his son Jean-Claude as his successor, hundreds of young Haitians from the middle class found themselves in North America. Life basically threw them there, for reasons that were complex and sometimes unrelated: economic difficulties; fear of the dictatorship that could attack anyone at random; worries about daily life and the future; students who had gone off to study in Europe and who, in the face of these difficulties, had decided to emigrate to the United States. At that time, without exception, the initial movement was a parental decision. I'll never forget the morning of '68 when Anne-Marie said to me, 'Wake up, and go give your regards to Rolph'. I learned, as I told him goodbye, that he was leaving for New York that same day (which he himself must have learned only a few hours before I did). Three years later, it would be Evelyne's and my turn.

New York. 'Mini Jazz', 'factories', regular taxis, and 'gypsy' taxis. The general feeling of a country adrift. Right-wing politicians fixated on the myth of return, leaders of so-called parties of which they were sometimes the only members, gathering their handful of followers at the hairdressers or in their apartments. The traditional conservatism of the

Haitian petty bourgeoisie, of reproducing social and linguistic prejudices; choosing assimilation, for many. The choice of university studies among young people. But with some hesitation. Especially since one has to do something, like choose a job or pursue a diploma. It was within this blur, along with the idea of a country that we wouldn't see again anytime soon, that was born this vast, diverse ensemble which we would later call Patriotic Action. Young people with a social conscience must do something, set themselves in motion, join a movement or take some kind of action. Rolph wrote and composed songs. Along with Jean-Baptiste Obas, Jean-Edouard Morisset, Frantz Saint-Hubert, and Ernst Bruny, he formed a group, Les Ménestrels. It was kind of like mini jazz, which was all the rage. But they couldn't just be like the others and accept this lyrical hollowness. A little like the founders of the Kouidor troupe, who at almost the same moment couldn't simply restage their theatrical passion as they once had. We had to do something different. Especially since many groups—most often small groups—were getting going, singing the hymn of the revolution, claiming to be Maoist or Leninist. At first, they were the only ones taking themselves seriously. Some practiced in basements; some spoke of supporting the 'home front'. But by combining this existential stalemate (a twenty-year-old dictator who was in good health, protected by a regular army and an army of Tontons Macoutes – as long as he was there, we weren't likely to see the country again) with a critique of capitalism, this Patriotic Action that suffered from every imaginable growing pain, was resolutely left-leaning.

Here were brilliant former students, sons of public figures who became construction workers, illegal taxi drivers, laborers, anonymous people, giving up their free time to improvise as cell leaders or grassroots activists, in a hostile environment, along with a large part of the Haitian diaspora at the time promising to have nothing to do with Haiti. Rolph was one of the editors of *Le patriote haïtien*, the newsletter for the MHAP, the acronym of 'The Haitian Movement of Patriotic Action'. In 1971 he was also (done with mini jazz), along with the very same Jean-Baptiste Obas and Jean-Jean Morisset, and Kettly, Edwidge, and Guy-Gérald Ménard, one of the founding members of *Tanbou Libète*, a musical group that pioneered patriotic song. He wrote half of the group's repertoire in Creole. (Later on, in the same vein, came *Solèy leve, Atis endepandan* ...). These experiences were fundamental to his decisions and his development.

He would speak very little about his necessary break with the MHAP and the newspaper, which must have been painful to go through. In the background, in addition to the minor power struggles within the small group, lay the obscurity of dogmatism and a rejection of a nonetheless Marxist principle establishing the connection between individual and collective achievement. A suffocating structure, doomed to sclerosis. For Rolph, being on the left meant being able to think. His *Tanbou Libète* experience was formative in other ways. When Evelyne and I joined the group, he had already produced a record and made many public appearances. Here again, traces of Stalinism asserted themselves as a threat. The group was criticized for being overly autonomous with respect to the actual 'political' groups to which it should have been 'related'. Rolph was also criticized for doing things that were not always 'accessible', that were too modern, or too elaborate. To affirm the autonomy that made him proud, the group transformed itself into the '*Tanbou Libète* Revolutionary Organization', thus appending to his practice a broad-based theoretical research program that specifically engaged questions of ideology, form, and the production of meaning. For a group that focused solely on culture, this rather pretentious name, 'revolutionary organization', denoted two related principles: the production of collective thinking and the institutionalization of that approach, as well as the choice of the cultural domain as a battleground in the same vein as politics. The *Tanbou Libète* moment was, for us, the most beautiful free university that we could have imagined: readings, discussions, arguments, collective creation—by day and night, for the most robust. I remember that one time, while working on an article for *Lakansièl*, we spent two days and nights writing, quarreling, discussing, and rewriting. We had a long conversation on the phone with anthropologist Jean Coulanges, who lived in Montreal. We weren't happy with our hypotheses. In the afternoon we got another phone call from Jean asking us to pick him up at the station, without having told us he'd taken a train to New York to continue the discussion. He left the next day. We still weren't satisfied. Rolph had a VW bug in very bad condition, with no license plates. We screwed 'borrowed' plates onto the vehicle, borrowed twenty dollars from our friend Cauvin Paul, a member of *Tanbou Libète* and the magazine, and we left in the night for Montreal where we arrived ... right in the middle of a snowstorm. That was living. The creation of *Lakansièl* (1975) answered a need to establish a written record of our collective and individual quests, but it was also a set of principles: breaking with the old dichotomy between form and content, the production of meaning implied thinking about the question of the language of this production; the modesty to admit that we didn't know very much about Haiti's history, structures, and social practices, and that we had to ground ourselves in reality instead of slogans; free discussion as a form of learning and everyone's availability to support the others' areas of interest. Within the group, Rolph favored History, group logic, and the structuring effects of contradictions among groups and their expressive modes. (As he himself recounted, the evenings or afternoons spent listening to our father, Ernst, and our uncle, Hénock, summoning individuals and events of the past, had nourished the child he had been.) Strongly marked at the time by Gramsci, Poulantzas, and a little Althusser, but also by so many others—this man had the strength of a reading machine. He labored daily at building an impressive theoretical arsenal: he was convinced that he needed to look into the conditions surrounding the birth of the Haitian state in order to understand the contradictions in Haitian society and the process that structured it, as well as the relation between state and society. The book *Ti difé boulé* was born from an article published in the journal *Lakansièl*. The magazine gave a large place to the Creole language and thus departed from the 'Creole corner' approach that prevailed within the pages of 'progressive' productions.

Creole was not really seen as a working tool for reflection, it was placed in a category that often consisted of bad poems (accumulations of proverbs and imitations of the perception we had of 'popular' language). Two groundbreaking books had just come out, signaling a rupture and an evolution: Franketienne's *Dézafi* and Georges Castera's *Konbèlann*, a novel and a poetic exposé accompanied by a theoretical text. Work within, on, and through Haitian Creole language was progressing. In literature. Rolph's article in *Lakansièl* (under the pseudonym L. Raymond; it was the time of pseudonyms for most of the editorial staff and few knew who was behind L. Raymond, Michel Amer, Jules Laventure, Henriette Saint-Victor …) was one of the first attempts at an in-depth reflection within the social sciences field.

An article was good. So why not a book? With his unbelievable energy he put himself to work, knocking out an enormous amount of research, inviting us constantly to discuss it, obsessed by the question of language, not as an ornament but as a constituent element of the theoretical process: drawing from the popular imagination, oral philosophy, rhythm, and popular symbolism, transforming the appropriated material to produce the text, which was at once thought and writing. What makes this book more than a repertoire of lucky finds—which it also is—is above all a restitution of the dynamics of popular language fused with the production of critical thought. The audience, the tale, the chorus, the allusive charge, the myth, the figures (synecdoche, paronomasia, awakened metaphor …), everything is called forth, not as a background presence but as an element intrinsically connected to the gravity of the hypotheses. One could say, though it would be parroting the work and overly simplistic, that it was a 'marasa' (Divine Twins) approach.

At that time, we tried our hand at publishing, Rolph writing and me (and sometimes Evelyne) 'setting' the texts. There was no existing publisher whom such a text would really interest. Almost all the books published in the diaspora were printed at the author's expense, except for a few titles published in France and Canada. The 1,000 copies quickly disappeared. I don't recall articles in the diaspora newspapers, but word on the street assured the book enormous success. As of 1976 we had renewed contact with the home country, having realized that we wouldn't overthrow the Duvalier regime from New York apartment 'basements'. Meanwhile the echoes of the book's publication drew the attention of some high school teachers who used it, at their own risk, as a reference book or even as a textbook. After the fall of Jean-Claude Duvalier in 1986, *Ti difé boulé* finally became a reference that could be openly named. Handmade versions and photocopies abounded. And Rolph had become Mister Ti difé boulé. In 2014, the Université Caraïbe Press, directed by our sister Jocelyne, had the excellent idea of republishing it. The requests are many, and I often receive calls from individuals or groups wanting to obtain it.

It is impossible to conceive of *Ti difé boulé*'s production without connecting it to the collective adventures of *Tanbou Libète* and specifically *Lakansièl*, for which Rolph played the role of natural leader. His approach was enriched by something that has been lost today within intellectual and 'progressive' circles: thematic conversation consisting of informal exchanges about a given proposal, text or draft text. The crew at the time included the constant presence of Evelyne, Cauvin Paul, Jean Coulanges, and myself, along with other sporadic or ephemeral members, Karl Toulanmanche, Guy-Gerald Ménard, Julien Twin, and a few others present from the beginning in *Tanbou Libète* but absent from *Lakansièl*. Later, when Haiti's gates reopened for us, encounters with Pierre Buteau and Michel Acacia would become essential in Rolph's life as well as theirs. It was through *Ti difé boulé* that they first knew him, it was like his passport to Haiti; they could trust the man who had done this work. Buteau and Acacia, both editorial staff members of *Les Cahiers du vendredi*, and later *Lire Haïti*, became privileged conversation partners with Rolph, and it wounded me that doctoral students organizing a symposium on Rolph's work had declined to invite them.

But memory is unfaithful. I have probably forgotten some names and encounters, so I apologize to those whom I haven't mentioned here. I will finish this overly long introduction by highlighting two elements that are important for understanding the 'conditions of production' (one of Rolph's favorite expressions) for *Ti difé boulé*. Rolph's own approach to writing and to creating form and meaning in the Haitian Creole language was enriched in ways that were indirectly connected to this book but which helped him situate it within a movement and a trend. These included his contact with Guy-Gérald and the songs of Tanbou Libète; sisters Kettly and Edwidge Ménard; the guitarist Jean-Edouard Morisset, himself an author-composer; and also the collective writings of theatrical performances, especially *Si kacho pran pale*. From this point of view, this book is a contemporaneity, like the summit of a moment. The second point, undoubtedly the most important one—and here I return to what I was saying at the beginning of this presentation—is that this broad group, and Rolph in particular, harbored an anti- or rather a counter-academicism, with a vast knowledge of the 'academic' literature in the areas under study. They firmly insisted on the originality of the knowledge to be produced, on the need to undo (the verb 'deconstruct' wasn't yet in vogue) in order to proceed differently, to oppose the knowledge embargo imposed by the 'official' venues of knowledge production and dissemination. The propositions Rolph put forth in *Ti difé boulé* contain a virulent criticism of a set of propositions dear to traditional historiography. 'Trickster', in terms of the academic whose approach and subsequent work tacitly continued desacralizing discourses and producing a discourse intent on subverting an order that produces harm and injustice. *Ti difé boulé* was born from a political intention: through which groups, which collective subjects, could Haitian reality be transformed? To do this it was necessary to generate knowledge tracing the formation of these groups in order to track how they developed.

I think that all his life, Rolph remained this politician and this writing-writer … Besides, he had a Creole novel in his head: *anba pla pye lanmè*. His songs, his thinking, his scholarly work, his activism, the journals: all that comprised a whole for which *Ti difé boulé* constituted a distinct moment and launched his entry into the history of Haitian thought, more exactly the history of revolutionary thought in Haiti.

Thank you, brother,

Forever

Lyonel Antoine Trouillot

Translators' Note

Mariana Past and Benjamin Hebblethwaite

We consider this translation of Michel-Rolph Trouillot's first book to be a vital point of departure that is in no way definitive. Our objective was to produce a readable and clear English version of *Ti difé boulé sou istoua Ayiti* that would shed light on complexities within the original text while respecting its cultural and linguistic subtleties. Across a decade-long collaboration, our approach entailed reading, translating, writing, revising, striking out, mining dictionaries and thesauri, studying history books, analyzing lexical entries and their sentential semantic effects, soliciting feedback from countless colleagues, friends, and family members and constantly exchanging our work. This spiral-like method enabled many discoveries and improvements, yet as we came to understand the intricacies of Trouillot's writing, we were seldom fully satisfied with our renderings. We trust that engaged readers of this first-ever English translation of *Ti difé boulé sou istoua Ayiti* will help shape spirited conversations about Trouillot's first book, and we hope that it may eventually be possible to publish a facing-page bilingual edition.

Our work on this project took a winding path (see Past and Hebblethwaite 2014). The impetus for the translation came in 2009 in the context of the 'Creole texts and contexts' working group at Duke University's Haiti Lab, organized by Deborah Jenson and Michaeline Crichlow. Mariana Past subsequently sought Michel-Rolph Trouillot's permission to undertake the English translation. She invited Benjamin Hebblethwaite, who teaches Haitian Creole at the University of Florida, to collaborate and a team was formed. In December 2011, Trouillot granted permission for the preparation of an English version of *Ti difé boulé sou istoua Ayiti*, and our work began in earnest. We regret not having had the pleasure of meeting him personally before his untimely death in 2012. However, we are very glad to have had the opportunity to communicate with other members of the Trouillot family. Evelyne

Trouillot was an especially generous advisor during the final stages of manuscript revision, and it was she who suggested the translation for the title, *Stirring the Pot of Haitian History*.

As Lyonel Trouillot notes in his Introduction, Michel-Rolph Trouillot laid the groundwork for *Ti difé boulé sou istoua Ayiti* in an exploratory essay that he published in the journal *Lakansièl* under the pseudonym of L. Raymond, titled 'lindépandans dévan-dèyè: dapiyanp sou révolision' ('Independence Upside-Down: Seizing Revolution') (*Lakansièl* 4, Spécial nouvelle année, 1976, pp. 46–50). Although the short but provocative piece—which has flown almost entirely under the radar—merits greater attention than we can offer it here, we are pleased to be able to include this foundational text in the Appendix to this translation, alongside the similarly germinal 'Ki mò ki touyé lanpérè' ('What bad spirit killed the emperor') (*Lakansièl* 3, 1975, pp. 37–39).

We received thoughtful feedback on our work from Jacques Pierre, who teaches Haitian Creole at Duke University; contemporary Haitian writer Makenzy Orcel; Boaz Anglade and William Blanc, former and current Haitian Creole instructors and graduate students at the University of Florida; and Nathan Dize, a doctoral student in French and Francophone Studies at Vanderbilt University who assisted with the preliminary manuscript review. Jean Jonassaint also provided important insights along the way, and he kindly consulted with his own networks of Haitian friends and colleagues regarding translations of some tricky expressions. Our mainstay reference works were bilingual dictionaries, Valdman *et al.* (2007) and Freeman *et al.* (2004). The National Endowment for the Arts' Literature Translation Grant (2013–15) and various research awards from Dickinson College further supported our work on the translation.

Differing and overlapping interests have moved each of us. Mariana Past engaged with *Ti difé boulé sou istoua Ayiti* while studying Haitian Creole with Jonassaint in 2000. She was drawn to the ideas of Haitians as revolutionary catalysts (i.e. Alexandre Pétion's assistance to Simón Bolívar), and Haiti's Revolution as exemplary rather than exceptional—a fundamental part of Caribbean and Latin American identity. Benjamin Hebblethwaite found *Ti difé boulé sou istoua Ayiti* in 1999 on the shelves of the Indiana University Creole Institute and quickly became absorbed by the book's marvelous illustration of Haitian language and culture. As budding Haitian Creolists, both of us were excited by the provocative and creative style of this Haitian Creole text about the Haitian Revolution. Trouillot's book underscores the transformative potential of the Haitian language for the purpose of development and scholarship in Haiti while raising important questions about how to view Haitian history.

Translating *Ti difé boulé sou istoua Ayiti* inevitably presented us with many challenges. Our approach was more circular than linear in nature since new features and questions surfaced at each stage of reading and review, requiring continual reworkings spanning the entire manuscript. When we initially considered the text, our translations were overly literal. Over time we carried out multiple revisions to ensure consistency and accuracy, occasionally choosing an alternative wording that would resonate better with readers of English. For instance, we opted to render *sinzinosan* ('holy innocents') as 'innocent angels', *déchinnin* ('to unchain') as 'to fly off the handle', and *sévré* ('to wean') as 'to cut one's teeth', among other desiderata. On the other hand, we retained and modified some literal translations. For example, a section of Chapter 6 begins with the adage: 'Rat, rat, rat / min youn bèl ti dan / mouin ba ou / ou-a ban-m / youn vié ti dan'. Our English rendering offers a cultural translation in citing the parallel figure who gathers children's lost teeth in the anglophone world: 'Tooth fairy / what a nice little tooth / I gave you / you're going to gyp me'. Within his chapter, Trouillot deploys the proverb in a critique of the 'bait-and-switch' tactics of the French colonial army.

Our initial drafts included extensive notes explaining and exploring Trouillot's references to historical figures, events, proverbs (and his many creative riffs on proverbs), geographical features, religious practices, and other elements that seemed likely to pose interpretation problems for non-Haitian readers. From 'Onè—Réspè' to 'té koton', 'Minis Zaka', 'twòkèt', 'blan mannan', 'Ayiti Toma', 'Mr. Mbarouli', 'mazon', among so many other terms, we sought to clarify all we could. While we enjoyed spirited conversations with Haitian friends and colleagues about all these topics, the resulting parallel discussion in the notes weighed down the English version of *Ti difé boulé sou istoua Ayiti*. We decided on a form similar to the translations within *The Haiti Reader* (Dubois et al. 2020), retaining primarily footnotes containing essential historical information so as to leave the text as unfettered as possible. We opted not to comment on the wide range of potential meanings conveyed by numerous expressions within the text. Therefore, given the difficulties of translating *pale andaki* (ambiguous Creole replete with innuendo), our translation offers *an English version* among versions.

For historical anchoring, an important source was Thomas Madiou's *Histoire d'Haïti*, especially the first three volumes that address the time period of *Ti difé boulé sou istoua Ayiti*. Madiou's 1987 edition includes a helpful index of the names of people (pp. 371–431) followed by an index of place names (pp. 433–64) as appendices to volume eight. These indexes provided helpful answers to the many historical questions we had to answer to be able to translate accurately. Other valuable references were Michèle Oriol's *Dictionnaire de la révolution et de l'indépendance* (2002) and François Roc's *Dictionnaire de la Révolution haïtienne* (2006), along with personal correspondence with the historian David Geggus.

Spelling was another translation issue, and we purposefully adopted a hybrid approach maintaining key features of the original text but prioritizing readability. In rare instances where notes contain Haitian Creole terms and expressions independent from Trouillot (1977), we used the Kreyòl Ayisyen spelling system that predominates in Haiti and the diaspora today. Lyonel Trouillot directed the publication of a second edition of *Ti dife boule sou istwa Ayiti* (2012) through Edisyon KIK to reflect this updated spelling. In our English translation, when particular Haitian Creole words are retained, we deliberately use the original spelling from *Ti difé boulé sou istoua Ayiti* (1977) so that citations remain unambiguously identical to Michel-Rolph Trouillot's first edition, and especially so that his original text and its ideas and expressions can be situated within their historical context. However, the names of people and places appear in French within the English translation, because the French spellings are more recognizable in the English-speaking world. We reached these decisions through consultations with the Trouillots and Jean Jonassaint.

Besides questions about spelling, translating certain seemingly small words often required lengthy reflection. Notably, the Kreyòl pronoun *nou* can, depending on context, mean either 'you' (plural) or 'we/us', posing some sticky issues. Within Trouillot's narrative, the storyteller Grinn Prominnin primarily addresses his audience affectionately, as an extended family ('we/us'), but at times he employs a didactic tone to correct misconceptions that his listeners and readers ('you') may harbor about Haiti's history and its narratives. We fully realized that careful attention to the subtleties of *nou* was imperative in the English version or else the translation would lose significant shades of meaning.

Double meanings and wordplay throughout *Ti difé boulé sou istoua Ayiti* represented another challenge. We opted to preserve several key terms in Haitian Creole to maintain crucial complexities or connotations found in the original text. For example, in Trouillot's blistering analysis of the 1685 French colonial laws regulating enslavement known as the Black Code (*Kòd Noua*), he deliberately draws upon the double meaning of the Haitian Creole term *kòd*, which, as a homograph and homophone, can mean either, 'legal code' or 'cord' as in 'rope' (Jonassaint discusses this matter further in the Afterword). The *Kòd Noua* metaphor appears frequently in *Ti difé boulé sou istoua Ayiti*: it is simultaneously the 'legal code' (*kòd*) and a 'cord' (*kòd*) that binds and chokes the Haitian people by creating a legal and physical framework for torture and enslavement. While our chosen approach might slow down a few readers, we find it compelling to retain such phrases in the Haitian language given the symbolic resonances they provide.

Likewise, culture-specific references in Haitian Creole such as *marasa* (Divine Twins) also appear in the English version. The retention of these Haitian Creole terms within the translation immerses the reader in an unambiguously Haitian setting. Another phrase we retained was *koupé tèt boulé kay!*, meaning 'Cut off heads, burn down houses!' The expression was a rallying cry shouted by the black freedom fighters in 1791—a slogan that remains ingrained in Haitians' memories to this day. But when it came to translating Trouillot's original descriptive terms for formerly enslaved peoples, we used the French spellings *nouveaux libres* (black or mixed-race persons who were recently freed) and *anciens libres* (black or mixed-race persons who were either born free or who acquired freedom some time ago) because anglophone scholars commonly use those terms within studies on Haitian history.

Additional problems included translating terms such as *ésklav* and *milat*, which appear throughout *Ti difé boulé sou istoua Ayiti* and reflect a usage consistent with popular discourse and the historical period during which Trouillot wrote. Haitian scholar Jean Casimir (2009: xi–xiv) suggests that employing such terminology is akin to acquiescing to the mindset that Africans were inherent 'slaves', with European capitalists in the role of natural 'masters'. Casimir emphasizes that both positions were in fact temporary conditions for either group; moreover, some black and mixed-race people in the colony were born into, given, or purchased their own freedom. Most scholars now write in terms of 'enslaved people' or 'formerly enslaved people'. Daut (2015) comprehensively addresses the problematical implications of the term 'mulatto' as a racist racial category—a 'completely arbitrary, imprecise' term exposing a colorized understanding of Haitian history (19–20). While we in no way disagree, our translation refrains from superposing more nuanced contemporary discourse onto Trouillot's original text, as doing so would only serve to 'mask a reality that the book exposes', in Evelyne Trouillot's words. Despite what these fraught terms evoke today, we decided on a literal approach to translating both *ésklav* ('slave') and *milat* ('mulatto'), especially given the clarifications provided by the Trouillots. This English version of *Ti difé boulé sou istoua Ayiti* thus stays intentionally close to the book's original discursive content.

Yet another challenge we faced was deciding how to faithfully translate frequent 'false friends' in Trouillot's text. Depending on the situation, some of these terms can be appropriately translated in more than one way. For a few common terms we used synonyms to improve the intelligibility of the English: for example, *kontradiksion*, which literally means 'contradiction', is often more accurately translated as 'conflict' or 'tension', depending on circumstance. The terms *fòs* ('force') and *dominans* ('dominance') appear often, too, translating more accurately as 'power', 'strength', or 'authority', depending on the context.

In terms of formatting, we have maintained in bold typeface the myriad words and phrases that Trouillot published in that manner in the 1977 Haitian Creole original. To the degree possible, we also sought to reproduce his differential typography, which Jonassaint's Afterword discusses in greater detail. Also, for the sake of readability we have taken some very minor liberties in writing out 'versus' instead of employing slashes in describing dichotomies, as with 'France's supporters versus England's supporters' (instead of 'France's supporters/ England's supporters'). Lastly, we have spelled out most numerals, like '2' as 'two'.

A final, conceptual instance of a translation problem involves Trouillot's repeated use of the phrase *maladi nan san* (literally, 'sickness' or 'malady in the blood', or, technically, 'hereditary disease'). For decades, within international media coverage, discourses on diseases like AIDS and cholera have unjustly been associated with Haiti, reinforcing racism and xenophobia towards Haitians (Farmer 1992). Yet, in *Ti difé boulé sou istoua Ayiti*, Trouillot's expression *maladi nan san* refers instead to received and uncritical *ideations* emanating from fundamental tensions in the collective Haitian past, including the seemingly hereditary repetition of the patterns of political hero-worship, the racial genealogy of Haitian politics, and submission to authoritarianism. Trouillot's expression *maladi nan san* ('hereditary disease/ailment/malady/sickness') connotes an internal psychological and social affliction that is held and transmitted mentally through the community. We address the issue within a note and have translated *maladi nan san* alternately as 'malady', 'ailment', or 'sickness'. To be sure, every human family, community, and nation harbors harmful hereditary mental ideations, *maladi nan san*, that can stand in the way of progressive development.

As a young writer and political activist, Trouillot diagnoses, assesses, and treats the collective ideological hereditary *maladi nan san* of his fellow Haitians. His implicit critique of contemporary Haiti blames the perpetuation of failures on the cyclical repetition of behaviors and mentalities transmitted from the French colonists of Saint-Domingue and replicated by the builders of Haitian independence. Since Haitians' (hereditary) ideological malady is capable of mutating into new forms, constant vigilance is necessary: 'Fò jé nou byin foubi pou nou ka ouè maladi-a chak foua li réparèt figi-l' ('your eyes must be well scrubbed so you can recognize this malady when it rears its head again', p. 213). As in his later book, *Haiti, State against Nation* (1990), Trouillot shows that megalomaniacal leaders routinely mistreat the Haitian people; recent work by historians Dupuy (2019) and Fatton (2007) sheds further light on these issues. Due to the elite's long history of concentrating power in Port-au-Prince, and its self-interested support of a minority French language that is mastered by perhaps five percent of the population, the poor and rural populations have been excluded from opportunities and citizenship. And this systematic exclusion of Haitian Creole speakers from the state, education, services, and commerce limits economic potential and social cohesion (Hebblethwaite 2012). A recent *Boston Globe* essay argues that linguistic equality is fundamentally 'a precondition for political and economic equity' (DeGraff 2016).

Trouillot encourages Haitians to recognize and embrace the fundamental forces that surged to establish Haitian independence and identity: the farmers' ownership of the land and its cultivation, the national unity guaranteed by the Haitian Creole language, and respect for Haiti's liberating religion of Vodou. The potential and the responsibility for progress are latent in the *zantray* ('intestines') of Haitians themselves, not in the heads of foreigners or the NGOs that swarm in and around the country. Haitians can productively gather up this inner power, understanding that the 'bubble' of foreign aid, including its languages and cultures, tends to benefit powerful foreign interests, middle-class foreign aid workers, and a few local proxies (Schuller 2016: 223).

In 1977, Trouillot wrote in the context of the Duvaliers' dynastic dictatorships. Today, *Ti difé boulé sou istoua Ayiti* continues to resonate in an earthquake- and hurricane-afflicted Haiti in which NGOs from abroad, periodic military interventions by the United States, the embassies of the United States and France, and the United Nations' blue helmets have exerted an insidious foreign influence on the nation, including the latter's introduction of cholera in 2010 (Piarroux *et al.* 2011). In a country where Haitian Creole is becoming increasingly established in the domain of cultural production but is still marginalized within the state and educational system, *Ti difé boulé sou istoua Ayiti* is a major milestone in the effort to expand the corpus of Haitian Creole scholarly works capable of advancing and inspiring Haitians. This English translation seeks to make its influence accessible for a broader group of readers.

The Choice of Haitian Creole
and the Legacy of *Ti difé boulé sou istoua Ayiti*

The growing Haitian diaspora community has reshaped cities in the United States over the past sixty years (Charles 1998; Zéphir 2004). Nearly two million Haitians live outside of Haiti today, with trade and cultural exchanges between Miami, New York, Boston, Montreal, Paris, and Port-au-Prince creating a fluid transnational dynamic. Vexing fundamental problems remain, as Haitian-Americans find themselves threatened by structural poverty, underperforming schools in immigrant and black neighborhoods, an epidemic of gun violence, xenophobia from black Americans, racism from white Americans, and prejudice from other ethnic groups. In addition to these historical adversities—which expose the United States' own hereditary diseases—from 2017–2021 the executive branch of the U.S. government openly promoted white nationalism, white supremacy, and white violence. These noxious policies, incessant dog-whistling, and shameless verbal and physical attacks harmed Americans of every origin and shook the foundations of democracy.

Due to the second-class status of Haitian Creole in Haitian institutions, which is most damaging in schools, a portion of Haitians and Haitian-American immigrants have never learned thoroughly to read or write the Haitian Creole language. The prevalence of the English-only ideology within the United States, in turn, nips Haitian Creole in the bud, just as it suffocates the speakers of many other languages. The Haitian community's growing endorsement of Haitian Creole still lags in the domain of publishing in comparison to output in French or English. The imperative of earning an income, of reaching larger audiences, or of satisfying peer review requirements favors publishing in English and French for many Haitian and Haitianist authors.

The situation also impacts Haitian studies. Among established Haitianist scholars, Creole proficiency can be lackluster. Some time ago, a colleague who has published numerous French-to-English translations of Haitian literature, for instance, explained in an email to Mariana Past: 'I think this [English translation of *Ti difé boulé sou istoua Ayiti*] is a worthy project—I have a Xerox copy of the book but have never read it because of my limited vocabulary in Kreyòl'. Another Haitian-born linguist working at an elite university insisted that publishing in Creole would damage his career advancement given that academics disregard publications they cannot read. In academic circles within the United States, peer preference for English-language publishing, and to a lesser degree publishing in European languages, limits the potential for Haitian

Creole contributions from Haitianists. In many respects, the dominance of English-language publishing (and French-language in the francophone areas) within the Haitian community and beyond it has generated a subculture of 'Northern Haitianists' who have limited skills or interest in Haiti's actual majority language, Haitian Creole, and thus prevent themselves from understanding the majority of Haiti's people and their culture.

We believe that despite its imperfections, this first English translation of *Ti difé boulé sou istoua Ayiti* productively expands knowledge about Haiti and Haitians. Access to the land for farmers via land reform; publishing; instruction; and governance in Haiti's majority language, Haitian Creole; and a culture of coexistence among the nation's religious traditions reflect the book's leading ideals. Many authors have utilized Haitian Creole (in addition to French, English, or Spanish, as the case may be) to produce works of science or literature in recent decades (for example, Beauvoir and Dominique 2003; Casimir 2004; Dejean 2006; Beauvoir 2008; Pierre 2016; Trouillot 2017). Haitians and Haitianists alike should embrace these ideals in order to enable development and reconstruction in Haiti—especially in the wake of crises brought on by hurricanes, earthquakes, pandemics, famines, and hotter temperatures induced by climate change.

We hope that readers of *Stirring the Pot of Haitian History* will be inspired by Michel-Rolph Trouillot's incisive analyses of Haiti's culture, ideologies, languages, religions, and exemplary history. To consider but one example: as illustrated in Tarter's (2016) study on arboreal coverage in Haiti, overgeneralized media images, clichés, and stereotypical tropes distort the fact that one third of Haiti has tree cover. Fundamentally, Haiti needs new narratives, as Gina Ulysse (2015) argues. As both she and Trouillot observe in their work, the failure to develop institutions of knowledge and governance that prioritize Haitian Creole represents a flagrant and fundamental impediment when it comes to individual and collective progress in Haiti.

Encouraging the adoption of new narratives, new language policies, new practices, and new analyses of Haiti is an imperative project today, and Trouillot demonstrated his seminal leadership in these crucial areas through *Ti difé boulé sou istoua Ayiti*. His work excavates truths, exposes the manipulations of received history, and flexes the muscles of Haitian Creole. As Lyonel Trouillot's poignant preface points out, Michel-Rolph Trouillot demonstrated a strong commitment to these concerns from his days as a member of the *Tanbou Libète* ('Drums of Freedom') theater group in New York City, to his later contributions as a groundbreaking

Translators' Note xxxiii

anthropologist and political scientist (Bonilla 2013: 82). *Ti difé boulé sou istoua Ayiti* provokes an intensely original conversation, announcing important alternatives for thinking about Haiti and its heroes. Michel-Rolph Trouillot closes his narrative—one that suggests the potency of a *pèp tarodé* ('willful people')—by returning to the idea that Haitians must scour their eyes to search for the *maladi nan san* ('hereditary illness') each time it reappears.

The book concludes as it began, with concern and affection for people suffering hardship in Haiti. Along with the author's deep sympathies for the difficulties faced by Haitian people, and his tireless wrestling with calcified ideas within Haitian thought and historiography, Trouillot's Haitian Creole critique of Haitian ideologies provides Haitians and Haitianists with a powerful tool for understanding, representing, and constructing a framework for Haiti in which all Haitians can thrive.

Acknowledgments

It was our great joy to collaborate on this project. More than a decade of shared effort went into the production of this edited and annotated translation of *Ti difé boulé sou istoua Ayiti*. We labored over one another's drafts in multiple layers, in the company of generous consultants, and the outcome was a merging of minds. We consider ourselves to be students of Michel-Rolph Trouillot and his intellectual legacy as a Haitianist scholar. In our English interpretation of his first book, we recognize our limitations, and we welcome the feedback of our readers.

We extend the deepest gratitude to the National Endowment for the Arts for the Literature Translation Grant (2013–15) that we received to support our translation and editing of *Ti difé boulé sou istoua Ayiti*. This generous support and endorsement provided crucial momentum for our collaboration. Gina Ulysse was an exceptionally thoughtful sounding board as this project evolved, and we thank her wholeheartedly for the insights and support that she so generously provided. We also owe thanks to the two anonymous reviewers who provided extensive comments and suggestions, and to Dickinson College for its strong support.

We are grateful to the Trouillot family, especially Lyonel Trouillot for his willingness to bring this work to fruition and for generously contributing his reflections to this volume; Evelyne Trouillot, for her invaluable feedback and forbearance; and Nadève Ménard, whose kind assistance with communication (and coffee with Ben) at crucial moments helped us maintain hope for this project. We are profoundly grateful to Jean Jonassaint, who was the guiding light from the beginning, and the reason the translation took off. We fondly thank Deborah Jenson for encouraging Mariana to contact Michel-Rolph Trouillot regarding permissions in the first place (she has safeguarded his email reply ever since), as well as Laurent Dubois and Kaiama Glover for inviting us to publish excerpts of Chapter 4 in a special issue of *Transition*. Marlene Daut and Kaiama Glover's 'Enduring Questions, New Methods in Haitian Studies' conference brought welcome encouragement during the later stages of this collaboration. We also sincerely thank Eleanor Billington at the National Endowment for the Arts, Makenzy Orcel. We remain extremely grateful for all the additional efforts that have gone into copyediting this manuscript! Jacques Pierre, Claudine Michel, Robert Fatton, Jean Eddy Saint Paul, Anthony Cond, Charles Forsdick, Chloe Johnson, David Geggus, Nathan Dize, Erin Zavitz, Rob Taber, William Blanc, Boaz Anglade, Alyssa Goldstein Sepinwall, Cécile Accilien, Régine Jean-Charles, Philip Kaisary, Paul Miller, Mark Schuller, Natalie Léger, Julio Corbea, Grete Viddal, Kasia Mika, Linda Brindeau, Christopher Brokus, Ben Sweger, Jerry Philogene, Nathalie Dupont, Lesley Curtis, Katherine Smith, Aisha Khan, Claudy Delné, and Petrouchka Moise for their collective assistance, encouragement, and solidarity over the years. We are also grateful to copy-editor Alwyn Harrison, typesetter Rachel Clarke, and production editor Siân Jenkins, whose careful efforts saw this project through its final stages. Last, but not least, we are indebted to Joe Aufmuth, a geospatial consultant at the University of Florida's George A. Smather's Libraries, whose original and detailed maps provide a valuable geographical resource to augment the reading of the book.

Mariana thanks her husband Eric Bondy, her son Ray, and her daughter Ana, who grew up alongside this project, her parents, Al and Kay Past, and her sister Elena Past, who provided moral support and thoughtfully read drafts. Ben extends gratitude to his father, John Hebblethwaite, and to his mother, Meg, for her careful proofreading. He also thanks his wife, Julie Changhee Rhee, and his daughters, Chloe and Ellie, for their love and encouragement. Collectively, our deepest gratitude is felt for our families' support of our writing, translating, and editing over ten years.

*Stirring the Pot
of Haitian History*

with the courage of yesterday's teachers
and the considerateness of young people today
for the glory of tomorrow's children
    hand in hand
    with you
    my dear
        my wife
        my left flank
        steadfastly

            m-r. t.

I give a bundle of thanks to all the family and friends-comrades who helped me in every possible way to get this book on its feet. After expressing thanks to Kettly, I extend special thanks to Lyonel, Evelyne, and Jean-Robert for the strength they gave me.

            m-r. t.

'The habits of past generations are like iron weights on the minds of people today'.

1. I'm holding a gathering

*I'm holding
a gathering
to understand what's happened
to my brothers and sisters
oh yes!*

Night was spreading across the mountains. A woeful breeze was blowing, but the children didn't stop playing. Sédènié was running after Aséfi, his small belly bloated from bad fat, his wee-wee dangling in the darkness. Up in the sky, the moon was peeking under the petticoat of the stars, and close by, near the fence, three lightning bugs were playing hide-and-seek with hardship.

Lamèsi stoked the fire, threw on a piece of wood, then announced:

'Children, stop!'

All the adults raised their heads. Lamèsi looked at them. There were so many people, she couldn't count them all. Tipous was there, Roro was there, Fifi was there ... Voklin had even come with his drum. Timari brought coffee. Néréstan had a few stalks of sugar cane that he cut into tiny pieces so everyone could have a bit.

Lamèsi announced:

'Brothers and sisters, we're gathered here because Grinn Prominnin has returned. From the time of President Tibab, we sent Grinn Prominnin to sound the depths of our suffering. We sent him to find out what bad spirit killed the Emperor, what bad spirit killed Tipiè, Séfanm, and Marilis ... what bad spirit has been preying on the family up to this very day, as I speak. We gave him drink, and we gave him food. We gave him good clothes so he could make the trip easily. Days went by, water flowed under the bridge, my late father was long departed. Some people started saying that Grinn Prominnin must be dead. Other folks thought he'd given up. And then this morning, I had a big surprise; I was bathing upstream, and who did I see? Grinn Prominnin! His age was starting to show, his face looked tired, and ... it was like ... (I didn't like it one bit) he looked like a city person. But a weight came off my heart when he kissed me on both cheeks and said to me: "Sister Lamèsi, don't fear, you can summon the people. You're going to find out what's happened to your brothers and sisters"'.

'So, where is he? Make him talk then!'

Lamèsi glanced backward; she looked at the candelabra cactus thicket. The candelabra thicket parted. A man came forward, his head down.

'My family, I say: Honor'.

'Respect, Grinn Prominnin'.

The woeful breeze stopped blowing. The man rolled up his pant legs and sat down on a tree stump between Tisè and Fanfan.

'Brothers and sisters, I bring news. Since President Tibab's time, I've done nothing but travel. I've seen mountains, I've seen rivers. I've seen savannahs, I've seen the sea. I cast my eyes on other lands; I learned to speak ritual words ... But when I finally reached the realm of the past,

I realized that if we truly want to shed light on our condition, we must turn and look behind us ... We must confront all the crises the family's been through, we must study the traces they left in our blood.

'But, you don't understand what happened. Even Grandma Andrémiz, who was born years ago under President Sylvain Salnave,[1] doesn't know what the Emperor said.

'Well, that's what I've come to do here. That's the only thing I've come to do here. I've come from the realm of the past to tell you what went down. I've come from the land of the depths to speak the ritual words for you. I ... that's all I can do ... I've come from too far away ...'.

The woeful breeze returned, and it stirred up the flames of the fire. The flames rose up, lighting up all the members of the family. Grinn Prominnin turned and looked at Sédènié:

'That one was born while I was away, right?'

'Yes, he's one of those who were born while you were away. He's the youngest. The one born after him died. But Loulouz is pregnant again'.

The woeful breeze carried the words away. Sédènié put his head on Aséfi's shoulders. Grinn Prominnin cleared his throat. Up in the sky, the stars were challenging the moon, but close by, near the fence, seven lightning bugs were denouncing the hardship.

Grinn Prominnin said ...

In January 1820, General Jean-Pierre Boyer, President of Haiti, entered Jérémie. He sent a communiqué to proclaim far and wide that even though the army hadn't been able to capture Goman, Malfèt, and Malfou (the three main rebel leaders), they had managed to crush the last band of maroons who'd been sowing 'disorder' in the country.

In January 1820, Boyer entered Jérémie. In October 1820, Boyer entered Cape Haitian. In February 1822, he entered Santo-Domingo ... In April 1825, France recognized Haiti's independence.

A huge crisis was over. After thirty years of fighting, another kind of society—the society we inherited—appeared on Haitian soil. With another kind of leader. Another kind of slave. Another kind of maroon.

To understand that society, our own society, we must understand what kind of life disappeared into the wilderness with the three maroons

---

1 Sylvain Salnave was President of Haiti from 1867 until 1869, when he was executed (Nicholls 108).

of La Grand'Anse. For us to finally understand the malady we suffer from, we must understand the malady we've inherited.

Today, we're in charge, but we can't do everything we want to. We alone are responsible for tomorrow, but yesterday's chasing our tails. We alone have the power to choose, but the rules of the game were already written, and we didn't write them.

Between 1789 and 1820, Haiti was gripped by a **crisis that cut to the marrow**. And it was during that crisis, over the course of just thirty years, that the framework was built for the society we inherited. **The burdens of past generations are like iron weights on the minds of people today.**

Between 1789 and 1820, the Haitian people carried out the one and only slave revolution in human memory. But during those same thirty years, a native-born class pulled a fast one on the people, and it took over the revolution. And if we want to fully understand the malady that we suffer from **today**, we must retrace the path of that crisis. On the left hand, a revolution; on the right hand, a coup.

So, when all the ashes were cool, when Boyer took Jérémie … I myself … they themselves … he himself … you **yourself!**

Sister Lamèsi, please, give me a little cotton tea. All these ideas call for refreshment …

2. *A Kòd Noua*
to tie up little pigs

*Ay ay
Janpétro
broke
a real-life
chain
like a rope.*

School has its rules, work has its rules, the state has its rules. The Bible has the Ten Commandments.

Traffic has its rules, war has its rules, peace has its rules, and the cemetery has its rules: hey, stiff, move it! The cemetery has room …

Latin has its rules, English has its rules, Creole has its rules. Farming has its rules, speechwriting has its rules. A dance worthy of the name has its rules: if you don't have a tie, you can't go in.

That's to say, when we raise our eyes, we see the sky's full of rules. People give them all kinds of names. There are commandments, there are regulations, there are *kòd*. (Not the type of *kòd* you tie the pig up with, but that type would've been nicer.) There are *dèkrè*, decrees, there are *dèkrè-loua*, legal decrees, and there are *laloua*, laws. (It's not the bitter *laloua*, aloe, that they use for remedies, but that type would've been nicer.)

What if all those rules were there for nothing? No, director! What if they were all innocent? No, your Honor! What if that's just life? Stop, pastor, stop!

Let's seek out the truth, leaving no stone unturned …

What could it mean for *laloua* to be bitter?

The first major law that took shape in Haiti was the regulation they called the *Kòd Noua* that went into effect in 1685. Who wrote the *Kòd Noua*? Why did they write it? They say 'la loi est une pour tous' ('the law is equal for all'), but we all know those French words are just for show! Was the *Kòd Noua* the same for everyone? My friends, what could it mean for *laloua* to be bitter?

As any regulation does, before the *Kòd Noua* showed up, it took a scented bath. It donned the costume of justice, supposedly to keep slave owners from mistreating slaves. But General History shows us that it wasn't what they said that mattered, it was what they did when they finished speaking …

The person who had the *Kòd Noua* written up was a French minister named Colbert, the only major player in the government of Louis XIV who strongly believed in commerce. So, when they told us the *Kòd Noua* was there to improve the slaves' situation, we were shocked …

Since when have hawks cared about chickens' fate? *Laloua* didn't serve everyone's interests the same way. *Laloua* primarily served the interests of the classes controlling the State … Since the colonists were the ones controlling Saint-Domingue in 1685, you can bet millions that the *Kòd Noua* served their interests. And since the colonists were dependent upon French merchants, you can bet a million bucks that the *Kòd Noua* wouldn't upset the merchants. Let's dig in a little further …

little cucumbers and eggplants

France began its assault on Haiti in 1625. But, at that time, the French weren't really interested in business. Most of the Frenchmen in Saint-Domingue were a ragtag bunch of thieves who pirated Spanish, English, and Dutch boats that they came across in the region. Haiti (Tortuga island especially) was like a barracks where they came to rest after each raid.

Besides the **freebooters**,[2] there were other French folks who didn't often take to the sea. Either they hunted pigs and cattle, or they worked the land. Those who hunted were called **buccaneers**[3] because they roasted the animals over big **bonfires**. The **farmers** worked the land. When I say they worked the land, you shouldn't assume they worked as hard as Haitian farmers do today, because both farmers and buccaneers had gazillions of slaves working for them.

The buccaneers and farmers had two types of slaves:

indentured ones (white slaves who were there for a short time)
black ones (who were slaves for life).

Even so, the freebooters, buccaneers, and farmers all got along like co-wives, and they also got along with the slaves, whether white or black. Though the slaves worked really hard, the slave owners at the time protected them.

Are the offending parties surprised? As though I'm telling lies? As though I'm not serious? Troublemakers start grumbling …

Whoever wants to speak, speak. Whoever wants to listen, listen. I'm not selling out to whites here, and I'm not saying slavery was a good thing. But if you want to understand why Lamèsi gave Magrit a dirty look, you must understand what's gone on since colonial times, when they were living together with our old buddy Jérilis …

---

2 The seafaring freebooters or *flibistye* were the original pirates of the Caribbean.
3 The buccaneers or *boukànye* built *boukan dife* 'bonfires' to *boukannen* 'roast' and smoke meat for sale or trade. Many of the animals they hunted had been released into the wild by the Spanish colonists on the eastern side of the island more than a century before.

Words right and left
Words inside out
Words here and there
Words

Every five-cent coin has two sides: heads isn't tails. All that exists has an opposite. There's life, there's death. Day isn't night. Yet a lot of nights and a lot of days make life move forward. Considerate older folks always tell me: there's no proverb without an opposite …

> Rotten teeth beat ripe bananas
> [but] the runt is the fiercest.
>
> The early bird gets the worm
> [but] getting an early start means nothing—what counts is knowing the way.
>
> The worthy ones don't ask
> [but] the squeaky wheel gets the grease.
>
> Don't fake it if you can't make it.
> [But] big bark, small bite.
>
> Might makes right
> [then again] the strongest have weak spots.

Every coin has two sides. Heads isn't tails. All that exists has an opposite. If there were no life, there'd be no death. If there were no high, there'd be no low. If there were no front, there'd be no back. If there were no mountains, there'd be no ravines. If there were no rich people, there'd be no poor people. If there were no exploiters, then there'd be no exploited.

War inside and out, war between life and death, war between slaves and slave owners, between large landowners and fieldworkers; they call this **conflict**. It's a war where anything goes. But it's this war that makes life move forward. A conflict is the flames under Sister Lamèsi's bean pot. At some point, the cauldron explodes: teeth get stuck in rotten bananas, slaves slit their owners' throats, death talks behind the back of life, day chases off the orb of night.

Yet if we look closely, when dusk's about to fall, the battle between day and night is caught in between. Like when the dew hasn't formed, and it's not totally night, but it's not yet day. Or when the moon hasn't gone away, and it's not daytime yet, but we can't call it night because the rooster has already crowed for the third time.

At that moment we can say: the young conflict hasn't yet unfolded its wings. It's swaying from side to side. It's emerging. But we know it will take off. It's either night or day. Twilight doesn't last long. A conflict goes through three stages: **the growing stage, the entangled stage, and the unbound stage**.

I know you can understand now why the buccaneers and farmers living in Saint-Domingue around 1650 didn't mistreat their slaves. It wasn't because they were nicer than Caradeux or Praloto.[4] It was because a slave in a field didn't scare them. In 1680, amidst the whites in Saint-Domingue, there were 1,400 men. Amidst the slaves, there were 1,100 men. The society was growing. The slave versus slave owner conflict was still cutting its teeth. Don't forget: **a conflict goes through three stages: the growing stage, the entangled stage, and the unbound stage**.

If you understand that fact, you'll also realize that a static situation doesn't last long. Social conflicts are like gangs on the offensive: they don't stay put. Dusk doesn't last very long. Why do slave owners force slaves to work? So they can make money. When they start making money, how can they make more money?

There are two things they can do:

1. go find more slaves to add to those already working
2. make the slaves work harder.

Saint-Domingue's whites did nothing less. In 1665 there were a lot of black slaves. Yet, the more time passed, the more the whites piled the slaves up, and the harder the slaves worked … The unhappier the slaves got. In 1680 there were already more than 1,000 slaves in Saint-Domingue. In 1679, when the conflict hadn't yet entered the second stage, Lamèsi's pot started bubbling over: a group of slaves took up arms under the orders of Padre Jean.

This is a fact of History: **social conflicts must move forward**. For factory owners to make money there must be lots of people working and they must work harder every day. For slave owners to turn a profit they always must get more slaves and they must mistreat them.

For a society to move forward, the productive forces must expand. But the more these forces grow, the harder the slaves work, and the unhappier the slaves become.

---

4 Caradeux and Praloto were officers in the French military in Saint-Domingue during the Revolution. See Ros, *Night of Fire*.

So in 1680, both in Saint-Domingue and on other islands under French control, the conflict was moving forward. In 1685, it started getting entangled.

When the productive forces start to swell, the conflict gets more complicated, and foreigners show up with *laloua,* **orders, and regulations to tie the little pigs up with** *kòd.*

In 1685 the foreigners let the *Kòd Noua* loose on the streets.

The *Kòd Noua* contained sixty articles. Some parts of it repeat other parts. So we won't go through it line by line, word by word, like some people would want us to study it. Instead, we're going to sort out what we're reading, we're going to mix it up together, and we're going to unravel it to see the truth behind all that French talk.

no pain, no gain

For a system to be sustained in a society, the society must reproduce itself. It must keep producing the same types of people and social classes as it did before ... For the bourgeoisie to eat meat, there must be cattle, there must be goats. To have cattle and goats, the cattle and goats must bear offspring. In the same way, for a slave owner/slave society to be sustained, the slaves must work constantly. Therefore, they can't die for nothing. That society, **at the same time as it crushes the slaves**, must preserve the slaves' physical strength. If all the slaves worked so hard that they died in three months, the slave owners wouldn't have enough time to recover their investment, and they'd lose money. If factory workers worked so hard that they died like flies in a trap, the big bourgeois types wouldn't have a proletariat to work for them, and they wouldn't have customers to buy their products. That's why they give workers Saturday and Sunday off. It's certainly not because they 'like' them!

And so we discover a big conflict that's within every society. **For the upper class to fully exploit the lower class, the upper class must preserve the lower class's physical strength.**

He sells meat ...
... with all the spices inside it!

A bunch of articles in the *Kòd Noua* were there to preserve the slaves' physical strength, so the society could continue in the same way. Louis

XIV decreed that slaves mustn't be dismembered for no reason, their arms mustn't be crushed, and slave owners should give them food, drink, and rest (articles 22 through 27). He ordered that slaves rest on Sundays and for slave owners to not separate babies from their mothers (articles 6, 7, 12).

In truth, while the *Kòd Noua* required slaves to be fed, at the same time it clamped down on them. A slave had no rights. Owners considered him like any other kind of property: like a horse, a dog, a chair, or a table. The *Kòd Noua* put it like this: **a slave is a piece of furniture**! The slaves weren't allowed to buy or sell anything (Article 18). They weren't allowed to complain to the authorities about anyone, even if that person had harmed them (Article 31). They couldn't carry weapons or 'big sticks' (Article 15). If they raised a hand against the owner of the house, the woman of the house, or the children of the house, the owner of the house had the right to kill them (Article 33).

So, my friends, we uncover the *Kòd Noua*'s two functions in Saint-Domingue:

1. preserve the physical strength of the lower class
2. prevent the lower class from getting agitated.

Yet that still wasn't enough for the parties concerned. Because, for slaves to take up arms, to assault the plantation owner and his wife, the devious notion had to occur to them, and there had to be backup. Thus, the *Kòd Noua* tried to prevent the idea of revolution from getting into the slaves' minds. Article 16 bluntly 'outlaws the assembly of slaves from different communities, whether in daytime or nighttime, whether for weddings or for other reasons, whether in a white person's house, or elsewhere. As for gatherings on the main roads, or in the backwoods, out of the question'. The article required slaves who disobeyed *laloua* to be beaten, and if they did it again ... to be killed. Article 17 upheld the charge: if slave owners allowed slaves even a little leeway to hold a gathering, the owners had to pay the consequences.

suppressing human dignity

I don't know if you understand. The people who wrote this article were intentionally seeking to transmit eye disease to all the slaves for thirty-three generations. Scholars studying human intelligence have shown us that talking helps men and women think! Conversations between whole neighborhoods help neighbors think. But for neighbors to talk, they must meet up, they must come together. To outlaw gatherings is to outlaw speech. To outlaw speech is to outlaw thought. To outlaw thought is to outlaw freedom ...

The *Kòd Noua* suppressed the human dignity of the Haitian people. To fully understand this form of takeover, you must know the ways colonists split up slaves in Saint-Domingue. The colonists intentionally separated slaves who came from the same African nation. So the slaves in a given community didn't serve the same *loua* (spirits) or speak the same language. The colonists did that so they could force their own ideas and their own language into the heads of Saint-Domingue's African slaves. But the slaves outsmarted the slave owners. They took the colonists' language, folded it into a bunch of African languages, and produced Creole. They took the colonists' religion, folded it into their own religion, and produced Vodou ... That's what made a lot of troublemakers hate Creole and Vodou.

Careful now, I'm not taking a stand for either Creole or Vodou. No language is better than another. **Native-born crooks stand by to tell the Haitian people bad lies in good Creole.** No religion is better than another. **Some people also use Vodou to take advantage of the Haitian people.** But like it or not, Creole and Vodou were the first two battles Haitian workers won against the foreign colonists. But let's get back to the *Kòd Noua* ...

When you know how they separated Africans in Saint-Domingue, you see more clearly how the *Kòd Noua* sought to tie up the slaves. When the *Kòd Noua* declared that slaves couldn't gather, even for a wedding celebration, it was like stealing the people's soul, putting it in a jug, and burying it underground.

Speaking is one of the basic rights all men and women are born with. It's a basic right to say: 'Good morning, sister', and for her to say: 'How are you?' It's a basic right to answer happily, 'Not bad, my dear, but if we go forward together, tomorrow will be brighter'.

sweep it under the rug

So we discover the three important functions the *Kòd Noua* sought to perform for Saint-Domingue's upper classes:

1. The *Kòd Noua* was there to preserve the slaves' physical strength

2. The *Kòd Noua* was there to prevent the slaves from taking up arms
3. The *Kòd Noua* was there so the colonists could suppress the slaves' intellect and keep them from reflecting on their problems.

For that same reason, the *Kòd Noua* required slave owners to baptize the slaves. Numerous articles in the *Kòd Noua* sought to make the colonists convert the slaves, because the parties concerned knew that lots of ideas in the Bible could help make the slaves be more submissive. But the Bible has its own contradictions, too. It says people must obey *laloua*, but it also says: everyone is a human being (as children of God). The colonists of Saint-Domingue understood this contradiction. They knew that parts of the Bible weren't made for the slaves. They knew that many articles in the *Kòd Noua* were there just for show.

To take control of Africa and America, and to mistreat slaves at will, European colonists acted as though they only wanted to convert the other people on earth. Just like today, to prey on smaller countries at will, lots of predatory countries act like they're coming to help the poor people ... They make the sign of the cross with the left hand, and they scarf down our food with the right hand. The articles in the *Kòd Noua* about religion were sweet, flowery-smelling pieces of crap, policemen's tricks. They were there to let Saint-Domingue's colonists and the French bourgeoisie confess and take communion with clean consciences, without protests from other countries (or other classes in their own country). They were there to help uphold slavery with the blessing of the church.

This contradiction is present in many *laloua*: besides bloodthirsty rules, **there are also rules to make the upper class look good, to sweep things under the rug.** The fourth function of the *Kòd Noua* in Saint-Domingue was to cover up the exploitation of slaves.

every man for himself

But that still wasn't enough for some of the parties concerned. They didn't want slaves to gather together, but they also didn't want freedmen to help slaves. To the contrary: the *Kòd Noua* enflamed tempers so slaves would hate freedmen. Freedmen had the right to kill a slave who raised his hand against them (Article 34). And if a freedman helped a slave escape, the freedman would pay a heavy price.

Given that three quarters of the freedmen were mulattos within the society of Saint-Domingue, that article drove a wedge between black people and mulattos. It made blacks hate mulattos. It made mulattos stand apart from blacks. As for blacks who were free, either because their mothers were free or because their owners had set them free, this law ended up making them scorn their old friends, so everyone was out for himself. The sixth function that the *Kòd Noua* sought to carry out in Saint-Domingue, was to **sow division between slaves and free blacks** so the *grand blanc* (wealthy white) colonists could gallivant around at will.

But the question of the freedmen didn't end there. The secretaries to Louis XIV knew that the freedmen were a double-edged sword. If they cooperated with the slaves, it wouldn't be good for the colonists, but if they fully cooperated with the colonists it couldn't be good for France. They could join forces and exploit slaves in a way that kept France from skimming the cream off the top. So even though articles 57–59 said that freedmen and whites were equals, Article 58 (in the middle) said: if freedmen disrespect their former owners, they must be severely punished.

breaking the *kòd*

My friends, I don't know if you realize this, but *laloua* isn't as simple as they want you to think. **Laloua is a weapon in the hands of the classes in power, to keep society in check.** And this weapon strikes on many sides, in various ways. In Saint-Domingue, the *Kòd Noua* was there:

1. to help preserve the slaves' physical strength
2. to keep slaves from finding ways to revolt
3. to keep slaves from reflecting on their situation
4. to make slaves be more submissive
5. to sweep all the abuses and the colonists' crimes under the rug
6. to keep other classes (and other groups) from siding with the slaves
7. to keep free blacks from joining with whites against the French bourgeoisie.

My friends, this is the essence of the *Kòd Noua*. The question we should ask now is, did they follow that *laloua*? And this question begs another: why did they follow one rule, and why did they ignore another?

We already know that *laloua* is a *kòd* the upper class (or upper classes) puts in place to tie up the lower class. Yet we also know that the more Lamèsi's bean pot heats up, the more smoke rises.

In the same way, the more entangled a society's inner conflicts become, the more the lower class starts ignoring *laloua*.

At the time in question, the first gesture of the exploiter class was to have the lower class beaten up. Everyone knows that if Ti Piè doesn't follow *laloua*, he goes to prison. That's one thing. But they can't put a whole class in prison. So if the lower class keeps on resisting, the class in power has two options:

1. It can further tighten the *kòd* to avoid giving the lower class any breathing room, like what happened in Chile,[5] for example.
2. It can lengthen the *kòd* to mislead the lower class, to make the lower class think it can go where it wants to. But that's bogus, the *kòd*'s never untied, it just gets longer, like how it's done in New York,[6] for example.

Between 1700 and 1791 in Saint-Domingue, the upper classes (the powerful colonists) tried to play with the *kòd* like a little child that loses control of his kite in a whirlwind. They let it loose, they pulled it back, and they pouted. Nothing worked. They pulled harder on the *kòd*. They showed up with articles even stricter than the *Kòd Noua*. But the conflicts were still stewing, and the class that they were exploiting was not just any kite! It was a kite with razor blades on its tail! In 1791, what happened? The tail of the kite broke the *kòd*.

Do you want to know how that happened? Do you want me to tell you, my friends, what kind of hurricane Hazel[7] went through Saint-Domingue? Well, sit down, and listen … Lamèsi, give me another spot of cotton tea. All these ideas call for reflection …

---

5 This refers to the brutal authoritarian dictatorship in Chile (1973–90) that began on September 11, 1973, when the government of democratically elected president, Salvador Allende, was toppled by a CIA-backed military coup led by General Augusto Pinochet. Widespread political repression and persecutions followed.
6 *Ti difé boulé sou istoua Ayiti* (*Stirring the Pot of Haitian History*) was written in New York City, where—as mentioned by Lyonel Trouillot in the Preface—Michel-Rolph Trouillot and his siblings participated in anti-Duvalier activist efforts.
7 Hurricane Hazel struck Haiti in 1954 and left more than 1,000 dead in its wake.

3. Keep reading and you'll understand

Jakomèl, you have the authority
you have the authority
minister Zaka
but there's no justice!
You'll lend me a chair
so I can sit down
so I can take a look
so I can watch them ...

Primary school teachers instruct all schoolchildren that there were three classes in Saint-Domingue: WHITES, SLAVES, AND FREEDMEN. And it's not the teachers' fault ... That's what they learned at school, and that's what's written in the book. But if you think about it, my friends, you'll see that names of classes are out of sync. When someone shows me a white person, I don't yet know what that white person contributes to society. Is he a merchant? Is he a teacher? Are merchants and teachers the same? No. So when people say WHITE or MULATTO, they tell you the person's **RACE**, or what his **COLOR** is, but they haven't yet told you his **CLASS**.

Sometimes people say, 'freed slave' (or freedmen) instead of 'mulatto'. That's not bad, they're making progress. But that term's still not totally right. When I hear that Jacques is a 'free man', I know he's not a slave. But I still don't know if he goes around begging or if he moves merchandise. He's a free man, okay. Is he a shoemaker? Does he own a plantation? Are shoemakers the same as plantation owners? No. So when people say **freed slave** or **freedman**, they tell you the person's legal status, but they haven't yet told you what work he does within the society he lives in. They haven't told you what CLASS he's in.

By the same token, I don't know if you recognize the tribulations with students' (and teachers') education [in Haiti]—how many beatings they endure (and inflict) to learn a whole litany of lies.

one island, two countries

It's one thing to dismiss people's social class, and another thing entirely to identify what classes actually existed in Saint-Domingue. The first effort we must make is to carefully figure out how the society operated: which industries were profitable, where the money came from to start those businesses, and into whose pockets the profits went.

The whites from France occupied Saint-Domingue from around 1625 onward. But the island was never legally theirs. Christopher Columbus took it over in 1492. At the time Christopher Columbus was working for Spain, so the island supposedly belonged to Spain. But after the Spanish had finished stealing all the indigenous peoples' land, Hispaniola—that's what they called Haiti—didn't interest them much anymore. Little by little the Spanish cleared out, and French colonists started pushing in further. In 1697 Spain signed a deed giving part of the island to France, the part that is our country today. The other part, which Spain kept, is what we call the Dominican Republic today.

The piece of paper that Spain gave to France in 1697 in the village of Ryswick[8] is important because it gave the French colonists free rein and complete license in Saint-Domingue. It was the first time the land of Caonabo[9] got divided, and that scalpel cut would traverse our entire history along with the history of the Dominican people. That scalpel cut would make Dominican blood flow under Boyer, under Souloque[10] ... That scalpel cut ripped open the guts of Haitian laborers under Trujillo, under Balaguer[11] ... That scalpel cut has been chasing us up to the present day because there are troublemakers who want us to see the Dominican **people** as our enemy.

one, two, three plantations ...

The 1697 agreement gave France the green light to exploit the section of Hispaniola that the Spaniards had left to the pirates and buccaneers. Thus, at the start of the 1700s, Saint-Domingue looked completely different.

8 In the Treaty of Ryswick (1697), signed within what was at the time the Dutch Republic, Spain formally recognized France's control over the island of Tortuga and the western third of Hispaniola, where the colony of Saint-Domingue had been established by French settlers.
9 Caonabo (d. 1496), of the Maguana nation, was an indigenous Taíno chief on Hispaniola. Supported by his wife Anacaona (who became legendary because of her resistance to the Spanish and her choice of execution over surrender), he attacked Columbus at Punta Flecha (1493) and was subsequently captured and sent to Spain; he died in a shipwreck.
10 Jean-Pierre Boyer (1776–1850) was one of the leaders of the Haitian Revolution, and he served as President of Haiti from 1818 to 1843. After the 1806–10 civil war that had split the north and south of Haiti, Boyer unified the country in 1820. In 1822 his armies occupied Santo Domingo, the eastern part of Hispaniola, unifying the island under Haitian rule until his ouster from the presidency in 1843. Faustin Souloque (1782–1867), elected President of Haiti in 1847, had himself proclaimed Haiti's Emperor, as Faustin I, in 1849. During his reign, Souloque organized a black noble class and sought to take control of the Dominican Republic, without success; General Fabre Nicolas Geffrard ousted him in 1859.
11 Rafael Leónidas Trujillo de Molina (1891–1961) ruled the Dominican Republic from 1930 to 1961; his abuse of power led to some of the most violent episodes in Caribbean history, including the 1937 massacre of some 25,000 Haitian laborers in the border region. Trujillo was assassinated in 1961. Joaquín Balaguer (1906–2002), a close supporter of Trujillo, was himself elected President of the Dominican Republic seven times. He published numerous volumes of poetry and history, many of which contained racist and anti-Haitian discourses.

Plantation owners stopped planting cacao. Instead of continuing to plant a lot of indigo, cotton, coffee, and vegetables, most of them started imitating Portuguese and Dutch colonists who were planting sugarcane in Brazil. They planted sugarcane, they planted sugarcane, and they planted sugarcane. They didn't plant just a little. All the other crops declined. They built mills on the plantations, they bought cauldrons to produce sugar. The importers living in France happily invested their money in sugar coming out of Saint-Domingue. In the blink of an eye the country's industry was transformed. In 1717 there were 100 sugar cane mills in Saint-Domingue. In 1724 (seven years later) Cape Haitian alone had 200. In 1789 there were around 800 plantations based on the sugarcane business. As a result, whites stole land from one another. A plantation worthy of the name was never smaller than 319 acres. There were plantations measuring around 1,595 acres! Furthermore, a sugarcane field couldn't be maintained by just one or two slaves. Soon enough the French went looking for more in Guinea, in the Congo, Dahomey, Angola, and many other African countries. In 1680 there were 2,000 slaves in Saint-Domingue. In 1700 (twenty years later) there were 20,000 slaves (ten times more). In 1726 there were 100,000. In 1789 there were around 600,000 slaves working like mules in Saint-Domingue from five o'clock in the morning until eleven o'clock at night!

the joker doesn't win the game

In truth, the sugar industry changed the face of Saint-Domingue.

1. one **single** commodity replaced a lot of others
2. **big plantations** replaced **a lot of** smaller plantations
3. there were more **sugar mills**
4. there were more **slaves** (indentured workers disappeared)
5. the slaves worked **harder**.

But that didn't mean the cards had gotten reshuffled. It didn't mean a revolution had happened, either. To the contrary. All change is change, but not all changes are the same. Every change of clothes is not a revolution. Instead of improving Saint-Domingue's situation, the changes that happened only helped the upper classes get richer. Plantations got bigger, and slaves worked harder.

Still, high school teachers call that period the 'Sugarcane Revolution'. I never understood why. Did the sugarcane stalks arise and carry out a revolution? Did the class that was controlling the country collapse?

Because a revolution is when the class that's been controlling the country collapses, and another class rises: 1789 in France, 1804 in Haiti. Is it called a 'revolution' when the upper class maintains its own power with its own money? Is that what 'Sugarcane Revolution' means; 'Industrial Revolution'; 'scientific revolution'; 'electronic revolution'; 'revolution here, revolution there'? Or has a **revolution** become a skeleton key like the joker in the bezique card game, that lets any old 40-point set of jacks get onto the table? Luckily, the joker doesn't win the game …

hereditary illness

But let's leave that aside and come back to reality … In truth, the sugar plantation system appeared in Saint-Domingue with specific features:

1. BIG PLANTATIONS
This feature drags a big problem along with it: there can't be many little fields, and the people working the land can't enjoy the benefits of their work within the system.

2. SLAVERY
Slavery is a characteristically Brazilian system. For sugar plantations to be profitable, **there must be many laborers working like mules**. At the time, slavery was the easiest way the white colonists could get lots of laborers to toil away for free! The big Portuguese landowners who launched the system in Brazil went around saying: 'If there weren't any slaves, there wouldn't be any sugar, if there weren't any sugar, there'd be no Brazil'. Likewise, if there weren't any slaves, Saint-Domingue wouldn't be Saint-Domingue.

3. COMMODITY CROPS
Sugarcane fields take up a lot of space. Sugar mills do too. All in all, they're very profitable. Also, when the sugar plantation system takes shape in a country, plantation owners don't have any **room** or **interest** in planting other crops on their land. They don't plant any vegetables at all.

4. DEPENDENCE
But if a country plants only sugarcane (or only sugarcane and coffee), it's not destined for native farmers. The country must sell the sugar (and coffee) abroad. It must buy most of the goods that

the native farmers need from **abroad**. It's inevitably at the mercy of the big countries who are selling them those goods.

The pirates and buccaneers didn't overrun Saint-Domingue so the French bourgeoisie could reap all the benefits. But once the sugar plantation system took shape, Saint-Domingue was completely under the control of the French bourgeoisie. They sent commissioners to keep order, sell slaves, sell goods, and buy sugar.

These words are very important! In order to set up this plantation system within a country:

- there must be big plantations
- there must be slaves (or free people laboring like slaves)
- the country mustn't plant lots of different crops, and it mustn't plant vegetables
- it must be under the control of other countries.

These ailments were in the system starting in 1570, when it started developing in Brazil. Those ailments are still there in Brazil, in Colombia, and in Haiti, etc., wherever the *engenhos*[12] system continued, even if it came into fashion, wherever it left its stamp, even if the society's not exactly like 1600s Brazil or 1700s Saint-Domingue.

easy, driver …

Now we've discovered the **primary industry** of Saint-Domingue: plant sugarcane, make sugar, sell sugar. We've seen the industry's four features and all the problems they drag behind them. So, in fact, we're getting closer to seeing the **primary conflict** in the society of Saint-Domingue and the social classes living out this conflict. **The primary conflict in a society is rooted in that society's primary industry. It bears that industry's features and it can't disappear unless the society is completely overturned.**

Let's look back at the primary industry's features:

Feature number one: big plantations
Feature number two: slavery

12 'Sugar mill', in Portuguese.

In fact, within these two features we find two of the classes living out the primary conflicts in Saint-Domingue. If there are 'big plantations', there must be **big plantation owners**, and if there's 'slavery' that means there are **slaves**.

Thus, among the classes that were contesting Saint-Domingue's primary conflict, there were:

1. Slaves; people who produced sugar (and coffee), planted sugarcane, worked mills, and boiled syrup
2. Owners of the (big) plantations; people who profited from the sugar, who were forcing the slaves to work on the plantations.

You can now easily see that it's a mistake to think of **whites** as a **class**. You'd be sidestepping the primary conflict, because **whites weren't all plantation owners and plantation owners weren't all white**. You'd also miss the hidden conflicts entangled with the primary conflict. But the hidden conflicts are important. They're no less important than the primary conflict. Don't you believe me?

If someone points out Philogène's truck, the one that makes trips from Port-au-Prince to Cape Haitian, and they ask you which of the truck's parts is most important, like the motor, the steering wheel, or the brakes, what are you going to say? Don't answer, because they're trying to trap you. It's true, the motor gives the truck the power to climb Mount Puilboreau, but without the steering wheel and the brakes, that power's not useful at all. The truck would fall off a cliff! So the bundle of hidden conflicts is like the steering wheel and the brakes on Philogène's truck. The day they start fraying, the primary conflicts collapse.

hit the brakes!

So it's all well and good for us to identify two classes contesting the primary conflict. But we must dig deeper into the trough. We must find out what other classes were operating in Saint-Domingue's society. And we must look within the classes to be able to situate each **group** within its role, within the specific category where it serves its class. Because a social class is like a soccer team: it contains several groups.

The (big) plantation owners' class had two groups:

1. white plantation owners
2. mulatto plantation owners.

Some white plantation owners crossed over to France to go enjoy their money, and to start businesses with their profits. Most mulatto plantation owners lived in Saint-Domingue.

if a poor mulatto is black is a rich mulatto white?

You shouldn't be surprised if I come back to the words 'white', 'mulatto', 'freedman'. We don't use those words to define a social **class**. We use those terms to say what group they belong to within the same social class. Because within a given class there are always several categories. There are always a few hidden tensions stewing. Plantation owners in Saint-Domingue didn't have the same opinions (or the same interests) on various issues. Whites who owned plantations hated the rich mulattos. And the day the party got wrecked in Saint-Domingue, the white plantation owners didn't travel the same path as their comrades, mulatto plantation owners. Neither one followed the path of their class, but rather the path of a specific category within the class of plantation owners.

There were lots of **hidden conflicts** within the society of Saint-Domingue, and it's because all the conflicts frayed, the steering wheel didn't work, and the brakes didn't engage, that Philogène's truck crashed on the first of January 1804.[13]

all slaves are slaves but not all slaves are the same

Just as plantation owners weren't all the same, slaves weren't all the same either. It's true, most of them worked in fields and mills, but there were lots of other categories, and it's because of those categories that a lot of the uprisings happened the way they did. There were **domestic slaves**. Some of them had trades under their belts. They heard the owners talking. They knew something of the goings-on in other countries. There were also **overseers** who beat their fellow slaves, but who had more leeway to run through the woods because whites paid less attention to them.

---

13 Philogène's truck personifies French colonialism in Saint-Domingue. On January 1, 1804, Jean-Jacques Dessalines declared Haiti's independence from France.

There were **urban slaves** who knew the value of money because they worked as shoemakers, tinsmiths, cooks, masons ...

These categories are very important because they explain a lot of questions in the History of Haiti. Where did the leaders of the revolution come from? Why were Boukman, Toussaint, and Biassou[14] among the standard-bearers? Why, out of all the leaders, were they the ones who rose to the top? Why did they overtake the maroons? Why, when they came to power, did the rest of the former slaves get upset?

Well, we shouldn't be afraid to admit it: because they had connections, the urban slaves and the domestic slaves were better informed than the others, but it was **their position in society** that allowed them to learn more than the others. For example, they learned to enjoy freedom.

What happened? Is anyone surprised? You don't think they 'learned' to enjoy freedom? Well, you don't understand the system they called slavery. When a people are in a situation in which they can't even blink an eye without getting beaten, when generations have grown up and died under that tyranny, under rules like the *Kòd Noua* that kept slaves from gathering even for wedding ceremonies, the day comes when the people forget the taste of freedom. Careful, that's not to say they like their fate! It means that twenty-year-old men and women had never gotten to experience freedom in any capacity, or say what they wanted about rich folks, even if it was true. The situation was wretched, but you shouldn't believe it didn't exist, because it answers a lot of questions about the History of our country. But also, a situation like that couldn't last forever. There's no prayer without an 'Amen'. For the system to be sustained, the kite had to fly. That's why overseers had to have a longer *kòd* ... But once a zombie tastes salt, Bois-Neuf looks different. Indeed, when slaves who knew trades started fluttering their wings, when urban slaves heard what was happening in other countries, when people saw how rich folks lived, the desire for freedom grew. There's no denying that.

---

14 Boukman Dutty was a Jamaican-born Vodou priest who led the Bwa Kayiman Vodou ceremony that launched the Haitian Revolution in August 1791. Toussaint Louverture (1743–1803) was a Haitian revolutionary leader and the Governor-General of Saint-Domingue between July 7, 1801 and May 6, 1802. He published his own Constitution in 1801. Georges Biassou (1741–1801) was one of the original Haitian revolutionary leaders. He fought against France on the side of the Spanish, was defeated by Louverture, and then left Saint-Domingue for Florida.

there are no small sins in history

And so, in Saint-Domingue, a lot of revolutionary leaders were in the category of slaves who'd begun to know and enjoy their freedom again. Boukman was a former coachman, a former overseer. Toussaint had been a courtyard watchman and ultimately became a coach driver. He came and went between plantation and town. What's more, his owner eventually made him responsible for the work of all the other domestic workers, a job often held by whites on certain plantations … Lots of the overseers from Morne Rouge, Linbé, and Lacul resembled Boukman, and Bryan Edwards[15] said: '**Most of the leaders (rebel slaves) had been domestic workers with better positions than the rest. They were born and raised right under the owner's nose, in their family's house**'.

We must think carefully about this because there's a contradiction hidden under the fancy clothes. It's because of their superior position that domestic slaves, urban slaves, and overseers were able to lead the others. And if today we're asking serious questions, if we're squeezing the sores to get out the pus, we shouldn't fear this fact. This is not to say that urban slaves, domestic slaves, and overseers were more revolutionary. This is also not to say that for a slave to join the revolution he had to have groveled at whites' feet. We shouldn't forget that **the primary conflicts were what pushed Philogène's truck**. It's the field slaves and skilled slaves who were the revolution's engine. Likewise, the other slaves got themselves involved, in their own way, according to their specific position within the society.

If we consider what recently happened in Vietnam and Cambodia,[16] we see that many former sergeants from the reactionary army joined the revolutionary camp. That doesn't mean that they weren't real sergeants. Yet, with no majors, there aren't any sergeants, and it's not every day that sergeants break away from majors … History has no minor sins.

History has no minor sins, but the cat that falls into hot water rushes to find cold water. Those who aren't on their toes can get left behind. My

---

15 The bibliography of *Ti difé boulé sou istoua Ayiti* includes a title by Bryan Edwards: *A Historical Survey of the French Colony of San Domingo* (1797). Bryan Edwards (1743–1800) was a witness to the events in Saint-Domingue between the years of 1789 and 1794 (Library of Congress from wdl.org).
16 From 1975 to 1979, Cambodia's Khmer Rouge regime, led by Pol Pot (and assisted by North Vietnam), sought to establish Stalinist policies in the country that resulted in a genocide which left nearly three million people dead.

friends, we know that every contradiction has two sides. We must now look at the flip side of these words.

A category or a class with more political awareness stands a good chance of taking charge of a revolution. But at the same time, it's also likely to take advantage of others. At the end of the game, it also stands a good chance of running away with the ball in order to form its own personal team … That's why, in many revolutions, certain classes and categories reappear, with masks on their faces, to enjoy the advantages they'd dreamed about before the battle grew hot. That's what happened in Saint-Domingue. Under Toussaint's government, a group of former domestic slaves and urban slaves, combined with some other people from other classes (artisans, plantation owners), started seizing power. This seizure of power lasted throughout the war for independence. The jackpot was won on the people's backs. Therefore, when we hear people cheering: long live the 'middle class', long live 'progressive intellectuals', long live 'experts', we shouldn't forget for a moment that those people are counterparts to the domestic slaves, urban slaves, and artisans in Saint-Domingue … They're anxious to take the lead, but nobody's ever sure where they're leading the band.

ace marble players don't stay in the circle

'-Krik?
-Krak!'

Once upon a time there was a little boy watching a marble game. But instead of watching the circle and the marbles inside it at the starting line with all the other marbles, he'd been keeping his eye on the top marbles from the start of the game. That one, hit. That one, knocked out. That one, out of the game. His eyes never left the top marbles. Well, what happened in the end? The game ended, and he didn't even notice. To be sure, each time the top marbles scored points, he saw another marble leave the circle. But he never tried to tell how many marbles there were overall, or how many marbles were still there. Because his eye was glued to the top marbles, the game took place right in front of him and he couldn't make heads or tails of it.

Likewise, when we look at dog-eat-dog tendencies surfacing in a society, if we only focus on the top marbles, we're not going to understand anything about the game itself.

People who are ace marble players never stay crouched down the whole time. From time to time they take a little break, they watch, they step back, they watch again, and they wipe their hands on the ground. It's not for nothing. If someone wants to understand, they must watch the whole game, from beginning to end. All the beautiful marble moves rest on the difficulties of the circumstances.

In Saint-Domingue, there were lots of people who weren't top marbles, but they played in the game. They didn't have plantations, and they weren't big traders, but they weren't slaves either. They weren't the ones managing the system, but they weren't the ones carrying the load either. Just about any society has a lot of people like that, who are neither on the bottom nor at the top. They're called the **middle class** because they sit in between. The middle class has its own features: it's always coming up short. The system allows it to live, but it could always live even better. It feeds on the leftovers of the upper class but bears the burdens of the lower class. It's at the center of the argument going on within the primary conflict. This position is crucial because the middle class plays in the game with both major social classes. Each one was pulling on one end of the *kòd*, and the middle class was smack in the center. It was like a double-edged sword: the candy was theirs, and the soap was theirs, but the room they stood in wasn't theirs ...

In Saint-Domingue, the middle class consisted of whites, mulattos, and blacks: carpenters, barbers, police, masons, minor State employees, washerwomen, coast guards, and seamstresses ... If we look closely, that's a range of professions, but they form a single class because all those jobs have the same features: they aren't the ones in the society's primary industry, but they must be there for society to be sustained. **The middle class's labor is a tangle of activities that allow the primary industry to continue.** The middle class isn't **peripheral**, its efforts are intertwined with the primary industry. There must be carpenters to build the mills, there must be mechanics for factories to function, there must be police to clown around, there must be teachers to make us obey, there must be doctors to tell us what ailments we suffer from. Which is to say, society drops a lot of burdens on the back of the middle class so the upper class has free time to go enjoy their money and so the lower class has free time to go work like mules.

On account of this circumstance, of being stuck in the position of coming up short, the middle class is constantly stewing.

In Saint-Domingue, the middle class had its own hidden contradictions. It harbored heaps of prejudices. Mulattos hated blacks, blacks hated mulattos, and whites hated both. The middle class's prejudices were always stronger than those of the other classes, because a middle-class white or mulatto person knew that by appearance alone, they had an advantage over a black person in the same position. In the same way, even now, many light-skinned women exploit their light skin color to cross the threshold into wealth. And some neighbors have told me: a lot of men do the same thing.

... But that's not all. The middle class didn't just have its own hidden problems, it also had a problem with the other classes. Black people and mulattos looked down on the other classes, but at the same time, they hated the fortune of plantation owners and big traders. And quite a few middle-class blacks were there alongside the slave masses from the very start of the war against the colonists.

In the same way, **middle-class whites didn't always side with the big landowners or big foreign traders**. To the contrary, they were continually struggling, and they were helping sustain the system. Many educated people call middle-class whites *petits blancs* (little whites). (We also call them **po' white folk**.)

you'll take me
for everything
I've got ...

Let's go back over what we've learned before going further.

We've learned there were two classes in Saint-Domingue who were disputing the primary conflict: the **plantation owners** exploiting the **slaves**. We also see that at the center of the struggle there was a **middle class** out of kilter. We recognize a tangle of conflicts:

1. the primary conflict within the society:
   plantation owners versus slaves
2. the hidden social conflict:
   middle class versus slaves
   middle class versus plantation owners ...
3. the hidden class conflicts:
   big plantation owners versus small plantation owners
   urban slaves versus field slaves
   lower middle-class whites versus middle-class blacks, etc.

But are those all the classes? There's no work within a society that isn't the work of a class. There's no position which lacks the features of

3. Keep reading and you'll understand   33

its class. The plantation owners' feature was the land they had and the slaves they were exploiting. However, a lot of *grands blancs* in Saint-Domingue didn't have the features of that class. Either they sold slaves to plantation owners, supplies and other goods that they sent abroad, or they collected plantation owners' commodity crops to send to France, or they conveyed the orders France sent to plantation owners and the middle class. Whether they were traders, warehouse managers, lawyers, or army generals, they were in Saint-Domingue to make society function the way France wanted it to. In all truth there weren't many of those people, but their work made them so particular, their **position** so distinct, we can't lump them together with plantation owners. We must try to see if they didn't have their own features.

seven-headed serpent

> Collect Saint-Domingue's sugar **bound for France**,
> bring products **from France**,
> transport slaves **on France's behalf**,
> impose order within Saint-Domingue **for France** …

All these industries bore the same features on their foreheads: the features of **French interests**, the features of the **CLASS** interests controlling France.

Therefore, in Saint-Domingue there was a group of big shots whose positions weren't equal and who didn't have the same interests as the plantation owners. Their work was to serve as **commissioners** for France, either in **business** or **politics**. Their interests lay in sustaining the kind of social order that France favored because their profits depended upon the provision of these services.

A commissioner class was never native-born because it had its seven heads abroad. Long ago, those heads rested in France: Bordeaux, La Rochelle, Saint-Malo, Paris … Today they're in Washington, Montreal, Tel Aviv, Tokyo, Bonn, Paris …

In Saint-Domingue there were two types of officials:

- economic commissioners (high-up officials, big traders, and warehouse bosses)
- political commissioners (governors, army generals, and political leaders)

all the port's power is abroad[17]

Among the economic commissioners, the big traders were central because they headed the industries of Saint-Domingue. It's true, they didn't own plantations, and they didn't plant sugar or coffee. But **they were the ones who sold sugar and coffee to France**. It's true, they didn't have lots of slaves working like mules for them, but **they were the ones who sold slaves to plantation owners in Saint-Domingue**. It's true, they weren't directing the primary industry **in the fields and mills**, but without them the primary industry was meaningless, and they enjoyed the country's profits even more than plantation owners did.

How did this come about? Where did the Port get so much power that big landowners allowed it to run things? Why did the class that had the primary industry in its clutches let big traders seize control of it?

These aren't simple words. The road is narrow. And when the road's narrow, we must ask questions: it's by asking questions that they catch the wild horse. Little, easy questions like water ...

What did Saint-Domingue produce? Sugar, right? Who bought the sugar? France, right? The capitalist traders in Bordeaux, Le Havre, Marseilles, La Rochelle, Saint-Malo ... And who worked as salespeople for those people on the island? The Port traders, right?

And so, even though plantation owners controlled the sugar industry within the fields and mills, they had to bow down to big traders because the big traders had France backing them, and France was buying the sugar.

It's when we identify the serpent's seven heads that we learn why its tail is so long ... All the Port's power is abroad.

What do you call a donkey's mother?

But, the way I see the Port's power, if the Port's power is abroad, just imagine how powerful the foreigners are!

In fact, if the commissioner class was able to control Saint-Domingue's plantation owners, **it's because Saint-Domingue itself was under France's control**.

---

17 This refers to the central harbor areas in Cape Haitian and downtown Port-au-Prince.

1. When a society produces things to serve foreigners,
2. when the foreign commissioner class has free rein over the country,
3. **that society is under foreign control**. It might have a declaration of independence in its pocket, and it might have the legal right to appoint any governing section chiefs, but if its economy—how money is made, and how money is divided up in the country—is under foreign control, like it or not, the society isn't totally **independent**. Accordingly, if it's not **independent**, we can't say it's independent. Let's not lie to ourselves, okay? If it **answers to** another, we call it **dependent**. Don't you agree? What do you call a donkey's mother? A donkey! A dependent society answers to the other country (or several other countries) that's controlling it.

Dependence/control comes about in two ways.

1. Either the society has a declaration of independence in its hand (in that case, economic control is official, but political control is secret),
2. or the society totally lacks self-government. In that case, the commissioner class has the specific role of giving orders to the country on behalf of foreign powers.

Saint-Domingue had no autonomy. It was totally dependent, whether in words or on paper. As a result, the COMMISSIONER CLASSES consisted of two distinct categories forming the sole State in Saint-Domingue: **big bureaucrats** pushing pencils and **big military types**. Those men were there to help traders turn a profit for France. They were the ones making laws in Saint-Domingue, whatever laws France desired.

twin[18] plantains ...

My friends, I'm going to see if you remember. We've discovered another class within the society of Saint-Domingue. We've seen the power that class holds, both in the country's economy and in its politics. We've seen

---

18 The Haitian Creole term *marasa* refers to the patron *lwa* of twins in Vodou and, by extension, to biological twins in general. In reference to twins, *marasa* coexists with the French-derived words *jimo* (male twin) and *jimèl* (female twin).

that this is the class who's selling **the country's main commodity crops** to France. We've seen that this is the class who's keeping the country **under France's control**. What does that remind you of? Two more features of the primary industry:

Feature number three: **commodity crops**
Feature number four: **dependence**.

Therefore, the **commissioner classes who** sold the main commodity crops to foreign countries, who kept the country under foreign control, were enmeshed with the features of the society's primary industry, just as were the plantation owner classes and the slave classes. And so, just like the two other classes, **it was a primary class**. The conflict between this class and the producer class (slaves) is a conflict within the roots of the society. It's a conflict that can't be eliminated if the society's foundations don't change. It's a conflict that's enmeshed with the slave versus plantation owner conflict, **and it's atop this entanglement that society is situated**.

In Saint-Domingue, the primary conflict was a conflict between slaves versus **plantation owners AND commissioners**.
In Saint-Domingue the primary conflict was a **twin conflict**.

twin limes ...

A twin (primary) conflict isn't just two single conflicts stuck together.
When you get a twin lime, what do you have in your hands? A single lime or two limes? You'd be wrong to say it's a single lime because it has two pieces, two inner parts ... But it's not two limes either ... two single pieces that aren't quite round. Each one's notched on the side to connect with the other one: it's the two **together** that make a whole. They're in the same skin, they're stuck both together and to the rest of the cluster, **you can't pick one without picking the other, and you can't peel one without peeling the other**.
Therefore, a twin lime is neither a single lime nor two limes stuck together. It's **a specific lime** that has

1. a specific form (it's swollen)
2. a specific size (it's bigger)
3. a specific feature (it's simultaneously one and two)

3. Keep reading and you'll understand   37

twin conflict

In a dependent society, when the primary conflict has two parts that are completely attached to the primary industry and to each other, so totally attached that you can't handle either one without handling the other, and you can't handle both of them without society capsizing, that's a **twin primary conflict**.

The primary conflict in Saint-Domingue was a double conflict: slaves versus plantation owners and French commissioners. Commissioners and plantation owners were joined together to exploit slaves, so the slaves' war against plantation owners was joined to the war against commissioners. And by the same token, their war against commissioners was joined to the war against plantation owners. And this twin battle was the one and only battle that could overturn Saint-Domingue completely. The slavery versus freedom conflict was joined to the dependence versus independence conflict, and both bore the primary industry's features.

all control comes from an invisible hand

It's true, the plantation owners' power was more visible than the commissioners' power. But when we trace that power, we find the tip of its head in Marseilles, Bordeaux, and La Rochelle ... and we discover the seven-headed serpent. The section chief's power isn't rooted in the section chief's specific role. All control comes from an invisible hand.

While traders and big landowners were fighting each other, they had to work together to exploit the slaves. While the big landowners were wrangling with France, they also had to lean on France, and they had to share power with the French commissioners. This balance wasn't easy, but that's where power resided in Saint-Domingue. And for a whole century, the commissioners and plantation owners maintained this balance. They reared up and they stooped over. They swung and they crouched. They stayed hunched over so they wouldn't lose ground.

Then, one day, a rumor ran through the streets of Cape Haitian. Saint-Domingue's solid block cracked. Plantation owners went over the edge, commissioners got scared, the middle class dug in, and slaves set things afire ...

A revolution was starting.

4. Fire in the house

Ago blows and blows
he blows the Nor'easter
he blows the Sou'wester
Ago rumbles and rumbles
Ago rumbles a thunderstorm
he blows and blows
Ago comes from Guinea
he blows and rumbles.

On the twenty-second day of August, in 1791, a massive whirlwind rose up on Haitian soil. A group of slaves in the northern region, on the **Tipine, Flaville, Clément, Noyé**, and **Gallifèt** plantations, broke the *kòd* of slavery and launched an offensive against colonists. In the blink of an eye, fire engulfed cane fields from **Morne Rouge** all the way to **Trou Bordette**. Traders and big landowners were caught in a tight spot. They asked Americans for help: zilch. They asked the middle class for help: zilch. They cried out for help from France: zero, zip, zippo.

On the twenty-second day of August, in 1791, a whirlwind rose up and wouldn't stop. A whirlwind that tangled its way across thirteen fiery years before reaching 1804.[19]

How did that war begin? What winds and ideas intensified it? How did slaves manage to turn Saint-Domingue upside down? What makes a revolution take hold?

For us to understand how slaves overturned Saint-Domingue, we must recognize the extent to which Saint-Domingue was swaying precariously.

A dog-eat-dog society is rooted in conflict. Therefore, to stay in power, the upper classes had to perform a constant balancing act. To keep that balance, they had to lean on other social classes and groups that could help them hold enough weight to stay in power. That didn't mean there were no conflicts between all those classes. It meant that the class at the very top (or the classes at the very top) exploited all the other conflicts that the classes and groups in the middle had with the very lowest class.

In any society, the primary conflict carries the most weight. Therefore, to maintain stability, the upper class must strike a balance with a lot of hidden conflicts. It leans on them to get strong enough to establish its own power. Which is to say, it forms a **solid coalition** to help it crush the lower class. Sometimes it forms several **coalitions**; that builds up its power even more.

---

19 As noted in Chapter 3, revolutionary leader Jean-Jacques Dessalines declared Haiti's independence from France on January 1, 1804, a date commonly referenced as an endpoint for the Haitian Revolution. Most contemporary accounts of the Haitian Revolution acknowledge that 1804 in no way marked an absolute conclusion, given that widespread social and political unrest prevailed in Haiti for several decades to come. For his part, Trouillot proposes 1820, the year of the fall of King Henri Christophe, as a closing date for the revolutionary era. Other scholars and historians have questioned whether the formation of the Haitian 'republic' preceded Dessalines's declaration, and whether a 'unified republic' was ushered in by Jean-Pierre Boyer (who served as president from 1818–43).

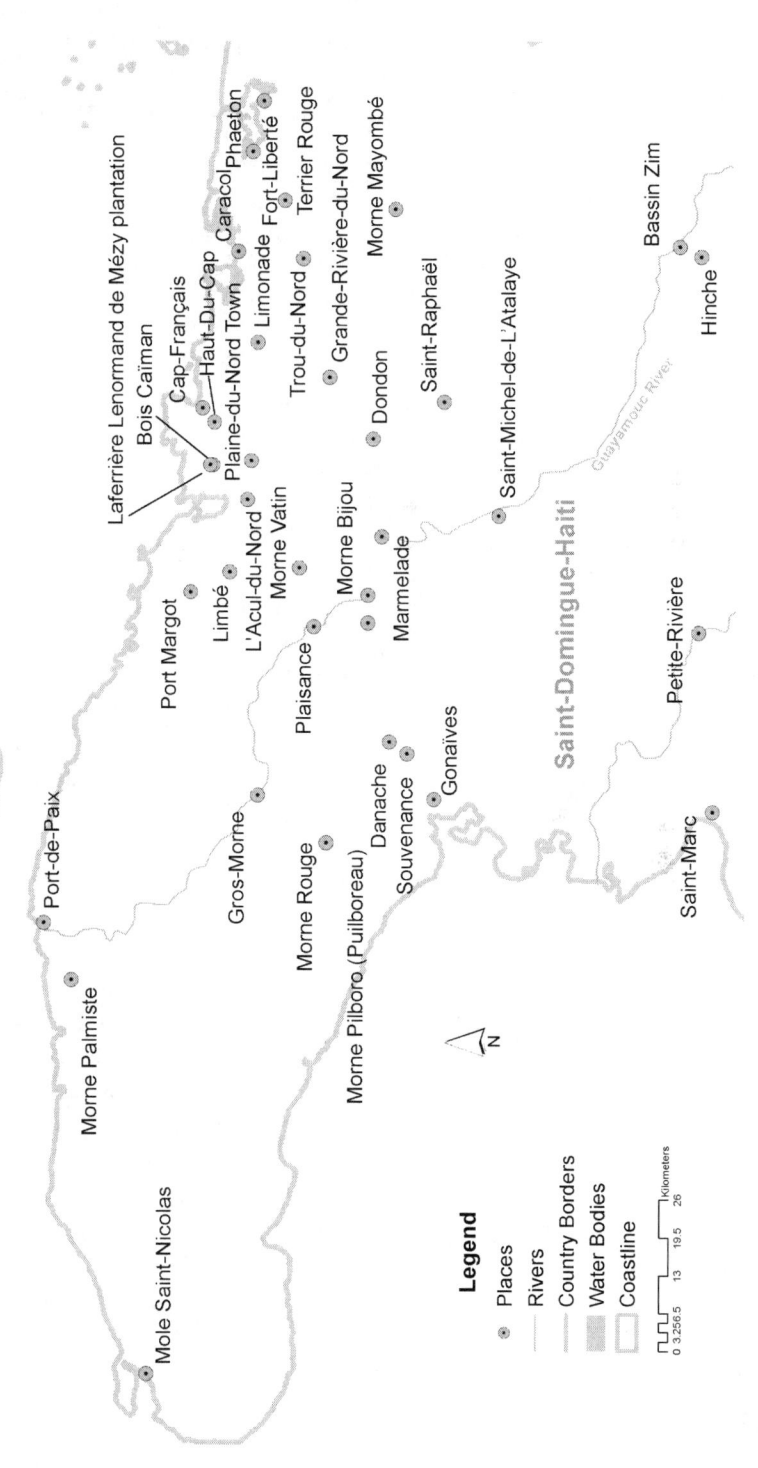

Saint-Domingue-Haiti, North, circa 1600–1810.

Map by Joe Aufmuth, Geospatial Consultant, University of Florida's George A. Smathers Libraries, 2020. Map depicts populated places. Water Bodies obtained from Open Street Map (© openstreetmap.org + contributors). Coastline, rivers, and country boundaries obtained from NOAA.

What solid coalition did plantation owners and French commissioners succeed in forming in Saint-Domingue?

1/THE BIG COLONISTS' COALITION

Saint-Domingue was a **dependent** society. In every dependent society, the class that's directing the primary industry must ally itself with the foreign commissioner class. In any dependent society, the class that's controlling basic production can't fully exploit the people without the foreign commissioners. That coalition is **unlike any other** scheme the upper classes can cook up. **It's a vital coalition**; no dependent society can exist without it. And since most of those societies are in agriculture-based countries, most dependent societies have a coalition between big landowners and big traders. The day that coalition got split up, society overturned, and another society rose up. By the same token, **the primary conflict couldn't be overturned if this coalition wasn't overturned**.

So, for plantation owners and commissioners to maintain power in Saint-Domingue, they had to form a coalition: the Coalition of Big Colonists. Power resided in that solid block. With France's blessing, the colonists schemed to appoint the society's head. The police were theirs, the money was theirs, and the law was theirs. Big Colonists were the same thing as the State.

2/THE FREE COALITION

Saint-Domingue's society was based on slavery. The class at the lowest end of the primary conflict was a **slave** class. Therefore, besides the twin primary conflict (slaves versus Big Colonists), there was **another** conflict between **free and enslaved** people. Slaves had interests that no free people could have whether they be white, black, traders, or skilled workers: **slaves had an interest in becoming free one day.**

What's more, besides the coalition they already had, the big colonists put another coalition in place: the FREE coalition, so they could form a massive and solid team against the slaves. The free coalition included French commissioners, white and mulatto plantation owners, and the middle classes (whether white, mulatto, or black). That coalition gave the big landowners and French commissioners a whole stream of services. It helped them push the middle class into a lower rank. It hemmed in the

42 *Stirring the Pot of Haitian History*

middle class to form a mass to control the slaves more effectively. It also helped keep the primary conflict out of sight. When someone looked at that coalition, he'd think the central struggle was a struggle of free people versus slaves. I say that's wrong, totally wrong! There were slaves because there were **slave owners**. There were slaves because the foreign commissioners needed donkeys to work so the rich could gallivant around.

Corralling the colonists and all the free people into this coalition served to pit slaves against all the middle-class groups, be they whites, mulattos, blacks, soldiers, or skilled workers.

In fact, besides the primary conflict, EVERY SOCIETY (every social formation) HAS ITS OWN FEATURES, THAT IS, HOW AND IN WHAT WAY DIFFERENT COALITIONS PUT PRESSURE ON THE PRIMARY CONFLICT.

It's the way distinct coalitions, distinct classes and groups combine to resist the primary conflict, it's the way social formations keep their balance, and the way distinct social forces get enmeshed, that make every society distinct from others. It's through the tug of war amongst those coalitions that the primary conflict sways like a rocking chair. It's through the same game that it overturns. In Saint-Domingue, the two big coalitions keeping things in balance so the primary conflict wouldn't overturn were the **colonist** coalition and the **free** coalition.

3/THE WHITE COALITION

When the hawk's chasing the chicken, it doesn't just use its claws. It uses its claws, it uses its beak, and it uses its wings. It uses all the weapons it can. So, to further expand their power, the colonists coated Saint-Domingue with a final dose of arsenic, a dose so strong that it's still in our blood today: **the color problem**. They made all whites believe they were better than everyone else, they made mulattos believe they were better than black people, and they made black people believe they were the most 'inferior'.

Color prejudice gave big colonists a huge advantage. It helped them form a coalition with middle-class whites. In this shifty **white coalition**, *petits blancs* (little whites) **positioned** themselves against black people and mulattos even though they were in a comparable **situation** ... Who was happiest? French commissioners and plantation owners. *Petits blancs* went after slaves with a vengeance ... Who benefited? French commissioners and plantation owners. Mulattos and black people clashed at the slightest provocation ... Who applauded? French commissioners and plantation owners. The colonists benefited enormously from this color prejudice.

1. It allowed them to form a solid WHITE coalition to reinforce their class's power.
2. It allowed them to drive a wedge between the other social classes to **keep them from forming their own coalitions.**

This is how plantation owners teamed up with French commissioners to maintain their balance on the backs of slaves in Saint-Domingue. These are the coalitions they put in place: the colonists' coalition, the free coalition, and the white coalition. These are the types of wedges they drove between the other classes. Yet in 1791, the whirlwind took off. How did that happen?

A revolution takes off:

- when the classes in power **can't keep their balance anymore**
- when the classes beneath them **don't want to do acrobatics anymore.**

From January 1789 to July 1791, distinct coalitions that had been propping up the primary conflict in Saint-Domingue cracked one after the other. The hidden conflicts got restless ... Trouble followed schemes ...

when dogs shiver, all the fleas get headaches

For us to understand how Saint-Domingue's coalitions split up, we have to think about France, since at the time France was undergoing a profound crisis that experts call: the Bourgeois Revolution.

Towards the end of the century, around 1789, the French bourgeoisie formed a coalition (bourgeoisie + workers + peasants) to launch an offensive against aristocrats at the head of their society. The bourgeoisie had been preparing that coup for a long time. From 1715 on, intellectuals wrote things to plant ideas in readers' heads. Certain teachers call that time the 'Age of Enlightenment' because knowledge and impressive writings were dazzling people's eyes.

Political pressure was mounting, too. Traders and mill owners were putting pressure on the King. In 1787, the King had to invite all the provinces to send delegates to explain their problems with the government. The bourgeoisie hijacked this big assembly. They wrote their own law and then made an arrogant declaration. At the opening of the declaration, the French bourgeoisie said: **before the law, all people are equal**.

To be sure, the French bourgeoisie were being dishonest when they swore upon that declaration. Without a second thought, when the bourgeoisie realized they were truly being taken seriously, they chopped off the head of their own child. The bourgeoisie leaned on the workers to get rid of the aristocrats, it carried out its revolution, and slowly but surely, it sent the workers packing. In 1871, after more than sixty years of turmoil, French bourgeois, weapons in hand, liquidated the last groups of workers who'd been threatening them.[20]

But, at the same time, a flash flood was rushing through Saint-Domingue.

1/THE COALITION OF BIG COLONISTS SPLITS

In November 1787, the politicians in Saint-Domingue caught wind of a large gathering of representatives taking place in France. In January 1789, the **white** plantation owners held a secret election to send representatives to France to **defend their interests**. They wanted France to give them the opportunity to trade with whomever they wanted, under the conditions they favored, so they could profit more. The matter of commissioners eating well and living well without even owning plantations didn't please big landowners.

But the big landowners' actions didn't make commissioners any happier. If France didn't hold a monopoly anymore, they'd lose their profits. They were, after all, French commissioners. The bigger the profit France made, the more turkey they'd be eating. They yelled at plantation owners. They forbade them to send representatives. They started shouting: France was supporting them.

The plantation owners defied them, and they sent representatives to France. A lot of them joined forces with *petits blancs* against the commissioners. In 1790, they held a big gathering in Saint-Marc. *Petits blancs*

---

20 This references the tumultuous events in France in the year 1871. After the four-month Prussian (German) siege of Paris was finally over, the irregular French militia that had been defending the city seized power and attempted to establish a government with socialist values (la Commune). Beginning on May 21, 1871, the French army violently suppressed this worker-led movement, leaving at least 7,000 dead on both sides.

took the lead at the gathering, and plantation owners had to follow. They wrote their own law. They told France to go to hell, and they fired the State army! They pretended to be supporters of the revolution in France, they put on red cockades, and so they called them **Ponpon Rouj** ['Red Pompoms'].

The French commissioners weren't afraid. They already had the army. To muster more troops, they pulled in two or three *petits blancs* and mulattos (either wealthy or middle-class). They joined forces with various white aristocratic plantation owners who supported the King. Wearing white cockades (*ponpon blan*) on their heads, they marched on the Ponpon Rouj. Even though the Ponpon Rouj had more supporters in the West and South of the country, the Ponpon Blan attacked Saint-Marc. The Ponpon Rouj ran for the hills ... It's true, several times after that battle, French commissioners and white plantation owners allied themselves again, against freedmen and against slaves above all. But it's also true that several times after that battle, one side pulled guns on the other again.

In March 1791, for example, the Ponpon Rouj killed Mauduit. They organized an army with Caradeux as sole leader. And most of the country was under their control when the slaves started setting fire to things.

And so there's no question that, from August 1790 onward, **the coalition of colonists split into two** and no miracle could save it, because two other conflicts had already broken out ...

2/ THE COALITION OF FREE PEOPLE SPLITS

While that struggle was solidifying, while commissioners and white plantation owners were clashing horns in Saint-Domingue, mulatto plantation owners took advantage of the situation. Vincent Ogé and Julien Raimond,[21] who were in France, spoke up for the mulatto plantation owners. Ogé invited white plantation owners to join forces with mulattos

---

21 Vincent Ogé (1755–91) was a free man of color from northern Saint-Domingue who joined the anti-slavery Society of the Friends of the Blacks in France and advocated for voting rights for free people of color in the colonies. Ogé is best known for having led an unsuccessful revolt against the white colonial authority in Saint-Domingue and in 1791 he was executed in Cape Haitian. Julien Raimond (1744–1801) accompanied Ogé to raise the question of equal rights for free people of color at the 1790–91 National Assembly. Raimond supported the idea of emancipation in Saint-Domingue but also advocated for loyalty to France.

so they could exploit slaves more effectively. He said: 'If someone's going to gain from this, mulattos must enjoy the advantages, too, because all landowners in Saint-Domingue must stand together'. He said: 'Sirs, you're sleeping on the edge of a cliff [...] In no time you'll see slaves raise the flag of revolution'.

Ogé's speech was enough to wake up people who wanted to believe **mulatto plantation owners** weren't prepared to join forces with their **white plantation owner** associates. At the end of his speech, Ogé promised the whites a strategy to prevent a slave revolution from taking hold in Saint-Domingue!

Thus, the **Declaration**[22] of the French bourgeoisie was fresh in the minds of mulatto plantation owners. But the French bourgeoisie, white plantation owners, and *petits blancs* in Saint-Domingue all did the same thing. When they shouted out loud: 'All people are equal', they said in a hushed tone, 'Only we count as people'!

However, the mulattos' scheme was like pouring water into a basket because race prejudice blinded the white landowners' eyes. They couldn't understand that Ogé was in the same **position** as they were, the position of plantation owners, exploiters, and slave owners. They took a **stand** against Ogé, they laughed at him, and they told him to go sit down. They treated him like an untrustworthy dog who hasn't yet acted up. Mulattos didn't miss a step with anyone! What were they thinking?

Ogé went back to Saint-Domingue secretly, and he hid himself away in Dondon. The mulatto plantation owners held endless meetings. One of them, Chavannes,[23] wanted to form a coalition with the slaves, but the others shouted him down. Ogé wrote to the governor (the French **King**'s commissioner), and the governor snubbed him.

When mulatto plantation owners saw that both white plantation owners and French commissioners took them for nothing, they finally rebelled. Two hundred and fifty mulattos charged on Grande Rivière, and they turned the village on its head. Mulatto plantation owners in other parts of the country felt encouraged ... Verrettes, Les Cayes, they

---

22 The French National Assembly passed the Declaration of the Rights of Man and of the Citizen in 1789. This document articulated the principles which helped launch the French Revolution: all citizens were free and equal before the law (though the category of 'citizen' was limited to white males).

23 Jean-Baptiste Chavannes (c. 1748–91), an educated freedman, participated with French troops in the American Revolution (including the 1778 Siege of Savannah). Upon returning to Haiti, he supported Ogé's struggle for political rights (Roc 61).

started resisting. Only the mulattos of Port-au-Prince and Léogâne were submissive for the moment. It's as though they knew ... In the blink of an eye, French commissioners joined forces with northern plantation owners. They put together an unusual army: 1,500 whites and 3,000 slaves to suppress the mulatto factions ... Ogé and Chavannes escaped to the Spanish part of the island. Colonel Mauduit himself, one of the leaders of the Ponpon Blan, appeased all the mulattos of Verrettes. In the end he went down to Les Cayes and drove all the rebels to their wits' end. In December 1790, the Spanish commanders returned Ogé and Chavannes to their French colonist cronies. The northern colonists took the two of them and beat them with batons in front of all the mulattos of Cape Haitian to 'set an example'.

In February 1791, the French colonists were confident that they had put the mulattos 'in their place'. But the bragging didn't last long. They'd pay heavily for that. Because from then on, many mulattos started to see the size of the hole in the chest of the **free people's coalition** in Saint-Domingue.

It's true, several times after the death of Ogé, mulatto plantation owners (and other existing mulatto factions) joined forces with white plantation owners or French commissioners to crush the slaves. But it's also true that several times after the death of Ogé, they pulled guns on whites again. For example, in late August 1791, they dragged a bunch of slaves along with them and marched on whites in Nerette, in Pernier.

There's no question that, as of February 1791, the coalition of free people in Saint-Domingue was in trouble.

And so, of three coalitions carrying weight for the upper classes in Saint-Domingue, two split apart.

3/ THE WHITES' COALITION SPLITS

It was French commissioners and white plantation owners along with the *petits blancs* in the middle classes who formed the WHITE coalition in Saint-Domingue. And so, the conflict among the colonists was a conflict within the bowels of the **white** coalition. **White** plantation owners were clashing horns with **white** commissioners. When the kitchen catches on fire, the living room can't avoid getting warm ...

And so this struggle made the *petits blancs* go prowling about. Some of them joined up with plantation owners at the gathering in Saint-Marc. They went to the side of the *grands blancs* because they weren't about to let

48   *Stirring the Pot of Haitian History*

mulattos score two points. Just as every other group had done, they'd read the Declaration of the French bourgeoisie through prejudiced lenses. Mulattos weren't supposed to have rights, yet *grands blancs* were supposed to recognize that all **whites** were equal. A lot of *petits blancs* saw past the plantation owners' games. They knew those men would never defend the interests of people who weren't in the same class as they were. And so they joined forces with the Ponpon Blan against most of the white plantation owners.

Therefore, even though the white coalition was willing to join forces to oppose mulattos or black people, the conflicts within their own various classes showed up more clearly. After two years of fighting, the white coalition was in shreds.

And so we can say that **at the end of 1791 all three coalitions supporting the power of the upper classes in Saint-Domingue were losing ground.**

> 1. Conflicts between classes (commissioners) and social groups (white plantation owners) that had formed the colonists' coalition had reached the unbound stage.
> 2. Conflicts between classes and groups that had formed the coalition of free people also came unbound. Specifically, the plantation-owning mulatto group and the middle-class mulatto group took up arms against other classes and groups within the coalition of free people.
> 3. Conflicts between classes and groups that had formed the white coalition were becoming more entangled each day.

The power of French commissioners and plantation owners was rooted in those three coalitions. Therefore, if those three coalitions split up in 1791, that meant that in 1791 the upper classes' power was unraveling. The first condition necessary for a revolution to get going is: the upper classes must lose their footing. In 1791, the feet of colonists in Saint-Domingue slipped out from under them ... Danger!

In 1791 the colonists' feet slipped. All three coalitions had fractured. But that stumble wouldn't have mattered if the slaves hadn't gotten involved.

For a revolution to take off:

> 1. the power-holding class must lose ground
> 2. the classes below must shove them.

4. Fire in the house

Saint-Domingue was leaning over, but it hadn't yet overturned, **and it wouldn't have overturned if the slaves hadn't pushed it**. They may say the scorpion stung itself, but to be sure the scorpion's really dead, you have to step on it. They may say weeds wither on their own, but whoever doesn't pull the weeds can't plant beautiful fields. For Saint-Domingue to truly produce big yields, **the slaves had to get involved.**

My friends, you already understand that no event in History has happened in vain. It's true, in 1791 the slaves decided to get involved. But **why** did they revolt? Which of the two reasons above made them decide at that moment to set fire to plantations?

For the lower class to revolt, the primary conflict must go beyond the entangled stage. The **situation** in society must reach the point of no return. But that's not enough. People aren't like the river, the river doesn't know anything; it doesn't understand what it is or where it's going. It does what its path dictates. It sees a slope, and it hurries down. It sees a crack, and it rushes in. It sees mountains, it goes in between them. It sees a cliff, and it comes unbound. If someone could count how many cracks, how many slopes, how many mountains, how many rocks, and how many cliffs are on its path, you'll know what the river has done in the past. **You'll find out where the river is going.** But you can never be sure what humans will do because humans make up their own minds. In the same situation, they can take various stands. Believe me or don't, but there are even times when they take a **stand** that's not in their interest, depending on the ideas that enter their heads, and the ideological situation of the society.

And so, for the lower class to revolt, not only must the political and economic situation be entangled, but the idea of fighting must also take root in people's minds. They must decide to defend their class. In Saint-Domingue, in 1791, there were three major events that put the idea of fighting into slaves' minds, three major events that made them decide to defend their interests, three major events that also made the ideological situation reach the point of no return.

Conflicts among the other classes showed slaves the power of the gun. The slaves reflected on the Declaration of the French bourgeoisie that said all people were equal. The slaves had already established a native-born culture. Several rebel slave leaders started discovering the rallying cry of freedom for all people.

in a rainy land the porch owner rules

Since 1789, slaves had followed the clashes between Saint-Domingue's other classes. They witnessed bloodshed. They learned the power of guns. They learned with their own eyes that in a dog-eat-dog society, the dog with the biggest teeth commands. In a rainy land, the porch owner rules …

Many slaves also fought. When there was a big skirmish, certain colonists put guns into slaves' hands to reinforce their supporting army. In the North, Colonel Cambefort marched on Ogé with 3,000 slaves and those 3,000 slaves made mulattos run for the hills. And so the slaves began to understand how much power they could have with weapons in their hands.

word spread like wildfire

The conflict in France led the slaves to reflect. Don't forget that slaves weren't all the same. There were city slaves in Cape Haitian and Port-au-Prince who unloaded ships. There were slaves who knew how to read. There were domestic slaves situated right under the master's nose. Mouth to mouth, the word spread. Word spread like wildfire. **A lot of slaves in Saint-Domingue heard about the revolution that was causing havoc in France.** They heard news of fieldworkers who'd taken up arms.

But the words that really shook up the slaves' minds were in the Declaration of the French bourgeoisie: **all people are equal!**

In fact, there's a conflict in the blood of the classes holding power. For a social class to take power, and for it to hold onto that power, it must act **as though** it's defending everyone. It must pretend that it's speaking in the people's interest, even if it's really defending its own personal interest. That conflict is the bourgeoisie's lifeblood. When the French bourgeoisie said: all people are equal, they knew what they really meant … but any conflict has a flip side: **the bourgeoisie couldn't stop other people from picking up those words.** In Saint-Domingue, white plantation owners picked them up, *petits blancs* picked them up, and mulatto plantation owners picked them up. **Slaves picked them up.** If everyone is equal, why are we in chains?

And so, conflicts between the other classes, along with the revolution of the French bourgeoisie, helped slaves in Saint-Domingue take their own positions on things.

But that's just the tip of the iceberg ... The main ingredient for the *lanmidon pouès* ['manioc pudding'] of the slaves' uprising was their own strength and courage: the native-born culture of Ayiti Toma.[24]

father's fields
granny's spirits
mother's tongue

Since the time of the *Kòd Noua* (1685), Saint-Domingue's plantation owners had sought to keep slaves divided. Slaves came from different African countries. Each of those countries had different tribes. Not everyone spoke the same language, not everyone served the same spirits. Some of them had been enemies since the beginning of time. Plantation owners took advantage of those conflicts. When they were buying slaves for plantations, they put bunches of mismatched Africans together. That way they could be sure the slaves wouldn't get along. They declared that blacks had betrayed blacks since the time of the Igelefe slave fort in Hueda, and that blacks would always betray blacks. History denies that claim. But Saint-Domingue's colonists had no use for History. Within the community of Saint-Domingue, despite what Ogé had told them, the colonists were carefree. Plantation owners went to bed with the door open so fresh air could waft in—right under the noses of all the slaves they'd mercilessly beaten for no reason the day before. Labarre, an important plantation owner, wrote to his wife and commented on how meek his slaves were. The guy said: 'This business of freedom for slaves is just a daydream. These people barely speak to one another'. In 1790, neither Labarre nor the other colonists had yet recognized that society's stomach was churning. Why?

In truth, in a dog-eat-dog society, the upper classes must intimidate the lower classes. But they also must fool themselves. **They must believe in all the threats they make against the lower classes. Their carefree attitude is necessary for them to maintain a tight grip on power.** And so, plantation owners in Saint-Domingue **couldn't** see that slaves weren't

---

24 'Ayiti Toma' is a Haitian Creole expression commonly used as a term of endearment for the land of Haiti.

mismatched anymore. They also couldn't see that a native-born culture with its very own features had surfaced in Saint-Domingue. What's more, they couldn't see that that culture gave slaves the **conviction** to fight.

The native-born culture that arose in Saint-Domingue had three major features. Those features passed into the very marrow of slaves' bones. Those features were so deeply branded that they traverse our entire History, from Bwa Kayiman[25] to this very day. Turn to the right, they're there; turn to the left, they're there. They were there in 1804 and they were there in 1918.[26] From Bwa Kayiman up to the present day the three features of the native-born culture have been: **land, the Vodou religion, and the Creole language**.

that sliver of land ...
that's all I need to say

For the very lowest class in a society to revolt, the primary conflict must reach the unbound stage. Which is to say, the economic, political, and ideological struggle between the upper classes and the lowest class reaches the point of no return. Very often, that class's economic situation within the society is the reason why it revolts. But, as we've already said, people aren't like rivers. They must have **conviction** to revolt. They must believe in what they're doing. They must **talk** about their economic situation. They must **hear** discussions about that situation. And among these various factors, there's one that speaks to them most forcefully. There's one they're especially **sensitive** to. When they revolt to transform their economic situation, they also revolt because the **ideological** conflicts have reached the unbound stage.

The economic situation of slaves in Saint-Domingue was interconnected with working the land. All Saint-Domingue's wealth lay in plantations, and slaves didn't have plantations. But to save money, plantation owners gave slaves a little sliver of land along the edges of the cane fields. Slaves planted their own subsistence crops on that little sliver of land. Sometimes slaves could even take their crops to sell at the market. And so that sliver of land **meant a lot** to slaves. In a society that

---

25 The Vodou ceremony of Bwa Kayiman in August 1791 catalyzed the general insurrection that ushered in the Haitian Revolution.
26 On January 1, 1804, Jean-Jacques Dessalines declared Haiti's independence; 1918 refers to the period of Haiti's occupation by the United States military, 1915–34.

gave them no opportunity, **their only opportunity was this little sliver of land**. In a society that gave them no rights, **their only right was to plant THEIR OWN field.**

In any society, the assets connected to the primary industry are always significant. But the more the water flows under the bridge, the more significant those assets are. They put together a cohort that wasn't just based on money. They start producing ideological conflicts that don't necessarily match up with economic conflicts.

In an **agrarian** society (based on field work), **land always means wealth**. For slaves in Saint-Domingue, in 1791, land meant Dignity. Land meant Respect. Land meant Hope. Land meant Freedom.

For slaves in Saint-Domingue, **for ¾ of the Haitian people today**, the issue of land is a *potomitan* [centerpost] issue. You'll come across some people who'll give you their food without a second thought, but they'll chop off your head if you assume you're going to enter their field 'as though it were your father's field' … Because land is unlike any other asset. It's where your family's entire memory resides. It's where all children's hopes grow. My grandfather's honor is within the land. Vièj's illness is within it. The stories I tell are within it. Service to the African spirits lies within it. What sets me apart from you, your brother-in-law, your wife, and your godmother is this little piece of land that my grandfather left to me. You don't have to believe me, that's your right. But ask Boukman for me, ask Goman and Akao,[27] ask the Caco leader, Charlemagne.[28] Or go ask Lamèsi then; she's right there, she can answer …

In 1791, Jean-François,[29] Biassou, and Toussaint asked the colonists for three things:

---

27 Goman and Akao were peasant leaders and insurrectionists. Goman, whose birth name was Jean-Baptiste Perrier, had served as a fighter in 1792–93. He led a peasant revolt between 1807 and 1820 in the Grand'Anse *département* in the South. He effectively controlled a region that was independent of the Haitian central government (Blackburn 254). Akao was a peasant leader who led the *pikè* insurrectionists between 1844 and 1848 in their struggle against the abuses of the Haitian State. One of the abuses was the manipulation of the prices of export crops in a way that benefited the Haitian government officials who controlled the ports but hurt the peasant farmers (Gilbert n. pag.).

28 Charlemagne Péralte was a defender of Haiti's independence who in 1915 led a rebellion of guerrilla fighters known as the Cacos against the United States' military occupation. Péralte, who was killed in 1919, and whose body was desecrated by U.S. Marines, remains a hero in Haitian society.

29 Jean-François Papillon was an African-born enslaved person who escaped from a plantation in northern Haiti before the Revolution, became a maroon, and

1. Freedom for rebel **leaders**
2. Forbidding the slave drivers' **whips**
3. Three additional weekdays for all **slaves** to plant **their own little sliver of land.**

That little sliver of land ... that sums it all up ...

The *calinda* rhythm is supposed to be drummed

But land wasn't the only sensitive issue for rebel slaves in Saint-Domingue. The Vodou religion was also very important because it gave them **conviction**. It made them take the chance of fighting, and it made them take the chance of winning. The Creole language was important, too. For us to understand the specific role Vodou and Creole played within the whirlwind of Saint-Domingue, we must be able to understand the conditions in which they developed.

When colonists invade a land, they bring along all their cultural baggage. They bring their language, their history, their songs, their laws, and their religion. When colonists invade a land, the native-born culture of that land enters a tireless war against the foreigners' culture. When the English left Europe to go invade the Hindu regions, that native-born culture clashed with English culture. But that culture was there before the English arrived. When the Spanish left Europe to go invade Peru, the native-born culture clashed with Spanish culture. But that culture was there long before the Spanish arrived.

Yet in Saint-Domingue, when French colonists arrived, **there was no native-born culture**. When the French showed up, the Native Americans had already died off. The Spanish destroyed both the Zemi spirit sculptures and the Samba poet-priests of the Caribbean Indigenous people, along with all their practices. After that, the Spanish cleared out. The Africans arrived together with the French. (The French were the ones who sent for most of the slaves in Saint-Domingue).

Almost any cultural war within a colony goes through three stages:

1. the native-born culture arises within the country on its own
2. the colonists' culture comes and attacks it
3. the native-born culture responds.

went on to become a leader in the Revolution; he allied himself with Spain for several years, then was abandoned by Spain despite his service.

In Saint-Domingue those three stages had disappeared. All three of those actions got entangled within a single day's storm:

- while the native-born culture was emerging
- the colonists' culture was attacking it
- the native-born culture was responding **while it was cutting its teeth.**

In Saint-Domingue, the native-born culture of plantation slaves **learned to fight while it was learning to breathe.** It was a culture born in struggle. It wasn't born before the struggle, and it fought right after its birth. **It was born because it was fighting.** And so both Vodou and Creole were baptized in discord. They bear all the scars of Saint-Domingue. They bear the scars of suffering, they bear the scars of resignation, but **they also bear the scars of resistance.** Vodou and Creole have in their marrow a degree of dissension that struggles against the upper classes.

beneath the arbor of my spirits
I say any words I wish

In the whirlwind of Saint-Domingue, Vodou helped the slave class in two ways:

1. it gave them more conviction to fight
2. it allowed them to organize themselves.

A week before the slaves started setting things afire, a bunch of rebel leaders held a ceremony in Morne Rouge, in a place called Bwa Kayiman, on the Lenormand de Mézy plantation. In that ceremony, Boukman, an *oungan* rebel leader, prayed to God beseeching support for the rebels. We know Bwa Kayiman the best, but a lot of other guerrilla leaders organized ceremonies before going off to fight. Biassou used to tell slaves: don't run from death, because if you die the spirits will return you to Igelefe fort in Africa. And that **concept** helped rebel slaves defy dangers. Colonel Malenfant was never so surprised as when he saw Yasint's rebels thrust their hands into the mouths of cannons, so great was their belief in the power of the spirits they served.

But that wasn't all. Many of the guerrilla leaders were *oungan* Vodou priests: Boukman, Biassou, Yasint, Lamour Dérance,

Romaine-la-Prophétesse[30] ... And three-quarters (3/4) of them were *oungan* **before** becoming guerrilla leaders. Their status as 'papas of the spirits' helped them organize the rebel slaves. We also mustn't forget that *calinda* dances in Saint-Domingue were the only '**meetings**' slaves had. And so a *calinda* dance was at the same time a cultural celebration, a Vodou celebration, and a political 'meeting'.

In fact, when Saint-Domingue's slaves were scheming their attack, they needed an organization. They drew on the only kind of organizations they knew of: Vodou organizations. The Ceremony of Bwa Kayiman can serve as our witness ...

People badmouth Bwa Kayiman in two ways. They say it was just a **political gathering**. They say it was just a **mystical** ceremony. Whether they take it seriously, or whether they take it for mumbo-jumbo, they don't take it for what it was. Beyond Boukman's invocation, four things happened at Bwa Kayiman:

- a *manbo* Vodou priestess killed a pig
- the rebels drank the pig's blood
- the rebels swore they wouldn't betray the cause
- they decided how they would attack.

People who've studied the religion of Dahomian spirits encounter a similar ceremony in Africa (killing pigs—drinking pig's blood—oath-taking). That ceremony has three meanings: solidarity, trust, and secrecy. That ceremony means: all initiates stand strong together, all initiates believe in one another, and all initiates would rather die than speak the secret.

Therefore, it wasn't a **political gathering**, which would mean wasting time, speaking French, and competing against one another. What happened was political, but it wasn't **only** political. In any case, it wasn't the **same type of politics known to most European people**. But the slaves weren't messing around either, and they weren't cracking jokes. It was a **Vodou ceremony** that was **simultaneously** the most important

---

30 Romaine Rivière or 'Romaine-la-Prophétesse' was a revolutionary and cultic figure in the Léogâne area in the 1790s (see Taber). He took the title 'prophetess' and raided towns with his troops while claiming to be the godson of the Virgin Mary. Romaine inspired his 12,000 fighters, recruited in the mountains, with features typical of Kongo religion (Taber 142). In the course of his bands' raids, he would perform the mass and torture his captives (Madiou 1989 2:128).

political oath they could mutually take before they decided to turn Saint-Domingue upside down.

In 1791, Vodou gave slaves more **conviction** to fight, but it also gave them more **organization**. It was like a sticky glue that bonded them together.

but why can't I be free?

Slaves had learned the power of the gun, they'd heard the news about the events in France, and they'd established a native-born culture. But that wouldn't have been enough if they hadn't found a **central rallying cry** for their struggle. In 1791, the central rallying cry was the command of **Freedom**.

In fact, the rallying cry of freedom didn't appear in Saint-Domingue in 1791. Ever since black people started arriving there, some entered the struggle, and others escaped to a plateau or the mountains. History calls groups of slaves who broke their *kòd*, or shackles, **maroons** because most of them simply fled slavery without trying to overturn the society. To be sure, in 1679 the group with *oungan* Padre Jean attacked plantations, in 1734 Plidò's group did the same, and in 1758 *oungan* Makandal and his group (on the Lenormand de Mézy plantation) set out to exterminate all whites. Other groups rose up in 1691, 1703, 1704, 1775, and 1778. But those groups weren't yet ready, the primary conflict wasn't yet entangled enough, big colonists maintained their power, the native-born culture had just started to grow, and the rallying cry of freedom wasn't clear enough.

In 1791, the rallying cry of freedom came upon fertile ground where it could grow. Slaves were more concentrated, their situation was worse, and it was easier for them to see the society's conflicts. In the North especially, many started realizing that the freedom they needed would never arrive on its own. They started realizing what this freedom meant: *koupé tèt boulé kay*.[31] The rallying cry was like the former maroons' rallying cry, but instead of freedom meaning **flight**, for slaves in 1791, in the North especially, freedom meant **fighting**.

In fact, those two rallying cries look similar but they're not the same. Pumpkins don't produce squash; and John's son isn't John. It's true,

---

31 This famous slogan, meaning 'cut off heads, burn down houses', is associated with Boukman Dutty and the Bwa Kayiman ceremony; it points to an early fighting strategy in the general insurrection of 1791.

maroonage was a way that a group could protest, a way to say it disagreed with the system. But the main feature of maroonage is escape. Escaping to the mountains, escaping field work or doing the work badly, escaping from the upper classes' laws, escaping their religion, their language, and escaping life itself (there were slaves who killed themselves, and there were female slaves who killed their own children). But there's a crossroads a class reaches: it either **can't** do maroonage anymore, or it **doesn't need** to do maroonage anymore, or it **doesn't want** to do maroonage anymore. In the North especially, in 1791 slaves had reached a crossroads where, instead of **escaping** to freedom they preferred **fighting** for freedom.

> O in La Plaine du Nord Saint Jacques calls for order
> let us go
> O in La Plaine du Nord Saint Jacques calls for order
> let us go
> Saint Jacques calls for strict ritual order
> let us go

Let's consider the differences that existed in 1791 between slaves in the North and other slaves in Saint-Domingue. In the South and West, there were many maroons. They were organized, and they were positioned on the biggest mass of mountains in the country: La Selle, La Hotte, Trou d'Eau ... But this advantage had its drawbacks. Those areas were so very high, so remotely mountainous, that those maroon slaves lost contact with the country's social conflicts. Those conflicts caused them to escape, but living on the mountain allowed them to ignore those conflicts. This was the same stance Cacique Henri (an Indigenous Caribbean Taíno chief) had taken towards the Spanish in 1530: whites can go hog-wild within the city, but leave the mountains for us.

Maroon slaves who were in the North of the country couldn't take that stance. The land itself didn't give them the option. Morne Rouge, Morne Beaubrun, Morne Bijou, Chaplèt, etc., high as they were, didn't rival the heights of Kabayo, Bois-Pin, La Selle, La Colline, or Macaya. While in the South and the West there are two true chains of mountains (the Massif de la Selle and Massif de la Hotte), the North has lots of spotty mountains, and the towns are right below. And so, a group of slaves couldn't support itself on a mountain and pretend it didn't need to know what was happening on plantations. Its members had to come down from time to time, either for the security of their stomachs, or the security of their territory. For those same reasons, whites in the North couldn't leave maroons alone.

And so in the North, maroonage couldn't provide the same things it provided in the South, or in the West in particular. But slaves in the North had certain advantages. They outnumbered slaves in other provinces (180,000, compared to 168,000 in the West and 114,000 in the South). Slaves in the North were also greater in number with respect to other classes in the province: there were seven times more slaves than free people. What's more, they weren't scattered all around. You could find tons of slaves on a single plantation. Plantations were stuck to one another, slaves crossed paths with other slaves, *calinda* dances were drummed in the dark, and the plot was hatched. On August 22, before the masters could even blink their eyes, fire covered the northern plain. The rallying cry **to fight for freedom** spread throughout the country. For thirteen more New Year's days of fire, that rallying cry grew, was subdued, and changed form. Malevolent types seized it for their personal interests. People died for it in 1795, in 1802, 1843, 1918, etc. That rallying cry is still around, but for us to seek it out and recognize it today, we must know what path it traveled from Bwa Kayiman up to 1804. We must understand the tribulations people have suffered, and the resistance they've put up, from 1804 to today. And so little by little, we'll lay rock upon rock until we establish the Vodou Temple of Freedom. Truly. Completely.

5. Open the gate

*open the gate
we'll open the gate
O, we must pass through!
master of three crossroads
master of three paths
master of three streams
we'll open the gate
O, we must pass through!*

On August 29, 1793, two years and two weeks after the Bwa Kayiman ceremony (while stray bullets were flying all around Saint-Domingue), the people of Cape Haitian heard an announcement that led men and women alike to tremble. The colonial commissioner Sonthonax decreed: **'all enslaved blacks and mulattos shall become free, so they can enjoy all the benefits that other French citizens enjoy'**.[32]

Some naive folks were taken by surprise, while others said they'd seen it coming. Some joined forces with Sonthonax, and some said he should be killed. Some were happy, some were angry …

So let's ask a few questions … Where did Sonthonax come from? What were his plans in Saint-Domingue? **Why did he free the slaves?** How was he able to make this decision? How did a young thirty-something man, fresh as a baby's bottom, get all that power within Saint-Domingue?

On July 28, 1792, a French government delegation set sail for Saint-Domingue. That delegation contained three people: Ailhaud, an aristocrat full of hot air, Polverel, a shifty bourgeois, and a prickly young bourgeois revolutionary: Léger Félicité Sonthonax (twenty-nine years old) was the delegation's president.[33]

The French government sent those three men to bring peace to the island—that is, the peace that France wanted. The French deputies were convinced that a coalition of **French commissioners, white plantation owners, and mulatto plantation owners** could make Saint-Domingue hale enough to resume the profit-making opportunities that French traders took complete advantage of before 1789.

Before those men left France, deputy Lagroce told them they had to 'make the *grand blanc* colonists understand that **their true interest was that of making free mulattos their equals** in order to secure the property that both groups possessed (in the country), to protect themselves against internal and external enemies, and especially **so they could jointly crush any movement by the [slave] rebels from plantation mills.**

---

32 For more information about Sonthonax's proclamation, see Laurent Dubois and John D. Garrigus's *Slave Revolution in the Caribbean, 1789–1804*.

33 Léger-Félicité Sonthonax (Madiou 1987 1:150–59, etc.) was accompanied to Saint-Domingue by Étienne Polverel and Jean-Antoine Ailhaud. Sonthonax headed this delegation of French Revolutionary Civil Commissioners who were sent to end slavery in the French colony. Polverel and Ailhaud were placed in command of the West and South, respectively.

For goodness' sake, the French government couldn't be any clearer than that. It sent the commissioners to form a coalition, and to bring the assignment to fruition it charged them with:

1. the power to appoint or dismiss whoever they wanted
2. the right to attack white plantation owners or any other group that disagreed with the coalition
3. fifteen ships
4. 6,000 soldiers to support the Civil Commission's decisions with the full force of arms.

The Civil Commission hypothetically had a lot of power. In the blink of an eye, it would hypothetically form a coalition of the upper classes. Hypothetically every day was a Sunday …

wanting
is one thing
being able to have
is another
the Gwayamouk River flows in between

So this is what the Second Civil Commission came to do in Saint-Domingue. This is what the French government wanted. But often, through the course of History, what people **want** to do is one thing, and what they're **able to** do is another … The Gwayamouk River flows in between …

The French bourgeoisie knew what they wanted, and they did all they could to find solid ground, but in truth there was too much water for them to cross. There was the French government's own internal conflict, there were the whites of Saint-Domingue, and (the runt is always fiercest) there were the masses of Saint-Domingue, lined up, worked up, fuming, like the Gwayamouk River about to take the Vincent Bridge by storm …

your neighbor's beard catches on fire
dip your own in water

The first river crossing that the Civil Commission had to traverse was the French government's internal conflict.

5. Open the gate

France had been upside down since July 1789. Two big camps were butting heads within the government:

1. Aristocrats (the King, big army leaders, big church leaders, and big landowners)
2. The bourgeoisie (businesspeople, factory bosses) who depended on craftspeople, factory workers, and farmworkers.

The French government couldn't maintain its balance. A decision was quickly made, and just as quickly, the decision was rendered null and void. But as the days passed, as factory workers, craftspeople, and farmworkers were putting pressure on the bourgeoisie, so too were deputies tightening their grip on the aristocrats. Bit by bit, the bourgeoisie was establishing its power in France, while also bit by bit the people started distrusting them. On August 10, 1792, while the Civil Commission was at sea, the people of Paris overthrew the King. Another government rose to power in France.

The Second Civil Commission bore the features of all the conflicts within the government that sent it there. The French King signed its paperwork, but deputy Lagroce wrote out all the orders. Just like the French state, the Commission had its own aristocrat (Ailhaud), but that aristocrat was there for show, just like Louis XVI in France was a puppet king. The bourgeois deputies were the ones controlling France, and two lawyers supporting the bourgeoisie were the ones controlling the Commission. There were even two camps within the army that had sailed with the commissioners. Of the 6,000 men, 4,000 were police officers supporting the bourgeoisie, 2,000 soldiers were in the king's camp, and the army chief, Despabès,[34] was a nasty aristocrat. Frankly, the cards weren't well shuffled.

case of mistaken identity

But the conflicts within the French government were nothing compared to Saint-Domingue's situation. What was that situation like? What does **political situation** or **political state of affairs** mean?

All politics are politics, but not all politics are the same ... We've gotten into a bad habit (bad habits are easy to get into)—which is to say, as soon as we're asked how Haiti's political cards got shuffled, we

---

34 Jean-Jacques d'Esparbès de Lussan (or Desparbès) was the Governor of Saint-Domingue (Oriol 195).

always assume the worst, and our political analysis is more like rumor-spreading. I say that's wrong, off the mark. Case of mistaken identity. When we find out who the only field guard was atop Mount Marinette when Sonthonax's carriage appeared … we don't know diddley squat. Of course, all of Saint-Domingue's leaders were involved in the country's politics, but when we take them up all together, we can sort them out. When we learn the birth name of Tirésias Augustin Simon Sam[35] we don't yet understand the country's **political situation**—we've only exposed the country's **political apparatus**.

I say **political apparatus** because all government leaders have their special roles, like magnets, buttons, needles, and speakers in a radio **apparatus**. They're all interconnected, and it's the whole combination that makes up the state, just like all the buttons, magnets, needles, and speakers make up a radio apparatus. So let's suppose I know what station the radio's set to. If I don't hear a song playing, do I know what kind of song the radio's playing? No.

Therefore, the **apparatus** is important, but **it isn't the song**. The apparatus has an impact on the song, to be sure. Some radios play louder than others. Some radios have more bass than others. Some radios pick up more stations than others. But the radio and the song are two separate things.

In the same way, even if the political apparatus is connected to the political situation, even if the apparatus has an impact on the situation, the political apparatus and the political situation are two separate things.

spinning
spinning spinning

In truth, a society's political situation is rooted in the position of the various classes, categories, and groups within that society. From August 1791 to October 1792, Saint-Domingue's political situation was a real mishmash because the social classes and groups weren't clear on their **positions**. To be sure, their **interests** hadn't changed, but it's not every day that a social class gets to take a stand and defend its true interests.

---

35 Tirésias Augustin Simon Sam (1835–1916) served as Haiti's president from March 31, 1896 to May 12, 1902; he resigned from office shortly before completing his term of six years.

5. Open the gate

Between August 1791 and October 1792 most of the classes and groups in Saint-Domingue had held fluctuating positions. When we follow the white landowners, for instance, we see that sometimes they teamed up with *petits blancs* to attack mulatto landowners, and other times they teamed up with mulatto landowners and *petits blancs* to crush slaves. Sometimes they teamed up with supporters of the King, and other times they supported the aristocrats' political commissioners. Mulatto plantation owners were doing their own spinning dance. In the North, they asked for rifles so they could go crush slaves, and in the West, some of them put rifles into slaves' hands.

In truth, when most of the social classes and groups were swaying back and forth, the political situation couldn't help but be a mishmash. But in October 1792, when Saint-Domingue got wind of what had happened in France, the situation got even more entangled. Social classes and groups rushed to take stands. But there were others that split in two. Each group tried to pull the society towards its own position.

When a society's future can't be decided without the partial consent of a particular social class, category, or group, and when that class, category, or group is pressuring the society to pull it towards its own position (even if that social class, category, or group isn't part of the political **apparatus**), it becomes a **social force**.

In 1792–93, a bunch of social forces took various positions in Saint-Domingue, they took various actions to make the rest of society accept their positions, and these various actions were what comprised the political situation.

each day's alike
no day's the same

A society's political situation is how the various social forces are pulling on that society. **A society's political situation is the specific combination of all the social forces at a specific moment.** Every time that combination changes, every time that moment changes, the situation changes.

What was Saint-Domingue's specific political situation in 1792? How were its **social forces** intertwined? What was their **position** on things?

In fact, there were six groups putting serious pressure on Haitian society: supporters of the new French government; aristocrats; freedmen; *petits blancs*; the leaders of the rebel slaves; and the slave masses.

There weren't many supporters of the new French government in Saint-Domingue. Within that group there were a few white plantation owners, bureaucrats, and big traders. The Civil Commission was leading that group: the French government that had just ascended had given it carte blanche ...

Not all the aristocrats came from the same social class or category. Their group was a coalition of political commissioners, economic commissioners, and white plantation owners who sided with the King. Most of them came from aristocratic families in France.

The freedmen were an important social force. Mulatto plantation owners were leading that social force, but middle-class mulattos and free blacks teamed up with them. When the news about August 10 reached them from France, mulatto plantation owners turned their coats. They, along with the other freedmen, sided against the aristocrats because they saw that the new government was determined to make all people **free** and equal to whites.

The po' white folks ('*petits blancs*') were a danger in waiting for both the Civil Commission and the freedmen. Sonthonax called them 'aristocrats of color' because, even though they were attacking the King's supporters, and even though they were carrying on like they agreed with the revolution in France, they hated freedmen, be they mulatto or black, whether they owned plantations or were in the middle class. They were attacking aristocrats, but only so they could take control of society, **because they too were white**. But what was even worse, since most of them didn't own property, was that they decided to crush, burn, and lay waste to everything along their path to power. *Petits blancs* were throwing rocks at every passing dog.

The Rebel Slave Generals were spinning around, flip-flopping the whole time. They supported the French King and the Spanish King at the same time, but they were attacking both aristocrats and supporters of the new government. Jean-François, Biassou, Toussaint, Desprez, Manseau, and Aubert[36] had promised the French leaders that they'd re-enslave all former slaves if they gave the slave generals the upper hand ...

But the Slave Masses had their own position, too. Above all, they were pursuing

- more time to work their own sliver of land
- freedom.

---

36 Jean-François was a rebel leader or a *chef de bande* (Madiou 1987 1:94, 96–99, etc.). Biassou was a rebel leader (Madiou 1987 1:96–99). Desprez led the rebel forces in the Northern region in 1791 (Oriol 188). Manzo (Louis Manseau) and Obèr (Aubert) were also rebel leaders (Madiou 1987 1:118).

Their **position** on freedom wasn't yet completely formed, but it was developing at top speed. In the end, the news about what the people had done in France, weapons in hand, further convinced the slave masses of the power they could have with a rifle in their hands. However, their position wasn't resolved on the issue of independence. Most of them understood that the French King or the Spanish King could give them freedom, and (just like the rebel leaders) they decided to maintain their allegiance to one or the other.

there are degrees of strength

My friends, let's stop and look back for a minute. When you know where you've come from, the path ahead of you becomes clearer ...

We've learned about the coalition that the French government sent the Second Civil Commission to establish, to **keep Saint-Domingue under French control**. We've heard what happened in France while the commissioners were at sea. We've laid bare Saint-Domingue's political entanglements to discover the positions held by most social forces vis-à-vis the country's central problem.

When we combine those three discoveries, we'll see that the Civil Commission was in deep trouble. In the wake of what had happened in France, Saint-Domingue's political situation wouldn't allow the commissioners to establish the coalition they'd come to put in place. Four social forces had blocked their path:

aristocrats
petits blancs
leaders of the rebel slaves
slave masses.

Between October 1792 and August 1793, the Civil Commission (and all the other supporters of the new government) set out to either crush or convert these social forces to solidify their own positions.

Since the 'new government supporters' were a weak social force, they propped themselves up on the other social force that had taken the closest position to theirs: the freedmen. They formed a **political coalition**.

A **political coalition** is when two (or more) social forces that don't have the exact same position, but who agree on a central position, unite to crush the other social forces in order to change (or to maintain) the political situation.

petits blancs
died in the boat

The first social power that the coalition attacked was the **aristocrats**, but the first social power that it eliminated was the ***petits blancs***.

In the North, in December 1792, the *petits blancs* plotted against the Commission and all the freedmen. Sonthonax attacked first. He started at the bottom and worked his way up to the leaders. On December 5, in the middle of the night, he captured four rookie leaders. On January 8, 1793, before the sun had risen, he captured nine others. The top leaders remained at large. On January 9, in plain daylight, Sonthonax attacked the very top. By leaning on the freedmen and their soldiers, he arrested Daugy, Raboteau, and the Archbishop Thibaut.[37] He sent them, reeling, off to France. In January 1793, the wings of the *petits blancs* in the North were broken.

In that same month of January 1793, the *petits blancs* in the West attacked. They tried to form a political coalition with the aristocrats, but the coalition was aborted. Sonthonax and Polverel got to Saint-Marc and assembled freedmen and the white soldiers supporting them. They added a few slaves to the group and greased the mouths of their cannons. On April 12, 1793, at nine o'clock in the morning, the Civil Commission's boat opened fire on Port-au-Prince. At six o'clock in the evening, the Civil Commission's 1,200 soldiers held complete control of the city. Borel[38] fled to Jamaica. In the West, the wings of the *petits blancs*' social force were broken. The *petits blancs* in the South were scared away.

By April 1793, the coalition was one-to-zero against the other social forces: it had destroyed the *petits blancs*.

---

37 Raboteau, Daugy, and Delaire belonged to the 'intermediate commission'; they were accused of agitation by Sonthonax, arrested, and embarked on the ship *L'América* (Madiou 1:122). Archbishop (Larchvêch) Thibaut attempted to intervene on behalf of those arrested and suddenly found himself arrested and embarked on *L'América*, accused by Sonthonax of disturbing the public peace (Madiou 1:122). This example serves as a reminder of the long-standing involvement of members of the Catholic Church in Haitian politics.

38 Borel, like the men mentioned in the footnote above, was a planter who fought against Sonthonax in Port-au-Prince and managed to escape to Jamaica via Jacmel (Madiou 1:130–31).

if at first you don't succeed, try, try again

The coalition eliminated the *petits blancs* to start with, but it struck the aristocrats first. Since December 1792, aristocrats in the North had been conspiring against the Civil Commission and the freedmen. D'Esparbès, their own military leader who'd come with the commissioners, was a raving mad aristocrat, 100 percent behind the King. When he heard the news about the French King getting overthrown, and when he saw the Civil Commission's decree to make freedmen equal to whites, he, along with a bunch of other soldiers, bureaucrats, and landowning aristocrats, decided to get rid of Sonthonax by force. But the plot was exposed. The coalition (the commissioners and the freedmen) shipped off d'Esparbès and several other aristocratic leaders. But if at first you don't succeed, try, try again. The aristocrats had property in Saint-Domingue. Either they were plantation owners, big traders, important bureaucrats, or big military types that the King had appointed in Saint-Domingue. They weren't about to lose their assets in this way. Anyway, if the King wasn't the leader of France anymore, they didn't need France anymore. Furthermore, they'd been playing footsy with Spain and England since 1792 so those two countries would help them crush the new French government's supporters in Saint-Domingue. Spain and England went along with it for a while. Then in 1793, twelve European countries declared war on France. The Spanish and English seized the opportunity to attack Saint-Domingue. A bunch of aristocrats went off to fight in the English and Spanish armies.

Galbaud[39] was a military leader the French government had sent to replace d'Esparbès as Saint-Domingue's commander-in-chief. He had a plantation there. As soon as he got to Saint-Domingue the *grands blancs* shoved him under their thumb. Galbaud took a stand and issued an order that was at variance with the Civil Commission's order. Sonthonax and Polverel (who had just defeated the *petits blancs* in the West) rushed back to Cape Haitian. They arrested Galbaud.

---

39 François-Thomas Galbaud (1743–1801), a French general, was appointed Governor-General of Saint-Domingue on February 1, 1793 (Oriol 201).

the monkey patted his baby so much that
he killed it

The aristocrats outranked most of the other whites, and they decided to march against the coalition of commissioners and freedmen.

On June 19, early in the morning, they clashed with the coalition's army that André Rigaud was leading in Grand'Anse. One day later, on the opposite end of the country, 3,000 men entered Cape Haitian, weapons in hand, shouting: 'Long live Galbaud/Down with Sonthonax'.

The commissioners had thought they'd resolved all their problems, and then all of a sudden they watched their arms get caught in the mill. The social forces they had teamed up with had neither the striking power nor the weapons to defend their position. On June 21, 1793, they issued a communiqué offering freedom to 'every black soldier who will fight for the Republic (the new French government) under the orders of the Civil Commission, whether against Spain or against other enemies of the French government, whether they be at home or abroad'.

Because the social forces that the Civil Commission had leaned on couldn't help them stay in power anymore, the Commission gave way to another social force: leaders of the rebel slaves.

On June 21, 1793, the commissioners' army was defeated. On June 21, 1793, the commissioners offered the slaves freedom. On June 22, 1793, 10,000 slaves poured into the city of Cape Haitian. On June 24, 1793, 10,000 colonists boarded ships without a thought of looking back. Galbaud's army was defeated!

In three days, the military situation had been turned on its head.

This is how Sonthonax himself put it: since they didn't accept that their basic interests were the same as those of mulatto plantation owners, and since they didn't accept the coalition that Ogé died dreaming of, Saint-Domingue's colonists helped 'crush the colonial system with their own efforts to uphold it'.[40]

Very often, over the course of History, hidden conflicts within the exploiter classes make those very classes contribute to blowing up the system they'd previously controlled. In truth, the plot among Galbaud and

---

40 David Geggus (personal correspondence) notes that the original quote, 'ils ont occasionné la ruine du système colonial, par les moyens mêmes qu'ils ont employés pour le défendre' ('they caused the ruin of the colonial system, by the same means that they used to defend it') comes from the 1795 'trial' that recorded the 'débats entre les accusateurs et les accusés' ('debates between the accusers and the accused') (Ardouin 2:39).

the other powerful colonists helped Saint-Domingue's revolution reach the unbound stage. The events of June 21 forced the Civil Commissioners to give way to leaders of the **rebel slaves**. But that wasn't all ... These events gave another social force the opportunity to advance its own ideas, demands, and positions: **the slave masses**.

gwayamouk flows in-between

In truth, even during the battles of June 21–22, the Civil Commission didn't talk about freedom for **all** people. The commissioners had offered freedom to soldiers who'd been fighting on their side, and they'd directed that communiqué specifically at Jean-François, Biassou, Toussaint, and the other big leaders. They'd offered those rebels freedom and plantations right away so they could raise an army as fast as possible; after that they'd see to other slaves. They would give them land and freedom, but gradually (Declaration of June 21).

The commissioners decided to pull out all the stops **to keep Saint-Domingue under French control**. But twice in a row, they'd leaned on the wrong social forces. The **freedmen** shared the Commission's position, but they didn't have enough military strength; the **leaders of the rebel slaves** had military strength, but they weren't on the Commission's side.

And you must understand why.

The commissioners had offered property to the slave leaders, but they already had property thanks to the Spanish army. The commissioners had offered them freedom, but they were already so free that they were involved in the slave trade themselves!

Besides, their decorations, titles, and ranks were longer than any police baton. In truth, that clique of big shots saw no advantage to this coalition. Especially since the commissioners' army had already fallen flat on its face. They told the commissioners to go to hell. (Declaration of June 25, and Declaration of July 6, 1793).

So, at the same time the leaders of the rebel slaves were sucking their teeth in contempt at the Commissioners with the full length of their chops, other social forces had been on the move. A piddling number of aristocrats and some leftover *petits blancs* had decided once and for all to hand the country over to foreigners (either England or Spain). They'd been plotting with their accomplices who were already in the North, and the English had been preparing to attack the South and Northwest of the country.

The freedmen had also been on the move. The major mulatto plantation owners had been throwing themselves on the English and

Spanish just like their white plantation owner comrades. A small team of mulattos who'd studied in France, who'd experienced the start of the bourgeois revolution over there, remained loyal to the commissioners. But in reality the country kept right on slipping out of France's hands.

Therefore, by July–August 1793, the Civil Commission had crushed two social forces in Saint-Domingue (*petits blancs* and aristocrats) but it had lost an ally (mulatto plantation owners), and the other ally that it had been pursuing (the slave leaders) had refused to recognize it.

The central mission of the Second Civil Commission was to **keep the country under French control**. Sonthonax and Polverel kept an eye on the only social force remaining, **the only social force that had enough strength to return the country to France**. But in politics, one very often must give to be able to take. To rally the slave masses, Sonthonax had to give them freedom, and all of a sudden, game on, anything goes.

On August 27, 1793, Polverel (in the West of the country) ordered that property in Saint-Domingue be split up so that slaves could have a little piece. He echoed the Commissioners' decision to give all slaves **who returned to work the land** the same freedom that all other French citizens enjoyed.

On August 29, 1793, in the North, Sonthonax decreed that all slaves were free. He gave all former slaves who'd been working on a plantation the right to split one third (1/3) of the plantation's profits among themselves.

Sonthonax and Polverel were making a last-ditch effort to keep the country under French control, but the conflicts were dragging them down. They had to rely on a social force that was daring and disjointed. They had to depend on a social class that had nothing more to lose. They'd given the steering wheel a sharp turn, but the Gwayamouk River wouldn't give them any more breaks: Saint-Domingue's revolution had reached the point of no return.

6. The little orange tree grew

The little orange tree grew
grew
little orange tree
mother-in-law's not mother

On January 26, 1801, Toussaint Louverture entered Santo Domingo and announced to all that the island was under his command, from the tip of Port-de-Paix all the way to the Spanish side. He wasn't making idle threats ... The Northwest was his. The Central Plateau was his. The Artibonite was in his hands. Les Cayes, Jacmel, and Jérémie had stopped complaining. Any Spaniard worth his salt was keeping a low profile ...

How did all of this happen? How was Toussaint able to take control of the North? When, how, and why was he able to seize the South? Where did all the government secretaries go? And the freedmen leaders?

In truth, Toussaint Louverture didn't hold this power on his own. While Toussaint himself was on the Spanish side, there was an enormous political organization that was able to control the country wherever its leader might be. Toussaint's power resided in that organization. That organization got him established step by step. And so, the day the organization was crushed, the day its coalition with the slave masses was broken (and we'll soon see why), Toussaint collapsed. But that's the grand finale ... In the meantime, at the beginning of 1801, Toussaint's organization was the only cock standing in the cockfighting ring of Saint-Domingue. We must seek to understand how the little orange tree grew as tall as a royal palm.

6.1 Mister I gave it to you ... Thank you, father!

Tooth fairy
what a nice little tooth
I gave you
You're going
to gyp me

In fact, when the Galbaud Affair[41] went down in Cape Haitian, the Second Civil Commission opened the government's doors to let the slaves come in. It was the last gamble Sonthonax and Polverel could take to keep Saint-Domingue under French control. They leaned on the slaves' social power so they could stay in power themselves. But neither the leaders of the rebel slaves nor the enslaved masses were ready to exploit the Commissioners' weaknesses. Instead, they were weakened of their own accord.

---

41 French general François-Thomas Galbaud (1743–1801) was appointed Governor-General of Saint-Domingue on February 1, 1793. Carolyn Fick (16) observes that when Galbaud 'refused to acknowledge the superior authority of the civil commissioners', riots ensued, resulting in the destruction of two-thirds of the city of Cape Haitian.

one flower
plus another flower
makes a bouquet of flowers
but it doesn't make
a laurel tree
like it or not

The rebel slaves had been hemmed in on both sides:

1) organization broke down for them

Many of the slaves didn't have proper weapons. Many others had weapons, but they didn't have any training. Instead of rebel groups seeking to team up together, though, scattered clusters of petty leaders ran around contesting one another. As the soldiers got dragged into the war, the leaders weren't even speaking to each other.

2) ideology broke down for them

But the biggest problem many of the rebel slaves faced was realizing they didn't actually know which of those two reasons had led them to fight. Naturally, they'd joined the rebel side, because at the time it was the only way they could win freedom. But once **they** were finally free, why had they kept fighting? They didn't know ... They didn't understand that freedom for **one** was intertwined with freedom for **all**.

Thus, many of them had stayed high up in the mountains where whites were afraid to climb. Many others had gone down to fight for their own personal interests. Jean-François and Biassou had been selling slaves.

This is something we all know (isn't it?): when every Tom, Dick, and Harry is out for his own self-interest, nothing gets done ...

Therefore, the rebel slaves were in a weak position, and the slave masses suffered from the same ailment:

--they had no organization
--they didn't understand the problem clearly enough. They didn't see that **all** slaves needed to fight for the freedom of all slaves.

But the slave masses had two big advantages:

--they were many, therefore they could become a major military force
--they had an **interest** in **all** slaves becoming fully free.

78   *Stirring the Pot of Haitian History*

mosquitos
watch out for
zombies

The group flanking Toussaint Louverture was unlike any other rebel slave group. In 1793, it showed what it was capable of.

On August 29, 1793, in Camp Tourelle, Toussaint issued a communiqué. He announced that he was fighting for **freedom and equality** throughout Saint-Domingue. He invited anyone seeking this freedom to join forces with his group.

This decree showed that Toussaint and his comrades had understood the country's central problem to be the conflict between slavery and freedom. The biggest demands they were making on Saint-Domingue's society were FREEDOM and EQUALITY for all people.

When an organization makes one or several demands, when it recognizes that demand as the fundamental demand that it's making upon a society, this demand [or these demands] become[s] the organization's political agenda.

By the same token, when we hear some crook speaking French, and we examine his words closely but still can't recognize the basic demand he's making upon society, we can be sure that he's dishonest. Towards the end of August, in 1793, Toussaint's group had scored two points more than all the other rebel slave groups. It had made one basic demand upon society, and therefore its political agenda was clear. It wasn't only clear, it was **spot on** because it dovetailed with one of the slave **masses'** basic demands: FREEDOM for all people.

Therefore, Toussaint's group had taken the **position** of defending one of the masses' basic interests. But in fact, his wasn't the only group that had taken such a **position**. On that same August 29, Sonthonax had already given the order for all slave owners to free their slaves. But Toussaint didn't join forces with Sonthonax, and there are several reasons for that. The main reason was that Toussaint's group and the Civil Commission had different **political tactics**. The Civil Commission had wanted to **give** the slaves freedom, while Toussaint himself wanted the slaves to **seize** freedom with their own strength, because that was the only way they could **maintain** that freedom.

Political agendas are one thing, and political tactics are another. Two organizations might have similar political agendas, but their tactics aren't the same. Two organizations might have similar political tactics, but their political agendas aren't similar. An organization's political tactics

6. *The little orange tree grew* 79

are how that organization situates itself to make society accept its basic demands.

Toussaint's group had seen only one way for Saint-Domingue's society to grant the basic demand of FREEDOM: there had to be an army of **slaves** that could seize this freedom, that could defend it with its own firepower, and that could control the government. Therefore, the organization had to be rock solid.

a fish
lays its eggs
at the bottom of the sea

Towards the end of August, in 1793, the group of rebel slaves flanking Toussaint Louverture scored two more points than all other slave groups in Saint-Domingue. He had resolved both the complications that had ensnared all the other groups: his political agenda was spot on, and his political tactics were spot on. They were spot on because both that agenda and those tactics dovetailed with the social class who had the greatest stake in overthrowing the society: the slave **masses**.

In 1793, Toussaint's group abandoned the position of the leaders of the rebel slaves in order to defend a basic interest of the slave class: **freedom for all people.**

But if Toussaint had clearly stated his political agenda, he didn't broadcast his tactics: his group was still weak. A fish lays its eggs at the bottom of the sea ... If we understand that tactic today, it's because we can look back and see the path that little group traveled until it managed to seize power. And so, we can't say exactly when or how Toussaint's organization was formed. But there are a few common stories in History that can make us think.

In 1792, Moïse, Dessalines, and Paul Louverture were already in Toussaint's army. In 1794, Christophe Meunier and Maurepas were already Toussaint's officers. In 1794, Toussaint's army controlled Gonaïves, Gros Morne, Marmelade, Plaisance, Dondon, Limbé, and L'Acul. It had four thousand (4,000) soldiers plus. It had a solid general staff: François-Dominique-Toussaint Bréda (called 'Louverture'), Jean-Jacques Duclos (called 'Dessalines'), Gilles Bréda (called 'Moïse Louverture'), Paul Toussaint (called 'Paul Louverture'), Christophe Meunier, Marcial Besse, Maurepas, Bonaventure, Clervaux, Desrouleaux, Duménil, André

Venais[42] ... In fact, it was a full-fledged organization that had allied itself with France!

making deals isn't a sin

Between 1792 and 1794, after plenty of narrow escapes, Toussaint's group had formed a full-fledged organization with a spot on political agenda, spot on political tactics, a solid avant-garde, and an army of 4,000 men to carry out its tactics, **and once the organization was able to stand on its own two feet, it allied itself with French political commissioners.**

The political coalition of Toussaint's organization was spot on because:

1) the organization already stood on its own two feet
2) the coalition benefited the organization more than it did France.

Let's take a close look at that deal, and we'll seek to understand what it offered both groups.

In July 1794, eleven months after Sonthonax's declaration that the slaves should be freed, the French political commissioners were in a weak position in Saint-Domingue. Because the big rebel generals' political agenda wasn't ideal, because they'd been advancing their own personal interests instead of fighting for the freedom of all slaves, and because they hadn't developed their political organization like Toussaint had, many of them (Jean-François, Biassou ...) had stayed in the Spanish camp. Others had turned around to join the French (Pierrot, Makaya, Pierre Michel[43] ...) but they lacked the military training that both the

---

42 Moïse (1769–1801) was Toussaint Louverture's adopted nephew, and Paul Louverture was his brother, who began as lieutenant-colonel and rose to general. Toussaint promoted other officers including Christophe Meunier, Marcial Besse, Jacques Maurepas, Bonaventure, Augustin Clervaux, Louis Desrouleaux, and Duménil (for more details, see Madiou 1987 1:269, 289–90).

43 Pierrot was a rebel leader or *chef de bande* who led a large army against Villatte in 1796 (Oriol 233); Makaya was another black general, and Pierre Michel was a rebel leader who rose to the rank of colonel, then general (Madiou 1987 1:182, 232, etc.).

Spanish and Toussaint's people had had. They weren't powerful enough to reinvent French protocols.

Therefore, in July 1794, despite Sonthonax's declaration, Saint-Domingue had been sliding back under French control. The English and Spanish had surrounded the country on all four sides. And so, the deal [with Toussaint] gave the political commissioners a solid army that was fighting 'for them' in the West and in the North of the country. Bit by bit, thanks to the organization, Saint-Domingue was returning to French control. But as we know well, my friends, life brings contradictions. Very often the wind stops blowing to catch its breath before a hurricane … Bouapiro sees far, it's true, but Grinn Prominnin sees even farther. If we look over the fence, we see that this deal was a total boon for the organization. While French generals and politicians were leaning on it to bolster themselves, the organization upheld its own independence. Besides, it got even greater traction within the political apparatus the French commissioners had put in place. The organization already had a solid team, a true avant-garde; the deal gave it the opportunity to position its own avant-garde at the heart of the country's political apparatus. Not only did some officers retain their rank, but many others got promoted. After each big battle they fought, Toussaint demanded that Lavaud[44] (the military leader of the French) give black people more responsibility in the army. And, given the situation that Saint-Domingue was in, military power was equal to political power. The organization was already an enormous military force, and it became the largest political power in the country.

To be sure, in the French commissioners' eyes, when Toussaint's army was growing, it was **France's** army that was growing. But when we look beyond the mountains, we see that Toussaint's group had been acquiring weapons, training, and status, along with **formerly enslaved soldiers who were already in the French camp**. We see that the army of former slaves had been growing. We see that Freedom's army had been growing. We also shouldn't forget that at that moment, the French camp was the only one where an army of former slaves could comfortably expand, because while the English and the Spanish had been making use of former slaves, they didn't depend on them as much. They hadn't felt very comfortable when all those black people had been carrying weapons. France was the only country that had recognized the slaves' freedom on a large scale, and the French had thus shut their eyes … When they made the effort to open them, it was too late to stop the action.

---

44 Étienne Lavaud was a French officer who originally came to Saint-Domingue with Sonthonax, Polverel, and Ailhaud (Madiou 1987 2:161).

Therefore, the deal had given the organization greater **political advantage** (it had more say in the government), **ideological advantage** (Freedom's camp was growing), and **military advantage** (Freedom's army was growing). And there were many other advantages, too, but those advantages were double-edged swords …

every donkey brays …

Toussaint's organization controlled some land within the country. According to how things worked at the time, when a general took a town, he took the best plantations for himself. The higher a man's rank in the army, the more land he got. And so, since before 1794, certain ex-slave leaders had land they controlled. But they couldn't flaunt it just yet … The coalition with France forced the State in Saint-Domingue to recognize the legal right of Toussaint's army leaders to many plantations in the North, on the Central Plateau, and the Artibonite Valley. In 1795, six months after the coalition was formed, Saint-Domingue's plantations lay in the hands of three groups: new French political commissioners (Lavaud's group), military leaders of the freedmen (Villatte, Beauvais, and Rigaud's team),[45] and the leader of Louverture's army.

These points are very important. We see that Toussaint's organization grew, and we see what its beauty, its discipline, and its power did for the **mass** of former slaves. But we must also see the thorns beneath the flowers. The deal with France allowed several of the organization's leaders to serve as plantation owners just like all the other plantation owners. Toussaint had his own land, just as Rigaud, in the South, had his own land.

… in the pasture next door

That episode had two major consequences.

A conflict emerged between *nouveaux libres* leaders (leaders of Toussaint's organization) and of *nouveaux libres* masses (masses of all the former slaves). Given that that conflict had only sprouted up in 1795

---

[45] Jean-Louis Villatte (1751–1802) and André Rigaud (1761–1811) became generals in Toussaint's army; Louis-Jacques Beauvais (1759–99), born in Saint-Domingue and educated in France, was a French general allied with Toussaint's army.

(it came unbound in 1801), we haven't studied it yet. But like Lamèsi says: even sworn secrets can leak out.

Another conflict emerged between *anciens libres*[46] leaders (blacks and mulattos who'd been free for a long time) and leaders of Toussaint's organization. To be sure, from the moment Sonthonax pronounced the freedom of the slaves, there was a conflict between *nouveaux libres* and *anciens libres*. But when Toussaint's vanguard seized their land, and France granted them absolution without confession, the *anciens libres* leaders—who had gone and appropriated most of the land that whites had left them—were not amused at all. Especially in the North, it was as though Toussaint had seized their fathers' land. Interests collided, and ever since those interests collided, we've traveled the path of conflict. In 1795, a conflict emerged between *nouveaux libres* **leaders** and *anciens libres* **leaders**, and this conflict couldn't be swept under the rug. This conflict combined with **another** (a bigger conflict): *nouveaux libres* versus *anciens libres*. Then both conflicts exploded like two-bit firecrackers, weapons were fired in the community of Saint-Domingue; and amidst all that smoke ... the little orange tree grew ... and grew ...

---

46 The *anciens libres* represent people of mixed race who had their freedom as a community for one or more generations, as opposed to the *nouveaux libres*, who had acquired their freedom after 1791 or in the course of their lifetime.

6.2 Come and pout

Come and pout
brother Jean
come and pout
come and see brother Pierre
who's pouting over you

On March 20, 1796, in the city of Cape Haitian, a bunch of General Villatte's supporters invaded the palace of Lavaud (the French general whom Sonthonax left as Major General of Saint-Domingue). They beat Lavaud into the ground, they arrested him, and they locked him up in prison. The Cape Haitian town council issued a communiqué saying that Lavaud was no longer in charge, and that Villatte was taking his place. Villatte sent notice to the other generals (Rigaud, Beauvais, Toussaint) about what was going on and asked them to join forces with him.

But in the early morning of March 22, Villatte received a letter from Colonel Pierre Michel—who had been under Villatte's command—and a letter from the general Toussaint Louverture. Both men said they disagreed with Lavaud's imprisonment and with Villatte becoming leader. They said that if the town council and Villatte did not immediately release Lavaud, they'd march against Cape Haitian. Villatte hadn't even finished reading their letters and Toussaint was on the move. In a flash, he sent a dispatch to French authorities in the United States to announce what he was planning to do. He ordered Dessalines and Belair to make haste to Cape Haitian with two columns of soldiers. Finally, Toussaint himself—the load always waits on the cart—took to the road with the rest of his brigade.

On March 20, 1796, Villatte and the leaders of the town council had Lavaud arrested. In the early morning of March 22, they read Toussaint's letter. On that same March 22, at nine in the morning, the magistrates panicked and released Lavaud; Villatte fled. On March 28, Toussaint entered Cape Haitian. On April 1, 1796, Lavaud rolled up his sleeves and proclaimed to everyone in Saint-Domingue: Toussaint was second only to him.

The little orange tree grew ... and grew ...

My friends, this is what happened. This tale burns like hot peppers, with episodes sprouting on top of other episodes. But History's not just a tale, History's a bunch of **whys** that stir up a society's guts. And so we have to ask the question: how did everything that happened, happen?

two mountains met

In fact, the episode they called the 'Villatte Affair' was rooted in several conflicts within the society of Saint-Domingue. In Saint-Domingue, in 1796, the army generals had seized nearly all the plantations that the colonists had abandoned in their flight. In the part of Saint-Domingue that was supposedly under French control, there were two tenacious groups of people who controlled the land: the *anciens libres* leaders and the *nouveaux libres* leaders. From the start, there was a conflict between **anciens libres leaders** (Rigaud, Villatte, Beauvais) and **leaders of the nouveaux libres** (Toussaint, Dessalines, Moïse) ...

It's true, some whites still had property in Saint-Domingue. But after the Galbaud Affair, many former colonists flew the coop. Most whites who'd retained control of their plantations had been on the team supporting the new French government, and their power rested in the hands of the *nouveaux libres*. And so the main conflict was the division between *nouveaux libres* leaders and leaders of the *anciens libres*. This conflict appeared in various forms: it was an economic conflict, it was a political conflict, and it was a military conflict ...

The *nouveaux libres* leaders controlled the Artibonite Valley, the Central Plateau, and the Northwest. They were forcing peasants to work, but war losses had taken their toll on those areas, and losses kept piling up, causing them headaches at times. In spite of the fact that Toussaint's organization was amassing wealth, it was still behind when compared to the wealth of the *anciens libres*.

But the political power and the military power of leaders of the *nouveaux libres* were not trivial. Their territory was in the center of the country. They could cast blows left and right. Their soldiers were well trained. Moreover, as of July 1795, the war between France and Spain was over. The group of rebel slaves who'd been in Spain's camp were crushed. Jean-François threw in the towel. Biassou melted away like butter in the sun, and no one ever found a trace of him. After that, most of the *anciens libres* rebels piled onto Toussaint's organization.

danmboua dédé
karidanm
O, corporal
O, division

The situation of the *anciens libres* was more or less the opposite of the situation of the *nouveaux libres*. In the South and in the West, plantation owners were enjoying their revenue.

But even though *anciens libres* leaders (especially in the West and the South) had money and supplies on hand, and even though their army stood on its own two feet, the political problem wasn't trivial. When the Second Civil Commission had disembarked (1792), the *anciens libres* had backed supporters of the new French government. But when Sonthonax departed (1794), he left Lavaud, a white Frenchman, as the country's leader. In July 1795, the French government promoted five military leaders in Saint-Domingue. So they gave Lavaud the highest rank (division leader) and they gave Toussaint, a former slave who'd just joined the team, the same rank as the highest mulatto military leaders (brigade general). The *anciens libres* weren't pleased one bit … In addition, from 1794 on, the French political commissioners (specifically Sonthonax and Lavaud) had withdrawn their support from *anciens libres*, and they'd propped themselves up on the masses of *nouveaux libres*. Lavaud had drawn blood from rocks to prevent the *anciens libres* from dispatching a commission straight to the French government, but he'd opened the door for Toussaint. On February 21, 1796, when two or three of Toussaint's and Lavaud's secretaries went off to France to make their voices heard, the leaders of the *anciens libres* were dumbstruck.

In fact, the problems facing all the leaders of the *anciens libres* in Saint-Domingue weren't trivial. But while every case may be worthy of its name, not every case is the same. The *anciens libres* leaders in the North (Villatte's team) had dealt with more problems than all the others. They didn't have the military advantages of the mulattos in the South. Lavaud had cornered them in Port-de-Paix, Toussaint was in Gonaives, and Pierre Michel was worming his way up inside them. It's true, Cape Haitian was controlled by Villatte and, it's true, Pierre Michel was supposed to control Cape Haitian, but Cape Haitian was nearly surrounded. Ultimately, because of the country's geography and because of their concentration specifically in the North, slave movements had always been strongest in those areas. In truth, the *anciens libres* were in a pinch. Thus, Villatte proclaimed: 'If I had … I would …'. He started undercutting Toussaint's organization. He sent spies and he rabble-roused, hatching little schemes here and there. He tried to cut off Toussaint's food supplies.

So while Villatte was giving Toussaint trouble, Lavaud was hitting the *anciens libres* in their weak spot. Before 1793, most plantations and estates in the North had belonged to white colonists, and mulattos' wealth was concentrated in the South. When the colonists took off, specifically in the wake of the Galbaud Affair, the *anciens libres* seized their property. But when the *nouveaux libres* entered the fray, when Lavaud's army gained strength (the strength of Toussaint's organization), Pérou,[47] who was Lavaud's secretary of finance, decreed those lands to be State property. He ordered the mulattos to pay rent and leases. The *anciens libres* protested that they'd spent a lot to rebuild those plantations, they hadn't seized more land than anyone else, and they hated any notion that would make them give the government their money. My friends, you'll remember this: ever since social categories or classes first started arguing about land in the country of Ayiti Toma, weapons have had to be fired. In 1796, Pérou demanded to see mulattos' land papers, and they attacked him. In 1805, Dessalines made the same demand, and they killed him. Well … (We'll come back to this.)

paper land titles/paper money

The issue of land titles wasn't the only economic problem the *anciens libres* had in the North. Paper for paper, there was the issue of paper money …

---

47 Pérou subsequently became a *chef de bataille*, or commander, in Toussaint's army (Madiou 1987 3:377–78).

Long ago, in Saint-Domingue like in many other places in the Americas and Europe, **silver**[48] was used to pay soldiers and officers. No, it wasn't painted pieces of copper like silver today. Silver! Real silver! Like the silverware in Madame Causédiau's cupboard, like the wedding ring on Madame Laristaux's finger. Silver! Yes, real silver!

But in 1796, trade was declining in the North, silver didn't circulate much from other countries, and Pérou paid officers with paper money. My friends, I don't know if you know this, but paper **money** isn't **money**. **Paper money is paper**. It's a sheet of paper that the State signs to promise Mister Joe, Miss Giselle, or absolutely anyone who holds that paper that there's one gourde, five gourdes, or 100 gourdes in their grasp. When the people take paper money from the State, they give the State credit. They're really saying that they believe in the paper the State signed, because they know the State has money. But what if the State doesn't have money? What if the State's credit isn't good? What if people stop believing the State's word? Paper money loses its standing. At that point, what you could buy for a gourde last year has become much more expensive; you bought it for four gourdes this year. Because foreign traders don't trust the State's paper anymore. Because people doing business transactions in the country don't trust the State's paper anymore. They take the State's paper to be a false promise.

And so, in 1796, the government in the North didn't have any money, and the *anciens libres* around Cape Haitian knew it. They weren't about to take soap for cheese. They told Pérou to get lost! They joined with white reactionaries, they joined with some *nouveaux libres* soldiers who weren't happy with the economic situation, they plotted with certain mulatto leaders in the South (especially Pinchinat),[49] and they launched an offensive against both Lavaud and Pérou. It was the only way they could take complete control of the government in the North. If they won that battle, the *nouveaux libres* were completely done for. The *anciens libres* were up, the *anciens libres* were down, the French commissioners were clearing out, and Toussaint's organization was like peanut butter on cassava bread: it couldn't even ooze out.

---

48 The Haitian Creole word *lajan*, like the French *argent* from which it derives, means both 'money' and 'silver'; an English translation cannot capture this double meaning.

49 Pinchinat was a freedman who was subsequently imprisoned along with André Rigaud. Bonaparte ultimately freed Rigaud but, according to Madiou's account, the 'virtuous' Pinchinat, whose 'only crime was to have been one of Saint-Domingue's apostles of liberty', died in prison in Paris (Madiou 1987 1:81, 83; 2:340).

grow, little orange tree

But the leaders of the *anciens libres* made a huge mistake: they hadn't recognized the amount of political and military power that Toussaint's organization had. They hadn't imagined that other leaders of the *nouveaux libres* like Pierre Michel (Toussaint's **personal** enemy) would be teaming up with the **organization**. And so, when Pierre Michel refused them, when Dessalines got raring to go, and when the whites of the Town Council fled, the *anciens libres* gave up. Instead of the Villatte conspiracy benefiting *anciens libres*, it bolstered the power of the *nouveaux libres* because it revealed that most of Saint-Domingue's whites, and Lavaud's general staff, couldn't budge an inch without Toussaint's organization.

After March 1796, French whites lost their remaining power in Saint-Domingue. The *anciens libres* were all washed up in the North. In the South, the conflict between the *anciens libres* and the *nouveaux libres* got even further entangled.

So the biggest consequence of the Villatte conspiracy was the power that it gave to the *nouveaux libres* **masses**. It's true, the masses hadn't been enjoying the lands controlled by Toussaint's organization. In the North, as in the South, they'd been working like mules so the leaders could run free. To be sure, there was a conflict between the **masses** of *nouveaux libres* and Toussaint's organization. Yet, in 1796, this was a hidden conflict within the **camp of *nouveaux libres***. The organization's political agenda was to defend freedom for all *nouveaux libres*. Its central tactic was to support this freedom with an army of *nouveaux libres*. In 1796, this coalition had more importance than the conflicts that were growing.

And so, when we size up the extent of the Villatte Affair, we see that the masses of former slaves benefited more than anyone else. The freedom they'd acquired in 1793–94 was getting more deeply rooted each day, and there wasn't a soul who could take it away from them anymore.

The little orange tree grew … and grew …

6.3 Iron cuts iron

Look at the mulatto's child
mister banjo
how do you think he's doing?
cane in hand
mister banjo
handkerchief in his big pocket
his boots are shining
shining

On June 17, 1799, Delva, Faubaix, and Desruisseaux[50] (three officers in André Rigaud's army) attacked Petit-Goâve in the middle of the night. They arrested Laplume,[51] the officer whom Toussaint Louverture had put in charge of that area. When Louverture heard that news, he put his army into motion and launched an offensive against Rigaud … The war that began on that day, June 17, the war that professors call '**the War of the South**', left many wounds on the Haitian people. Wounds turn into open sores, open sores get infected, and that's how you contract bad diseases …

---

50 Jean-Pierre Delva, Faubaix, and Renaud Desruisseaux (who controlled Léogâne) were army colonels (Madiou 1987 2:27, 44, etc.; 4:10, 12, etc.; 5:12–27, etc.).
51 Jean-Joseph Laplume was a *nouveau libre* who attained high positions within the French army under Lavaud and Sonthonax. Laplume was at the center of the Toussaint-Rigaud conflict; as French commandant of Les Cayes following the War of the South he took over Rigaud's property there but in late 1803 was ultimately sent back to France; he died en route (Oriol 214–15).

The first question we need to ask about the war between Rigaud and Toussaint is: how did that war come about? Saint-Domingue was supposedly under French control, and Rigaud and Toussaint were generals in the French army ... Had France been unable to prevent the war? And what about the other social forces in Saint-Domingue? ...

If we look back, we'll see that many of the social forces that had been pressuring Saint-Domingue in 1793 disappeared one after the other. The *petits blancs* had kicked the bucket. After the Galbaud Affair, many white plantation owners had fled, either to the American side, or to the English camp. The damage that had been inflicted upon the country, the problems that had arisen in France, and the English boats that were casting their nets in the sea, all amounted to pulling the rug out from under traders' feet. As for the *anciens libres*, in the North, they burned up their shrines during Villatte's conspiracy. And so, the social forces had gotten rearranged. Within the French-controlled part of Saint-Domingue, there were three big organizations butting heads:

Rigaud's organization (big military men and the mulatto plantation owners supporting France who controlled the South)

Toussaint's organization (which controlled the North)

The group of French political commissioners (who were making the most of the situation).

if the head goes faster than the body which comes in last?

I say French political commissioners, but in fact, three months after the Villatte Affair, whoever said 'French political commissioners' really meant Léger Félicité Sonthonax. Sonthonax had disembarked for the second time at Cape Haitian, on May 11, 1796, as president of the Third Civil Commission the French government had sent to Saint-Domingue. The goal for that commission, just like for the first two, just like any commission that a predatory country sends to a smaller country, was to keep Saint-Domingue under metropolitan control.

So just like the first two Saint-Domingue Commissions, the Third Civil Commission had received special orders regarding the ways and means to achieve this dominance, regarding the ways and means it would confront the various social forces. In 1796, the French government considered the English—along with the French who'd taken themselves for English—and the *anciens libres* to be France's major enemies on the island. Therefore, the Third Civil Commission received the orders: crush the English, crush the mulattos! Crushing the English had basically meant relying on the two generals' armies (Rigaud's and Toussaint's) to stop the invasion. But crushing the mulattos had meant relying on the *nouveaux libres*, and especially on Toussaint's organization. Crushing the mulattos had meant opposing Rigaud because however much he believed in France, André Rigaud would never crush a social force that was the only fence around the garden. And so, between May '96 and March '97 Sonthonax gave Toussaint a free pass, and the *nouveaux libres* got more traction within the government. At the same time, while Rigaud and his supporters were fighting against the English on France's behalf, the Commission clamped down unconditionally on ALL *ANCIENS LIBRES*. Sonthonax's secretaries descended upon the South and declared (rightly) that Rigaud was trying to set up a mulatto government in the country's basin. They said he wouldn't heed the orders of any commissioner. They declared (wrongly) that he was supporting the English. They went on and on and on interminably … Sonthonax declared Rigaud an outlaw, and he appointed Toussaint general-in-chief, the sole major-general of the French army in Saint-Domingue.

In truth, the Third Civil Commission did all that it could to keep the country in France's claws. But just as it was for the first two commissions, so was it for any hawkish commission in a country of clear-eyed little chickens, heading things off was no longer on the table. On August 25, 1797, once Sonthonax had given back the majority of the Commission's weapons to the *nouveaux libres*, major-general Louverture (who'd never broken ties with Rigaud) shipped Sonthonax back to France.

the extent of your fist is the extent of your anger

Many people who seem like experts on History have been baffled by the quarrel between Toussaint and Sonthonax. They've cited several causes that don't hold up to questioning … As if Toussaint got up one morning and stopped trusting Sonthonax. As if Toussaint Louverture couldn't tolerate another leader in Saint-Domingue. As if Toussaint had been jealous of Sonthonax … They've focused on the relationship or the personal disagreements between the two men, without looking deeper into their political differences.

To be sure, the relationship between Toussaint and Sonthonax had been off-kilter. Sonthonax dilly-dallied a great deal before appointing

Moïse Louverture general. He'd refused to promote several other of Toussaint's officers. But—and this is most important—despite any camaraderie between these men, they'd never been on the same page about major issues. Toussaint had favored letting many white plantation owners return to Saint-Domingue, and Sonthonax was against it. Sonthonax had wanted to exterminate the whole team of *anciens libres*, and Toussaint was against it. Toussaint had sought out trade with other countries (especially the United States), and Sonthonax dithered. Despite being white, and despite being married to a mulatress, Sonthonax had been fighting to keep Saint-Domingue's plantations under the control of a government in which the *nouveaux libres* masses and the Republic's commissioners were holding the bull's two horns. Despite the fact that Toussaint led all the *nouveaux libres*, he had been fighting so that all plantation owners (**nouveaux libres**, **anciens libres**, and **whites** too) could make Saint-Domingue walk the road to freedom without French interference in every speck of the government's business.

These respective positions hadn't been written down on paper, in the open, like we do things now, but they seeped into the words, letters, and actions of those two men, and they exposed all their roots under Toussaint's government (1800–01). So from 1797 onward those differences had mattered, and they'd fueled the fire of all the little personal jealousies that were simmering beneath the surface. Sonthonax's ouster was perfectly aligned with Louverture's political tactics and his stance on Saint-Domingue's situation during that month of August 1797. The people's anger is never slight (don't just eat the sauce, respect the cooking pot), and the extent of your fist is the extent of your anger. If Toussaint Louverture got rid of the French government's top commissioner, it's because the situation in both France and Saint-Domingue gave him the opportunity to be brazen.

In 1797 a lot of upheaval had gone on in France, and Toussaint Louverture had gotten the news:

Some of the deputies in the French government had demanded that Sonthonax return (June 3, 1797).

The English minister sent a delegation to France to discuss the ways and means the two countries could end the war (July 1797).

Saint-Domingue's former plantation owners were conniving within the French government. Some started saying that they had to reclaim their assets in Saint-Domingue. And when those people were counting their assets, they counted slaves like heads of cattle.

The Revolution in France was quickly losing ground of its own accord. The big bourgeois types effectively seized all the political power. They went along with former aristocrats, and they sent peasants, workers, and craftspeople packing. The slogan 'all people are equal' kicked the bucket ...

This news spoke volumes to Louverture. If former plantation owners and aristocrats were in the French government, France would clamp down on Saint-Domingue. The former colonists would try to reclaim 100 percent of their assets. They could even (because the revolution was losing ground, 'equal' had no sway anymore), **they could even take back people's freedom!** And if they didn't have English boats to impede them anymore, they could come back with as many regiments as they wanted.

Therefore, by ousting Sonthonax, Louverture

-eliminated a leader who disagreed with him on several of the country's economic, social, and political issues.
-pulled a fast one on the French government, acting as though he himself (Toussaint) were France's biggest defender.
-gave himself breathing room, so he could control Saint-Domingue in his own way, and so he'd have the upper hand in the event that he had to clash politically with France.

my mother had three little lambs
a thief came and stole one
two little lambs stood eye to eye

And so, Sonthonax's ouster had other political consequences, and Toussaint didn't necessarily anticipate all of them ...

After Sonthonax left, between August 1797 and April 1798, Toussaint's organization commanded all the territory in Saint-Domingue that belonged to France, **except for Rigaud's department**. Toussaint and his officers controlled the country's politics and economy without French interference, but **Rigaud was lone King in the South**. Rigaud and Toussaint didn't have anything against each another at that time. The two of them together were thrashing the English. Toussaint had sent weapons to Rigaud. Each one had kept the other up to date about how the war was going in the region that he occupied. But if we take a step back from that context to look at the heart of the problem, we'll see that **the war was what had forced the two camps to team up**. In 1797, the conflict between France's supporters and England's supporters was a

banner conflict, standing out so far beyond the others, despite not being a fundamental conflict, that it had to be settled before any other conflict. But once that conflict finally got resolved, once the war had ended, lots of other conflicts would of course crop up, and of course the two organizations would end up quarreling.

Therefore, at the end of 1797, although Toussaint and Rigaud were friends, and although their two organizations had joined forces to defeat the English, **the roots of the War of the South were already there, within the two organizations' political agendas and political tactics, and also within the primary positions held by the two massive social forces that were still standing face to face in the cockfighting ring of Saint-Domingue:** *NOUVEAUX LIBRES* **and** *ANCIENS LIBRES*. Sweet potatoes assuredly grow under the ground …

After the Third Civil Commission's visit, the three major conflicts glared even more harshly:

the conflict between France and *nouveaux libres*
the conflict between *nouveaux libres* and *anciens libres*
the conflict between Toussaint's organization and Rigaud's organization.

In February 1798, the French government sent one last special commissioner to gamble on those conflicts. Since he couldn't count on support from any social forces, he would take a blind gamble. He'd attempt to make *anciens libres* strike *nouveaux libres*, and *nouveaux libres* strike *anciens libres*, so that France could sing a requiem. Given the mistrust on both sides, he would attempt to trap either Rigaud or Toussaint, or both Rigaud and Toussaint! The he-man that the French Republic sent to pull off this underhanded maneuver was a powerful military leader, a pompous aristocrat with a big mouth: Gabriel-Marie-Theodore-Joseph Hédouville.[52] But like Lamèsi says, having a big reputation kills little dogs …

---

[52] Gabriel-Marie-Theodore-Joseph Hédouville was a French general sent by the Directory to restore French control over Saint-Domingue (Madiou 1987 1:325, 376, etc.; 2:38, 60, 99, etc.).

two poor people shouldn't marry

When Hédouville set out for Saint-Domingue, in March 1798, with 200 young officers who believed they were going to capture Limbé, Toussaint and Rigaud had already surrounded the English in every corner of the country. The English soldiers were retreating. So Hédouville slunk out of the way, and he kept a low profile. The people of Saint-Domingue were chasing the English out? Very well! That didn't bother him. What he'd come to do personally was to keep the country under French control—that is, to put Rigaud and Toussaint 'in their place'. He could either boot out both men or he could pit one of them against the other. This was the first time since 1791 that France had sent a commissioner who was supposed to decide **on the spot** which social force, and which organization, he would lean on.

The French government had given Hédouville the personal authority to choose between the two men. But even if someone shows a bias that may appear **personal**, that bias is rooted in the primary position the person holds within the society that he or she lives in. Therefore, when Hédouville chose Rigaud, it wasn't just because he favored Rigaud's gullet. And even supposing that he'd favored Rigaud's gullet to Toussaint's jaw, his bias was rooted in his social position. **Hédouville's position was closer to Rigaud than to Toussaint.** The position that Hédouville's government was defending was closer to the position of the social forces supporting André Rigaud. It's within these positions that we can see where the connection is made between Rigaud and Hédouville. And it's within these positions that we'll come to see how Louverture managed to be the last man standing.

round and round and round he goes …

Within any dog-eat-dog society, any society that has classes, there's always a social force (a social class or category) that's struggling to achieve its interests within the society. A class (or a category within a class) has several types of interests.

It has its economic interests, which is to say the most advantageous ways and means for money to be made, for wealth to be divided up, for work to be organized, and for goods to proliferate within the society. One of the economic interests of plantation owners in Saint-Domingue was the large plantation system.

It has its political interests, which is to say the most advantageous ways and means for running society, for organizing the government, for implementing ideas, and for condemning by the courts. One of the political interests of mulatto plantation owners was to have a voice within the State, equal to that of whites.

It has its ideological interests, which is to say the most advantageous ways and means for upholding (or changing) society's customs, the habits, beliefs, religious practices, and languages of the various sectors of the population. One of the ideological interests of *petits blancs* was color prejudice.

It's true, no class ever fully achieves all its interests, and it's also true that not all classes achieve their interests in the same way. Notice there's always one class that achieves more of its interests than the others, that achieves its primary interests. Those interests can be economic, political, or ideological, but we know they're pivotal for that class **when they're strong enough to drag the rest of the society in that class's direction**. Before 1791, one of the primary interests that the commissioner class managed to achieve was the total dependence of Saint-Domingue. In 1793, freedom for all was one of the primary interests that the enslaved class managed to achieve.

When one social force comes to achieve the majority of its primary interests within a society, and when that social force comes to drag other classes within the society in the direction of its own interests—whether or not it was within the government—that social force is in power, and that social force has **dominance** within the society.

The dominance of a class or category reflects the amount of leeway that class or category has for achieving its interests.

Before 1789, the class of French commissioners had the greatest amount of leeway for achieving its interests. But from 1789 on, the commissioners' dominance started to decline. It's true that no other social class could yet overthrow them. And we must understand why ... Dominance isn't built up in two days. A class can take a century to establish its dominance. (The bourgeoisie in Europe took several centuries!) A class can also take a century to lose its dominance. In Saint-Domingue, between 1789 and 1796, the commissioners' dominance was disintegrating further each day. At the same time, two other social forces were seeking to establish their own dominance, that is, they were seeking to achieve most of their primary interests. The *ANCIENS LIBRES* had added more land to what they already owned, they were equal to whites within the political arena, and they had their own small army. But the *NOUVEAUX LIBRES*, specifically the **leaders** of *nouveaux libres*, had managed to go even further: they had seized their freedom, they had secured freedom for ALL *nouveaux libres*, they were challenging other people for control of the plantations, and with the ouster of Sonthonax they successfully seized the country's political apparatus.

Without a doubt, while Hédouville was disembarking on the island, a brand-new power was making itself known within Saint-Domingue, and **neither Hédouville's government nor Rigaud's organization could allow it the chance to break through**. Even though Hédouville and Rigaud had been fighting for their own groups, in 1797 the interest of both groups was to crush Toussaint's organization. Hédouville and Rigaud's coalition was the only way that a declining social force and a shaky social force could hold back a mounting social force. Which is to say… if your enemy's my enemy, don't you think we can be friends? But, as Lamèsi says, it's better to have a good enemy than a bad friend …

… where he stops, nobody knows

Between 1789 and 1797, while French commissioners' dominance was decreasing, the conflict between Saint-Domingue and France was unraveling. That's not hard to understand: a society's dependence is tied to the dominance of the class that's serving foreigners. They're inseparable. Hédouville had come to Saint-Domingue seeking to patch up the commissioners' dominance, and to reinforce economic and political dependence. His position was clear: within the conflict between France and Saint-Domingue, he was 100 percent on France's side. Also, Hédouville hadn't intended to concede to the English. England was France's enemy, and Saint-Domingue was England's enemy. Saint-Domingue wasn't supposed to be whispering with the English, even if the English wanted to trade with the country. Besides, consider what trade Saint-Domingue was in! Saint-Domingue's goods were for France. No other country, whether England or the United States, had any right to come trade there. As for the **émigrés** (mostly white plantation owners who'd fled to the side of the English or to the United States), since they'd let themselves betray France, they could all just stay wherever they'd gone.

Without a shadow of a doubt, Hédouville's position was completely tied to the interests of France.

Bénoit-Joseph-André Rigaud was born within the Saint-Domingue community, but as soon as he was big enough to carry a tune, his father, a white man, sent him off to study in France. When he returned to

Saint-Domingue, Rigaud got involved in the camp of mulatto plantation owners, and from then on, he never stopped defending the *anciens libres* and the new French government. The *ancien libre* team flanking Rigaud believed that the interests of the Republic (the new government in France) were joined to the interests of the *anciens libres* in Saint-Domingue. That is why, when a group of mulatto plantation owners crossed over to the English side, Rigaud's team stayed loyal to France. France had given them an education, the French Revolution had made them equal to whites, and the Republic had given them ranks. So long as France didn't bother them in the South, they were shouting: Long live France. They were helping France. Moreover, in 1798, they had the same enemy as the French government did: **émigré** colonists. They were certain that if those whites returned to reclaim their plantations, mulattos would lose more than anyone else. Rigaud himself had clashed with several of those *grands blancs* before they bolted.

Therefore, his education, his manners, his history, and the interests of the group he supported pushed him into the same position as Hédouville. Within the conflict between Saint-Domingue and France, in 1798, André Rigaud set his eyes on: France!

In truth, all of this was 'France' for Toussaint Louverture. It's true that he called himself a 'child of France', but he was a child born out of wedlock. He was born in slavery, he'd fought against France, and his organization had grown up on the Spanish side. He'd joined the camp of the French Republic because that government had promised freedom to former slaves. He'd never taken orders from local princes or foreign generals. To the contrary, every time his own path crossed the path of those people within the cockfighting arena of Saint-Domingue, it was they who bit the dust. The *nouveaux libres* owed nothing to France, and Louverture owed nothing to France. He was France's illegitimate child, but he was an authentic son of Saint-Domingue. The war with France and other countries was something that affected folks in Europe. Once the English cleared out, and once they stopped threatening to revoke the freedom of *nouveaux libres*, there was no reason to bother with them, whether in Jamaica or anywhere else. Furthermore, Saint-Domingue needed the English to keep trade going, to unlock access to the Americans, and to unlock the door to émigrés. What would it matter if a few former plantation owners returned? They had money, and they had influence. If their businesses opened again in the country, money would circulate. Besides, the émigrés had a few slaves with them, and those people could come support the camp of *nouveaux libres*. With greater muscle comes greater courage.

my mother had three little goats

And so, these were the three men's positions on the question of dependency, according to the organization or government backing them ... Clearly, the Republican position of the *anciens libres* was closest to the position of the French government. It's just as clear that with each passing day, the conflict between the Republic and Toussaint's organization was growing. Hédouville had come to Saint-Domingue to re-establish dependence. Therefore, he threw himself at the group that most favored dependence: the *anciens libres* of the South.

It's also certain that the ideological climate in which Rigaud and Hédouville were immersed bonded them even more. In the French officers' eyes, Toussaint wasn't educated enough to be leader of Saint-Domingue. They saw Toussaint through their lens of prejudice ... The French Revolution had stated: all people are equal, but the revolution had retreated before it even grew teeth. Nine times twelve months wasn't enough time to change the mentality of former aristocrats!

In the same way, just like former soldier the Comte d'Estaing[53] and General Lafayette, André Rigaud had acclimated to an environment where it was 'normal' for Hédouville to be leader, since he was educated and had nice manners. It's true, the ideologies of the classes in power (whether in France or in Saint-Domingue) had influenced the mulatto general. It's also true that they'd influenced Louverture, and we'll come back to that issue. But what we want to expose right now is the connection that existed between the social and political positions of those three men and Hédouville's prejudice. Friendship, love, jealousy, all the feelings we know, they don't simply sprout up. They're rooted within each person's origins, within each individual's position facing the society in which he or she lives.

In July 1798, Rigaud and Toussaint went to see Hédouville. Hédouville spoke with each man separately. Some people say that on that very day Hédouville ordered Rigaud to help him crush Toussaint. Some people say that Toussaint hid behind a big cabinet and overheard the conversation. I don't know if that's true, but it doesn't matter! If that July day is important, it's especially because it strengthened **a series of preexistent**

---

[53] Charles Hector, Comte d'Estaing (1729–94), was the governor of Saint-Domingue from 1763 to 1766. He was executed by guillotine during the French Revolution's Reign of Terror (April 28, 1794) because of his loyalty to the royal family (Madiou 1989 1:36).

positions. A series of positions that hadn't needed a cabinet, a piano, or curtains to come into view.

In July 1798, Hédouville and Rigaud saw eye to eye. In July 1798, Hédouville went after Toussaint with a vengeance. At the slightest mistake that Toussaint made, and for the tiniest problem that arose in the North, Hédouville passed judgment on Toussaint. When Toussaint protested, Hédouville dug in. Hédouville cut off supplies for soldiers in the North, and then he wrote to France demanding that Toussaint be discharged. Toussaint offered to submit his resignation. By playing hide-and-seek, Hédouville was gaining strength. He was so certain of his success, that after a squabble within the fifth regiment (Moïse's regiment), he ordered one of his people (Manigat)[54] to arrest Moïse. Manigat clashed with Moïse's people. Moïse cornered Hédouville. Hédouville panicked and called for Louverture's help. Louverture sent his troops into action, he blocked the route to the South (nobody could budge), and then he gave Dessalines orders to immediately oust Gabriel-Marie-Théodore-Joseph Hédouville.

As Lamèsi says: having a big reputation kills little dogs.

my mother had three little goats
one little goat died
two little goats stood face to face

But Hédouville's ouster didn't solve all the problems within Toussaint's organization. To the contrary! Before Hédouville's departure, he'd promoted Rigaud over Louverture. Rigaud kept a low profile, and he kept it under wraps in case the game went bad so that he could always act like the law were on his side if he butted heads with Louverture. After Hédouville's promenade, the only hope that Rigaud's group had was to crush Toussaint with France's blessing. Whereas the only hope that Toussaint's group had was to crush Rigaud before France struck.

Given the positions these two groups held vis-à-vis the society, their political agendas and tactics were irreconcilable. Additionally, there was France's weakness, and beyond that, the underhanded dealings of

---

54 The *ancien libre* Manigat was a judge and senator who was promoted through the French military ranks by the Directory (Madiou 1987 1:415–18; 3:455, 459, etc.).

Manigat and Hédouville, and on top of that, the color problem that was singing a solo in the parade. **Starting in late 1798, the conflict between Rigaud and Toussaint turned bloody.**

what people do to one other makes God laugh

Thus, the War of the South had taken root within the two organizations' positions, but that didn't mean it didn't have other causes. In fact, besides France—which was going up in flames—there were two other countries stoking up the war: England and the United States.

Even though the English had been defeated by both Toussaint and Rigaud, Saint-Domingue never ceased to pique their interest. Their economic interests compelled them to trade with the devil if the devil's money added up. And Toussaint Louverture had decided to buy, even from the hands of France's enemies, if they sold fair and square. France was far away, France was fighting wars over in Europe, France didn't have any time to look after Saint-Domingue, and Saint-Domingue couldn't wait! Moreover, the English had thought they could play Toussaint. Balcarres, the governor of Jamaica,[55] wrote to the English government to advise them to get hold of Toussaint as an ally. Toussaint was a stupid person, and they could always chuck him away **later.**

As for André Rigaud, he was against large-scale trading with enemies of the Republic. What's more, rumors spread that he'd given his approval to attack Jamaica, which was under English control. As a result, the English isolated Rigaud. Even though they distrusted Toussaint, they supported Louverture as much as they could. They sold him the goods he needed most. They scattered thistles across Rigaud's path. They blockaded the passage to Jamaica to prevent other ships from bringing food and reinforcements to the *anciens libres* in the South.

But the responsibility of the English was nothing compared to the Americans' part.

In 1791, when the slaves rose up in Saint-Domingue, George Washington said: Crush them! The American coast guard that was near Cape Haitian rushed to help the French crush black people. Plantation owners in South Carolina and Georgia clasped their heads like it was

---

55 Alexander Lindsay, the 6th Earl of Balcarres, served as Jamaica's governor from 1794 to 1801.

the end of the world and said: I'm over here! They had many slaves, and they were the closest to Haiti (Florida wasn't yet in the United States), so they had immediately feared the revolution in Saint-Domingue. Rumors spread like wildfire, their slaves could rise too ... But while Louverture's organization was taking over the political apparatus, and while the war in Europe was keeping French boats from going back and forth at will, American capitalists in New England (the northeastern region of the United States) opened back-door channels to trade with Toussaint. Since those capitalist traders had **dominance** within their society, the American government gave them free rein. Therefore, **Toussaint Louverture's politics and economic strategy** (that of trading with any country with no regard for France's international politics) **dovetailed with the Americans' interests**. Meanwhile, Rigaud's position on total dependence (that of obeying France 100 percent) had made American capitalists write him off.

In 1798, although France and the United States were staring one another down, Toussaint wrote to President Adams, asking him to send trading ships to Saint-Domingue. The American consul to Saint-Domingue, Edward Stevens,[56] echoed the request. Toussaint assured him that nothing would happen to American ships that disembarked **in areas that were under his control**. Stevens told his bosses that he could fully handle Toussaint. Thus, even before the war started, Stevens asked them to cut off Rigaud's supplies (according to a letter that Stevens sent to Pickering[57] on May 3, 1799). Throughout the war Stevens maintained a political strategy that aligned with the English to support Toussaint economically and militarily. They gave him supplies, and they gave him weapons. President Adams took the chance of sending ships clandestinely.

The role the Americans played in the war between Rigaud and Toussaint was by no means small. It was clear, clear as spring water, how much their support for Louverture had added weight to the scale. France had leaned towards Rigaud, but only because Rigaud was weakening Toussaint for them. England had leaned towards Toussaint, but it wanted the war to continue, and it had no intention of seeing Toussaint climb too high. (If Toussaint acquired too much power, and if he really believed in the idea of freedom, he could attack Jamaica.)

---

56 Edward Stevens (1755–1834) was assigned to Saint-Domingue in 1799–1800 (see Johnson).
57 Timothy Pickering (1745–1829) served as U.S. Secretary of State from 1795 to 1800 (see Clarfield).

The American capitalists were the only foreign group with interest in having one of the two camps win the war quickly. And, just like the French and English hawks, those folks went all out to secure their interests.

Therefore, alongside the main reason for the War in the South (that is, the positions held by the two organizations), we mustn't overlook the competition between traders and foreign capitalists who were stoking the fires of their own personal interests.

three leaves
o three roots
throw it away to forget it
pick it up to remember

My friends, let's pause and see what we've learned. We've learned that the main cause of the War in the South lay within the positions of the two organizations, and the positions of the social forces supporting them. We've learned that those social forces butted heads about two fundamental problems within Haitian society: **dependence** (which is to say, the type of control that France held over the country) and **dominance** (which is to say, the kind of social class, or class-category, ready to pull the country towards its own interest). Besides that major conflict, we've learned how France's weakness (and Hédouville's prejudice) complicated that ugly situation. We've also discovered how foreign trader-capitalists were stoking fires to secure their own personal interests.

And now that we've gotten to this point, a lot of pot-stirrers might ask us: What do we do with the color question? We'll answer straightforwardly: **the color question wasn't among the main causes of the War in the South.**

by Saint Peter
by Saint Paul
where is the truth?

It's as clear as spring water, the color question couldn't be more important than any of the reasons we've previously mentioned. It's true, when we spoke of general prejudice, we spoke of color prejudice, too. But the personal relationship between Hédouville and Rigaud wasn't solely based

6. The little orange tree grew

on color, period. It was a prejudice embedded in education, in manners, in language, in origins and social status, to boot. Hédouville and Rigaud didn't get along solely because of color. There were mulattos who weren't mulattos in Hédouville's eyes, and there were whites who weren't whites in the eyes of Rigaud!

Did that mean color prejudice played no role in the war? I didn't say that. I said that it wasn't among the **reasons** the war broke out. However, it played an important role in its own way, and the role that it played has given Haitian History imbalance from 1799 until today.

Even though the southern mulattos had accepted the Declaration of Rights for all people and all citizens—the declaration of the French bourgeoisie—many of them sidestepped the question of equality for black people (which is to say, whether black people had the same rights as whites and mulattos). In 1795, when Sonthonax's delegates had surveyed prejudice within the South, André Rigaud declared: **'By preaching equality, those perverse people want to annihilate the mulatto group. The feat they pulled off in the North gave them hope they can do that in the South and the West, too, but they're wrong, you can bet on it'** ... In 1799, a squad of black people took up arms against Rigaud in the village of Corail. The mulattos arrested them, sent them into a cell smeared with lime in Jérémie, and those people died choking like flies in a trap.

Toussaint Louverture exploited the Corail Affair to denounce ALL mulattos. 'People of light skin, you who've been betraying black people from the start of the revolution, what do you yearn for today? Everybody knows ... You yearn for the extermination of whites, and slavery for black people ... I've raised my left hand. If I raise my right hand, **I'll wipe you all out'**. Toussaint Louverture gave this speech in the Cathedral of Port-au-Prince on February 21, 1799, at three o'clock sharp, and it was one of the biggest political mistakes a party leader ever made in the nation of Ayiti Toma. I say it's the biggest, because from that very day onward, it gave imbalance to our people and it's still making us unbalanced six generations later.

Why?

Rigaud's government was a mulatto government with clear-cut prejudices. In the South, no black person could ever become an officer. All the cavalry (soldiers mounted on horses) were mulattos. During the war against the English, black soldiers had walked on foot, in the infantry, where the fighting was hardest. Mulattos had treated them unfairly and the (mulatto) authorities hadn't batted an eye.

Meanwhile, in the North, Louverture's general staff had included black people (Dessalines, Moïse, and Christophe), whites (Agé,

Vincent),[58] and mulattos (Clervaux, Vernet).[59] Thus, in one camp color prejudice didn't have much importance, and in the other it could make or break you.

If prejudice existed in Rigaud's camp, why did we say that Toussaint made a major political mistake in responding to Rigaud tit for tat?

Color prejudice was not the main reason for the battle. Toussaint knew that, and Toussaint's organization was the best evidence that certain mulattos and black people could reach a mutual understanding on the question of freedom for all people. Bauvais,[60] who was still wavering in Port-au-Prince, submitted his resignation the next day. Toussaint tried to walk back his statement, but it was too late. It's a fact, though, that if Bauvais had adopted Toussaint's position (and he could have done it), many mulattos would have marched with him. It's also true that Toussaint's statement wasn't in vain because Pétion fled to join Rigaud.

Toussaint Louverture knew that all mulattos weren't alike. The mistake that he made was a tactical mistake. He'd been trying to exploit Rigaud's prejudice to make the masses rise against the clique of *anciens libres* in the South. But it was as though he'd thrown a rock that fell on his head.

Many people, black people and mulattos alike, didn't get trapped in color manipulation. A lot of mulatto officers had stayed in Louverture's army. A lot of black fieldworkers in the South had marched behind Rigaud. In the North, some had taken advantage of the war to rebel against Toussaint, because they said Toussaint was in bed with the English and the Americans who supported slavery. A few black officers in the North and Northwest (in Môle Saint-Nicolas and Cape Haitian especially) rose up on Rigaud's side. Those men weren't mulattos, but they knew well that the issue being disputed wasn't a color problem. Most of them hailed from *anciens libres* families (Gaulard, Carlo, Pierre-Paul) or were French supporters who'd joined the new government's camp before entering Louverture's organization. That heritage of black *anciens libres*,

---

58 Agé was a brigade general (Madiou 1987 1:353, 373, etc.; 2:41–44, etc.); Charles-Humbert-Marie Vincent was a colonel and army engineer.
59 Augustin Clervaux was an *ancien libre* lieutenant-colonel who became general (Oriol 176). André Vernet served with Toussaint Louverture in the Spanish army, subsequently changed to the French army, and was promoted to brigade general after the War of the South. He commanded Gonaïves and was a signer of the Acte d'Indépendance for the new Haitian Republic (Roc 387–88).
60 Louis-Jacques Bauvais was a brigade general of color who fought alongside Rigaud (Oriol 163).

who'd enthusiastically come to Saint-Domingue from other islands, lived in certain areas of the northwestern region and still do today. On many occasions in Haitian history, when Toussaint's and Rigaud's successors resumed their head-butting, several factions within the Northwest have taken themselves for Rigaud's successors. But let's leave aside the hymn and take up the prayer ... In 1799, many mulattos supported Toussaint Louverture. Clervaux, one of Toussaint's mulatto officers, had to run for the hills so mulattos wouldn't shoot him!

Thus many people, fieldworkers, soldiers as well as officers, black people as well as mulattos, didn't give the color discussion importance.

But many others had lost their minds. Because they'd heard the two organizations' propaganda, most people at the time had managed to convince themselves that the issue being disputed was a color problem. Color prejudice wasn't the cause of the war, but the war took flight by hitching a ride on prejudice.

Black people took varying directions. Rigaud answered Toussaint blow for blow. Insults piled on top of insults.

Rigaud declared: '**My brothers in the South, be well aware, there are two kinds of people in this country: the disgusting, good-for-nothing class, and the class that's thoughtful and intelligent. Let us stay in that second class, and let us chuck all the rest back into the mountains, where they were supposed to stay, far from our lives, amongst inferior beings who're incapable of living in society ...**'.

Toussaint declared: '**All people of color, join forces to overthrow Saint-Domingue**'.

truth is always in the people's interest

It's true, Rigaud was a racist opportunist. But when Toussaint answered him tit for tat, in the same manipulative streak, the people saw the war through the lens of color. Color served as an excuse. Color seized the day. Toussaint riled people up with his speeches, but he fell into Rigaud's trap. Before the War of the South, mulattos and blacks could ally against the French on certain issues when their interests coincided. After the war, countless times, crooks who were mulatto and black alike exploited color to defend their own personal interests. By answering Rigaud tit for tat, Toussaint Louverture let a poison take root in people's minds. He let a crooked path emerge amidst the battles over social class. He let blood

108 *Stirring the Pot of Haitian History*

spill as a result of this manipulation. And when blood bespatters words, it's not funny anymore.

Toussaint's backers might respond: how could Louverture have done otherwise? But History doesn't side with heroes who sit on the Champ-de-Mars looking down on regular people below. The only hero in History is the people.

What should Louverture have done? He could have come down among the people. He could have set free the poisoned trap that André Rigaud had set. He could have explained to the people what the basic problem was. In 1793–94, Toussaint's organization never told the slaves that it intended to kill **all** whites. And the slaves had trusted him. They marched with him down freedom's path.

Then again, in 1799, the *kòd* [rope] that attached Toussaint to the people's primary interests lacked the resistance that it had had in 1794. Because the interests of his organization were departing from the people's interests, Louverture was forced to join André Rigaud's demagoguery. He couldn't put all his cards on the table, either because he didn't trust the people or because if he had been transparent, the people would have stopped trusting him. He got caught up in demagoguery. And so his demagoguery allowed the poison that Vincent Ogé and André Rigaud got from their fathers to course through our blood for six generations. We've been dragging around an unsolvable problem that's left us badly unbalanced.

corn silks are one thing
Spanish moss is another
bearded face to bearded face
the truth comes out

Between February and June 1799, nasty hints pelted down in Saint-Domingue. Little conspiracies hatched here, little conspiracies hatched there. Rigaud stated that Grand-Goâve and Petit-Goâve should be under his command because that's what Hédouville had said. Toussaint stated that he wouldn't recognize Hédouville's law, and Grand-Goâve and Petit-Goâve would be staying under his command because that's what Roume (the commissioner who had replaced Hédouville) had said. Rigaud declared that he wouldn't take any orders from Toussaint, because before Hédouville had departed, he'd discharged Toussaint. After a lot of chatter, Rigaud was first to strike.

In short order Faubert and Delva[61] took Petit-Goâve. Roume declared Rigaud an outlaw. Hogwash. The southern people's army kept advancing. A lot of mulattos in the West of the country rushed in to boost their ranks. The beginning of the war was no good at all for Louverture. Rigaud's army was attacking Moïse's regiments in earnest. At the same time, a squad of black *anciens libres* and mulattos in the Northeast joined with *nouveaux libres* in the North who were ardent supporters of France; they took up arms against Louverture. But between July and November 1799, Rigaud waffled. During that time, Toussaint struck. On August 31, the *anciens libres* in Môle Saint-Nicolas surrendered to Moïse and Clervaux. The Northwest was losing steam, but the South didn't lay down its weapons. And for Louverture to take the South, he had to pass through the West. And whoever says the West is talking about Jacmel …

In 1799, Jacmel was under the command of Bauvais. Bauvais was a mulatto officer, a total republican who was acting as though he couldn't be bothered. But Jacmel's geographic position, along with the **political** position of Jacmel's *anciens libres*, made them sitting ducks for Louverture's army. While Rigaud sat on the fence, and while Bauvais sat there waffling, Louverture and primarily Dessalines made an agreement with a group of maroons who'd been strutting through the mountains near Jacmel. At the same time, Toussaint named Dessalines commander-in-chief of his regiments in the West.

On October 4, 1799, Dessalines took charge of the army. On October 22, 1799, he defeated Pétion and Desruisseaux[62] in the village of Bellevue (between Léogane and Petit-Goâve). On November 16, in the blink of an eye, Dessalines branched off to Jacmel. In the early morning of November 22, Jacmel was completely hemmed in: Laplume on the left, Christophe on the right, Dessalines in front, and the sea in back. Rigaud made as though he were going to go help his comrades, but he was only posturing. All the while, Dessalines and Christophe bombarded Jacmel relentlessly. Alexandre Pétion, a steely guy, said it wasn't going to go down that way. He

---

61 Faubert was a lieutenant colonel loyal to Rigaud who rose to the rank of colonel (Madiou 1987 1:81, 192, 193, 446–48, etc.); Delva was a colonel who also remained dedicated to Rigaud (Madiou 1987 1:427, 437, 446, etc.).

62 Anne Alexandre Sabès 'Pétion' (1770–1818) was a free man of color who was educated in France; he returned to Saint-Domingue to help expel the British, and he rose to the rank of army general. Following the assassination of Emperor Dessalines in 1806, and a civil war which divided the North and South of the new country, Pétion became the first president of the Republic of Haiti (in the South) (Oriol 231–32).

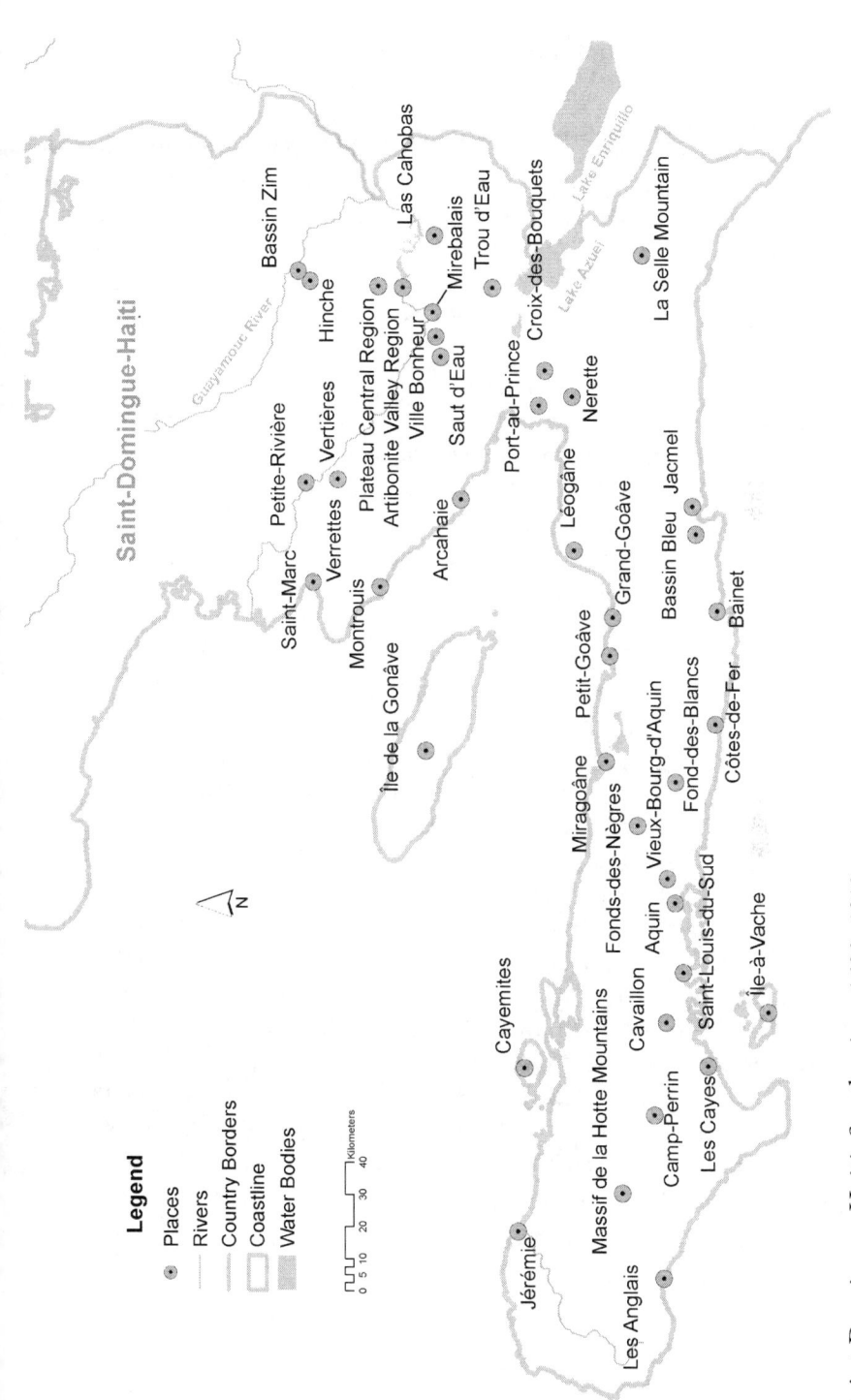

Saint-Domingue-Haiti, South, circa 1600–1810.

Map by Joe Aufmuth, Geospatial Consultant, University of Florida's George A. Smathers Libraries, 2020. Map depicts populated places. Water Bodies obtained from Open Street Map (© openstreetmap.org + contributors). Coastline, rivers, and country boundaries obtained from NOAA.

left Bainet, seized a ship, and entered Jacmel by sea despite the American ships patrolling the area. Pétion was an artillery expert. He answered the *nouveaux libres* cannon ball for cannon ball. But meanwhile, Jacmel's supplies were depleted. Hunger took hold of old people and children. People were eating shoes, tree stumps, donkeys, horses, and dogs. Any rat worthy of the name got devoured. Pétion opened the city's gates so that women and children could escape. Dessalines let them pass, he gave them water, he gave them food, and then he started bombarding the city again. Pétion realized that he was defenseless at this point, and he tried to pull a fast one on Dessalines.

Pétion ordered the soldiers to depart Jacmel via the left flank so they could get to Bainet. Early in the morning on March 12, he switched routes and made the men depart via the right flank. A foolish idea, since Dessalines had already sent Christophe to the area covertly. Christophe shot the place up. After six months of fighting, 700 *anciens libres* fled Jacmel, full of fear, leaving 3,000 dead in their wake.

On April 22, Dessalines seized Bainet. As soon as he was done, he dashed back to take Grand-Goâve. He turned around again, he seized Petit-Goâve, and he pushed for Miragoâne. He found himself face to face with Pétion. Pétion refused to retreat. Dessalines scaled the mountains, passed stealthily through them, and in the blink of an eye he'd reached Pétion's rear. On May 17, Miragoâne gave in. A few days later, Fonds-des-Nègres fell. Rigaud ordered his supporters to raze things to the ground, but he wasn't really in the fight anymore. Saint Michel fell, Fonds-des-Nègres fell, and Vieux Bourg d'Aquin fell.

In the middle of June, three special commissioners arrived from France. They announced that, according to orders from Napoleon, the French head of state, Toussaint was sole military leader in Saint-Domingue. When Rigaud heard that, he lost his last shred of conviction. As for Dessalines, he charged even harder. Wherever he went, he gathered up the best enemy officers and forced them under his thumb. Saint-Louis fell. Cavaillon fell. On July 29, 1800, Dessalines was knocking at the doors of Les Cayes. André Rigaud bolted. On the first day of August, Dessalines and Toussaint marched in step into the city. The little orange tree grew and grew ... But close by, on the sea, five American ships were winking their eyes in position ...

weapons give conviction
it's true
but there's no weapon more beautiful
than conviction

The question that we should now ask is why Toussaint won, and what Toussaint's victory did for the revolution in Saint-Domingue.

The first question isn't hard. Even though Rigaud's army was very well prepared (training, weapons, experience …), Toussaint Louverture won the war because of the political and ideological strength of his organization.

Toussaint's organization was nearer to the interests of the masses. Also, many peasants and fieldworkers joined the army. What's more, Toussaint and Dessalines managed to convince several groups of maroons to fight against Rigaud: Gilles Bambara, Masannga, Mentor Raison, Germain Lavalette, Joseph Aquart, et cetera.[63]

Toussaint's organization was nearer to the interests of the masses, but it was also closer to the interests of everyone in Saint-Domingue overall. A few whites had joined the battle, and as for those who didn't, Toussaint enlisted them directly. What's more, as the war went on, Dessalines made a crew of mulatto *anciens libres* join the army. Not only did that raise the morale of his own troops, but their enemies were terrified when they realized that their former comrades were shooting at them.

Toussaint's organization was nearer to the interests of the masses of former slaves, and he'd managed to draw a few people from other classes to his side. But that wasn't all. Given their political positions, Toussaint and his officers never had to wait, arms crossed, to see how France would react in the way Rigaud and Bauvais had to. Thus, they struck fast and they struck hard. They refused to accept Jacmel's detached position, as it could become a trap behind them. When they'd taken Jacmel earlier on, they had it made in the shade for waging a mobile war, or what's called a war-in-motion. They scaled mountains, they crossed waters. Women and men alike got involved. Between March and August, Dessalines was all over the South. He went right, he went left. He went front and back. He

---

[63] Gilles Bambara belonged to the Bande de la Vallée and became colonel (Madiou 1987 2:20, 63, 393, 477; 3:19, 22, 23, 65, 330); Germain Lavalette became a brigade general (Madiou 1987 2:235, 245, 363, etc.); Joseph Acquart's band sacked Marigot. Madiou mentions five individuals with the name Mentor, none of which is accompanied by a form of the name 'Rézon'; a thorough search of Madiou's index yields no reference to Masannga (Madiou 1987 2:6, 7, 11).

spun around like a spinning top. He took the towns one by one. In May 1800, the *anciens libres* were left patching up their regiments. By July, they no longer had the strength to stitch up torn pants.

three leaves
o three roots
throw it away to forget
pick it up to remember

What did the victory of the *nouveaux libres* bring to the revolution in Saint-Domingue?

The consequences of the war of the South were not trivial. We already know that war caused the color question to take on greater importance in the Saint-Domingue of distant history, and in Haiti today. Memories of that war weren't unimportant either, in the quarrel between Christophe and Pétion after independence. Likewise, the position held by many northwestern factions vis-à-vis Christophe was rooted in the conflict that came unbound in 1799. Along those same lines, after the War of the South, many *anciens libres* threw themselves into the French camp, into the camp of the revolution's enemy.

But we know that life's a chain of conflicts, right? Thus, you shouldn't be surprised if I say that the War of the South helped Saint-Domingue's revolution move forward.

After Rigaud's collapse, Toussaint's organization was the only top-notch fighting cock in Saint-Domingue. And despite the growing conflict between that organization and the masses, in 1799, the group of big *nouveaux libres* soldiers was the only robust political group defending **one** of the masses' basic interests 100 percent: freedom for all people. Louverture's victory supported freedom for all people in Saint-Domingue.

But that wasn't all. After André Rigaud's defeat, the part of Saint-Domingue that was supposedly under France's control wasn't distinct anymore, with tiny bits here and tiny bits there. Saint-Domingue became a bona fide nation under the control of a single political apparatus: Louverture's government. Coastal warehouses in all parts of the country sold commodity crops to foreigners under the same conditions. Food crops circulated from one province to another. Decisions about farming, trade, and the economy were implemented throughout the country without defiance from any department, without any clumsy fool trying to dance on his right foot while everyone else was dancing on the left foot.

That union was necessary before another important issue was proposed: the issue of independence.

But in truth, the War of the South didn't only bring political and economic union. Before the war, the segments of Toussaint's army had all been fighting single-handedly, in disjointed ways. Groups of half-brigades had never come together. The War of the South made them learn to fight together. It forced them to recognize that the acts of one person might disturb another, and that the acts of one might help another. It forced them to reflect on a military strategy; which is to say, a manner of fighting that would allow different regiments to synchronize instead of acting separately.

Furthermore, a steely general, better than all the others at putting his strategy into motion, employed a variety of high-speed warfare: it was Jean-Jacques Dessalines. It was Dessalines who gave the order to overthrow Rigaud's army bit by bit. It was Dessalines who served as commander-in-general of all the regiments. It was Dessalines who sought to calm down soldiers when certain men were eager to drink the blood of all mulattos, even breastfeeding infants. It was Dessalines who drove some of Rigaud's worthy soldiers (while he was thrashing them) into Louverture's own army. Even though Pétion himself fled after the war to join the French, the confrontation between Pétion and Dessalines at Jacmel forced the one to recognize the other as a man thoroughly experienced in matters of war. And that mutual respect would be very useful when the two black generals decided to take on Leclerc.

the little orange tree grew and grew

Therefore, the War of the South tainted the blood of Haitian history. It left scars on us, and it brought us imbalance. But in 1799, the War of the South helped the revolution move forward. It cut off the *anciens libres* before they could tear down freedom. It broke France's stride in terms of their two-faced deceptions. It allowed an organization of former slaves to trace signs of political freedom and equality before every entryway in Saint-Domingue. It allowed the army of *nouveaux libres* to fully immerse itself in preparations before it butted head-on with Bonaparte's soldiers.

Between June 1799 and August 1, 1800, Saint-Domingue was readying itself to take power. Despite the smoke of demagoguery, the revolution stayed its course and didn't lose its way. Despite thirteen months of devastation, the little orange tree grew ... and grew.

In the middle of the War of the South, before Jacmel was defeated, Toussaint Louverture sought Roume's approval for the army to take over the part of the island that remained in Spanish control. Since July 1795, according to conditions agreed upon by the French and Spanish governments in the village of Basel (in Switzerland), France had legal control of the entire island. But in truth, in 1795, the French didn't have the means to get a grip on the eastern portion of the island. The western part was now in real trouble! Besides, according to the conditions, **white** soldiers were the ones supposed to enter Spanish territory because those people were evidently super sensitive ...

But, for all the hypersensitivity, Louverture knew that Freedom for All couldn't be secured if the gate to the community were open behind his organization's back. Since 1795, he'd been saying to Lavaud: **'I'm warning you, people who have land in the Spanish territory, they don't want to hear any talk of freedom for all, and they're also die-hard supporters of the old regime, overseas ...'**. On top of that, the Spanish had continued the slave trade until 1800! Furthermore, if fieldworkers started profiting within the western portion, there was no reason why the Spanish lands wouldn't be cleared for planting just like all the others ...

But besides those reasons, Louverture knew that the French government was uneasy about his organization. He'd kicked out Sonthonax and Hédouville without hesitation because he controlled the biggest military force on the island. But what if France were able to send its commissioners and its army into the East before the *nouveaux libres*? Freedom for all could be in trouble. Full of mistrust, Louverture asked Roume for the army to enter Spanish territory. Full of mistrust, Roume said: No!

Philippe-Rose Saint-Laurent (known as Roume) had arrived in Saint-Domingue in 1791 as France's special commissioner with the First Civil Commission. The colony was in chaos, and the commission was in even more chaos, so neither Roume nor his colleagues had gotten anything done whatsoever. In 1796 Roume was still special commissioner, but within the Third Civil Commission, it was Sonthonax who did and undid things. After both Sonthonax and Hédouville were ousted, Roume theoretically had the upper hand, but in reality he was nothing more than a puppet in the hands of Louverture ... until the day Louverture decided to cross over to the East. At that time, Roume said: No! He

116   *Stirring the Pot of Haitian History*

sent Chanlatte,[64] an *ancien libre* mulatto, off to bluff on the other side of the island. But in April 1800, a quarrel blew up in the area of Plaine du Nord. Six thousand fieldworkers rose up and, **with backing from General Moïse**, they insisted on dividing up the plantations: half for the landowners, half for the workers. They said they were on the verge of massacring all whites. Toussaint used that impending threat to force Roume to approve his invasion of the East. On April 27, 1800, Roume resigned himself to his fate. General Agé, a white Frenchman, charged on the East. Chanlatte switched sides, and then he, along with Don García (leader of the Spanish), butted heads with Agé. Agé was defeated. Roume concocted a sneaky plan, proclaiming that he'd opposed the invasion. Meanwhile, the War of the South had reached the path of victory … In the blink of an eye, Moïse arrested Roume and locked him in a chicken coop at Dondon. A short while later, Moïse charged into Santo-Domingo. On January 26, 1801, Toussaint Louverture entered Santo-Domingo and announced far and wide that the entire island, from Môle Saint-Nicolas to La Romana, was under his command.

The little orange tree had reached the peak of its beauty. Freedom for All had spread itself across all of Saint-Domingue. English, Spanish, French, whites, and mulattos had all been defeated.

But far away, on the other side of the ocean, France was priming itself for action. And close by, inside the house, inside the very camp of *nouveaux libres*, inside Toussaint's own army, inside that same general staff who'd braved dangers in order for Freedom to blossom in all the gardens of Saint-Domingue, there were people who started saying: Cousin, is **this** what freedom is? … As if to say, that's not what you told us.

Sister Lamèsi, please, light the candle for me quick! These words require light …

---

[64] Antoine Chanlatte was a free person of color who served as brigade general in the French army; he supported the civil commissioners during Galbaud's revolt and rose to the rank of colonel in 1794 (Oriol 173).

7. Cousin
that's not what you told me

*Twins twins
twins two, three, four
I'm asking
what do you see here
are you happy?*

In January 1802, word spread through Saint-Domingue to the effect that France had organized a massive invasion to crush the people of Ayiti Toma. Toussaint Louverture was in Santo-Domingo, and he hurried up to Samaná to see with his own eyes. When he reached the mountaintop, he saw forty-seven ships bobbing in place on the water. He stated: 'We're done for! All of France is invading Saint-Domingue ... They've come to get their revenge'.

On February 2, 1802, Victor Emmanuel Leclerc, a French general who was Napoleon Bonaparte's brother-in-law, docked in the face of Cape Haitian along with twenty-three ships stuffed with soldiers. He sent a communiqué to Henri Christophe, announcing that he'd come to take the city and all the military garrisons under Christophe's control. Christophe answered in kind: You won't succeed! **'You aren't my boss, I don't know you, and therefore I am not accountable to you'. 'And if fate should happen to let your weapons prevail, you'll enter Cape Haitian only after it's burned to ashes, and I'll fight you right upon those ashes'.**

On February 4, 1802, as the sun was about to set, a red flame filled the sky: the army of *nouveaux libres* had set fire to the city of Cape Haitian.

On February 5, 1802, Cape Haitian fell into French hands. Just after Limbé fell, Plaisance fell. On February 10, Port-de-Paix fell. Meanwhile, in the West, Port-au-Prince fell flat on its face (February 5). Arcahaie fell, Montrouis fell. Meanwhile, in Les Cayes, Laplume acted foolishly, opening the door to the French in the South. Over on the Spanish side, Augustin Clervaux and Paul Louverture[65] bowed their heads to the French. A bit later, Maurepas[66] gave up.

On the morning of April 25, Christophe went to find Leclerc, and he doffed his hat. He stated that the 4,000 **fieldworkers** who'd been following him had cleared out, so he'd enlisted under the command of the French general Hardy along with 1,500 **soldiers** who'd chosen to stay with him. A bit later, Toussaint Louverture himself bowed to

65 Augustin Clervaux was born around 1763 in Marmelade and died of yellow fever in 1804. He was one of Toussaint Louverture's generals and submitted his region, Samaná, to French authority when Leclerc arrived with the French expedition in 1802. Clervaux was one of the co-signatories of the Haitian declaration of independence in 1804 (Madiou 1989, vols. 1–3). Paul Louverture was also one of Toussaint Louverture's generals on the Spanish side of the island.
66 Maurepas was a devoted general of Toussaint Louverture. He initially fought the troops of the French expedition in 1802 but ended up surrendering and being integrated into French forces, becoming similarly devoted to Leclerc (Madiou 1989 2:400–02).

Dominican Republic, circa 1600–1810.

Map by Joe Aufmuth, Geospatial Consultant, University of Florida's George A. Smathers Libraries, 2020. Map depicts populated places. Water Bodies obtained from Open Street Map (© openstreetmap.org + contributors). Coastline, rivers, and country boundaries obtained from NOAA.

France. On May 6, 1802, in the city of Cape Haitian, he doffed his hat before Leclerc. Bonaparte's brother-in-law invited Louverture to dine with him the next evening! A few days later, the one and only Jean-Jacques Dessalines joined the parade of grovelers. One month later, the French officers pounced on Louverture. They disarmed him, they arrested him, and they flung him off to France without uttering a word of French.

if the last card trick's not for the people the cards weren't well shuffled

How did what happened, happen? How did the French get Toussaint shipped off? Why did the generals give in? Why didn't the masses of fieldworkers budge? Since 1793, Toussaint Louverture had been defending freedom for every inhabitant of Saint-Domingue ... In February 1802, how did peasants in Saint-Domingue catch a whiff of this freedom? Since 1793, this freedom had remained in the hands of an organization ... In February 1802, when Leclerc invaded Cape Haitian, where was that organization? Toussaint's organization had dovetailed with fieldworkers on the issue of freedom since 1793 ... In 1802, what sort of castration shears cut the cord (*kòd*) of that collaboration?

In fact, the failure of Toussaint's officers and generals against Leclerc's army wasn't just a military failure. Some officers had switched camps without setting off a single firecracker. Toussaint's collapse was a **political** defeat, an ideological defeat, and a defeat which reflected the way Louverture's organization had sought to lead the country, and the way Louverture himself had sought to lead that organization. It was a defeat intertwined with the organization's agenda and tactics, and with how that agenda and those tactics hummed right along until they got beaten down before Saint-Domingue's up-and-down reality.

It isn't contradictory for us to say that the agenda and tactics of Louverture's organization were spot on between 1793 and 1799. And we must sing his praises for the way Louverture's army defended workers' freedom throughout that time. But, as we already know, freedom for all people was one of the slaves' primary interests, and the military organization of *nouveaux libres* was one of the requirements of that freedom.

When we look back, when we take the full measure of Saint-Domingue's primary industry, and when we seek out the interests of each social class within that society (before 1789), we uncover four conflicts which correspond perfectly to the four features of the primary industry (slavery, dependence, commodity crops, and large plantations):

a conflict between Slavery and Freedom
a conflict between Dependence and Independence
a conflict between Commodity goods and Food crops
a conflict between Big plantations and Food plots.

In Saint-Domingue, the primary twin conflict (slaves versus French commissioners and plantation owners) was interwoven with these four primary issues: Slavery, Dependence, Commodity crops, and Big plantations. But that didn't mean all those problems needed to be resolved at one time, with a single shot. **The contradiction between Slavery and Freedom had to be resolved before all the rest**. The problems of Dependence, Commodity crops, and Big plantations were important, but the conflict between Slavery and Freedom stood out from the rest as a **banner conflict**.

Thus, in 1793 the organization's political agenda was spot on because the major demand that it made on the society lay within the conflict between Slavery and Freedom. The political agenda of an organization is the central demand that it makes upon the society in which it's living in a specific situation. Within a society that has slaves and slave owners, the foremost demand for the people's organization is freedom in a legal sense. But this demand can't be consistent for all countries and for all times. Political agendas—thank God!—aren't carved in stone. There's no readymade political agenda that can be draped across the sky or spread across all countries forever and a day. Instead, the conflict is like a gang on the offensive: it doesn't stay put! History's judgment should be based on the ways and means by which an **organization** profited from the specific situation within which it lived. History's judgment should be based on the ways and means by which that organization put pressure on the various **social forces**, and the degree to which it forced them to recognize the central demand of the class at the very bottom.

It's upon that truth that we stake this claim: in 1793, the political agenda of Toussaint's organization was spot on (that is, Freedom for everyone before the law), and its tactics were spot on because only an army of former slaves could seize that freedom and be vigilant enough to guarantee that freedom without the people needing to sleep with one eye closed and one eye open.

We've charted how that army moved forward through seven fiery years, and how it rallied around the people so freedom could blossom on fertile land. But ...

But the conflict was like a gang on the offensive: it didn't stay put. In 1793, while Toussaint's organization was reaching out to help the people travel the path to freedom, heaps of other events were stirring up Saint-Domingue's economic situation: Galbaud had flown the coop with a crew of big colonists. This incident had several consequences: the French commissioners' power started to wane, and heaps of plantations were left to flap in the wind ... Therefore, the conflict between Slavery and Freedom wasn't the only one developing. The conflict between Dependence and Independence, that between Commodity goods and Food crops, that between Big plantation and Food plot, it was all shifting, raveling, and unraveling. Between 1793 and 1799, while the organization's position was spot on in terms of the freedom issue, **the position held by most of its leaders** on the three other major issues intertwined with the primary industry **had developed in the same way as the upper classes' position!**

The mistake committed by Louverture's organization was its neglect of the people in the face of those three conflicts. But if that error wasn't fatal in 1793, as the organization had gone about eliminating freedom's enemies, its own error weighed all the heavier. The more the organization sought to shore up its own power, the more disagreements seeped in between it and the masses. After the Galbaud Affair, after the Villatte Affair, after the expulsion of both Sonthonax and Hédouville,[67] after the War of the South, a tangle of conflicts (that had been developing since 1793) changed completely. With Louverture's organization now heading up the country, it couldn't pretend that freedom was in danger, and even the masses had come to believe that freedom was secured. There were young men and women who'd grown up under the shade of this tree, who'd never accustomed themselves to working like mules under the lashing whips of slave drivers. There were former

---

67 Gabriel Marie-Théodore-Joseph, Comte d'Hédouville (1755–1825) was a general sent by the French government to defend French interests in Saint-Domingue. He helped arm Rigaud and his troops of *anciens libres*. Hédouville made Rigaud the Commander-in-Chief of the Department of the South and encouraged him to fight against Toussaint Louverture as a means of weakening black fighting capacity in favor of French power. Louverture defeated Rigaud, precipitating the fall of Sonthonax and Hédouville. Ultimately, on October 22, 1797, Hédouville and 2,000 of his men fled the colony on three frigates (Roc 240–41).

maroons who'd refused to return to the grindstone ... In the blink of an eye, other conflicts sprouted up. They started settling in after the Galbaud Affair, after the Villatte Affair, after Lavaud put Louverture in power. At the center of the Freedom camp, the conflicts took on antagonistic tones: Dependence versus Independence, Big plantations versus Food plots, Commodity goods versus Food crops. These three conflicts split the camp of freedom in two, in three, in four ... At that moment, some people were surprised to see that Toussaint wasn't on their side anymore. Louverture and most of his generals stood atop the palace, looking down at fieldworkers with disdain. And so, Sister Lamèsi, who was a young child, got up and looked at her mother, and asked: Mama, was Toussaint ever on our side?

the alligator professes his love to the lizard and the anolis says scram

Not all the rebel slaves came from the same category. Most of the leaders were former overseers, house slaves, or slaves from the towns; and while they did suffer greatly, they didn't suffer in the same way as the slaves on the bottom rung of the ladder, who had the status of flunked out donkeys. Some of them even had their own savings. (Some experts say that Toussaint crossed over to the revolutionary camp with 40,000 piastres in hand.) They had more freedom to travel than any of the other slaves. And above all, they hung around the French and picked up all the ideas and words of the French big shots. Of course, they didn't make use of all those words at the same time, or under the same conditions. In 1791, they were all fired up about the idea of equality, and they planted that idea in the minds of many comrades. But they also picked up some prejudices. When Biassou appointed himself 'Viceroy of the Occupied Territories', the French nearly died laughing, as though they'd forgotten that Biassou had attended the school of the Brothers[68] in Cape Haitian!

Therefore, because of their social origins (the **category** they came from, within the **slave** class), the rebel leaders didn't view the country's

---

68 Some of Haiti's revolutionary generals had received a French education. This detail challenges the notion that the Haitian Revolution was won exclusively by masses who were enslaved and uneducated—a discourse that both renders Haiti's revolutionary history overly exceptional and also reinforces reductive perspectives about Haitians in general.

problem in the same way the slave masses did. That's why Biassou and Jean-François were selling slaves. That's why Toussaint waited until the cows came home before he started fighting for freedom for all. And that's also why we say that there were two **social forces** within the camp of *nouveaux libres*: military leaders (meaning Toussaint's organization) and the masses of former slaves. And there was a conflict between organization and masses.

Classes within a society don't stay put. They're rooted in conflicts. And so they move forward, then step back, as the economic, political, or ideological situation develops. When a class rises up, it turns the society upside down and carries out a revolution. After a revolution, the situation of the social classes is different. After the 1789 revolution in France, the bourgeoisie built up its power, and it knocked the big landowners on their backs. But those upheavals take time. A revolution goes through several rainy seasons. And so while the revolution is forging its path, certain categories or even entire classes figure out how to take advantage of the situation. For the slightest reason they move forward, and for the slightest reason they step back. At this specific moment they're straddling two different positions. Which is to say, they're moving from one class to another. That's when we say: they're changing class.

In everyday life, only individuals change class. Mister Clément got into politics, he stopped being a bus driver, he stole money, and he stole land. He enjoys his interest income, or he opens up a store. There he goes, he's changed class. Even if others turn up their noses at Mister Clément, Mister Clément is well aware that his grandchildren are going to grow up in a different class. Mister Clément also knows that his own personal change in class didn't resolve any of the problems of the social class that he came from. Mister Clément became a social climber.

But during a revolutionary crisis like the one that took hold of Saint-Domingue, it's not individuals who change class … Entire classes, and categories of classes, are caught with one foot in the door and one foot outside. The masses of former slaves were in this situation. They weren't slaves anymore, yet at the same time their freedom hadn't been completely secured, and until the fat lady sang, they weren't yet 100 percent independent farmers. The military leaders of Toussaint's organization also underwent this shift. They weren't slaves anymore, and they knew that freedom was under threat, but while anticipating those threats (if those threats materialized), they were managing plantations. If they changed class completely, they wouldn't be fieldworkers, they'd become **plantation owners**.

126   *Stirring the Pot of Haitian History*

This idea is very important. Within the camp of freedom, two groups of people who'd come from various categories within **one same class** were transferring to **two different classes**. Two classes that would inevitably butt heads once that freedom was secured.

After the Galbaud Affair, Saint-Domingue's plantations were under the thumb of three groups: Villatte's group, the group with Rigaud and Beauvais, and Toussaint's group. After the Villatte Affair, Saint-Domingue's plantations lay in the hands of two groups: Rigaud's group and Toussaint's group. After the Rigaud Affair, Saint-Domingue's plantations were under the control of one sole team: the military leaders of Louverture's organization. Pamphile de Lacroix[69] stated that Dessalines controlled thirty-two plantations, and each property brought in 100,000 piastres per year. Which is to say ... Dessalines was a millionaire! It's true, de Lacroix, a Frenchman, didn't like Dessalines, and his word wasn't Gospel. But nobody could pretend to say that Louverture's generals weren't rolling in money. A bunch of businessmen in the North offered Moïse Louverture 20,000 piastres per month for the properties under his control. Cathéart, an English spy in Saint-Domingue, proclaimed: Henry Christophe is worth 250,000 **dollars**. (What a lot of sway the guy had!)

Therefore, this same slogan of Freedom that had bonded the masses to the organization in 1793, had loads of conflicts tangled at its feet. **Because of their social origins** (specific categories that originated within the slave class), and **because of their ongoing transfer** (they were transferring into the plantation owner class), the military leaders of *nouveaux libres* tended to ignore the problems of Dependence, Food crops, and the Big plantations.

The Dependence problem had two branches: political dependence and economic dependence. At this moment, we're focusing on economic dependence, because that's what started to cut the *kòd* [cord] linking Louverture's group and the masses of fieldworkers. Also, the problem of political dependence was thoroughly intertwined with Leclerc's invasion, and you'll hear more on that from a reliable source once we've sought out the reasons why Leclerc came ashore, and the consequences of that

---

69 General Joseph Pamphile de Lacroix (1774–1841) traveled with general Leclerc on the expedition to Saint-Domingue and was one of the first French soldiers to arrive in Port-au-Prince in 1802. De Lacroix's memoirs were published in the book, *Mémoires pour servir à l'Histoire de la Révolution de St-Domingue* (1819), an important source for historians of the Haitian Revolution and War of Independence (Roc 265).

arrival. Meanwhile, let's take a closer look at economic dependence under Louverture's government.

In 1797, while Toussaint was taking over Saint-Domingue's political apparatus (he expelled Sonthonax in August 1797), John Adams became president of America. One of the features of Adams's government was the way he defended the interests of New England's big merchants. Toussaint understood those terms. And he decided to do business at any cost. He'd already made a secret deal with the English, which is to say that Saint-Domingue and England were trading goods. And so, riding on the coattails of that same exchange, he sent Joseph Bounel to tell the Americans that they'd never find a better customer than Saint-Domingue. Bounel (a white Frenchman) arrived in Philadelphia. He talked ceaselessly. The American deputies and senators rallied around the plan. They argued at great length. In the end, the American Congress sided with Adams, and gave the merchants carte blanche to trade with Toussaint. France was stuck in a war in Europe. Americans profited, the way they always had (in 1776, in 1782), and as they'd profit each time French ships had trouble traveling. Between 1804 and 1825, before France recognized Haiti's independence ... in 1915, while France was getting itself pummeled in Europe ... during the Second World War. Which is to say, those two characters have played 'hot potato' for ages, but we're the ones who feel the pain.

the dress coat racks up debt
the jacket pays for it

It's true, some people are always saying that the leaders of *nouveaux libres* couldn't turn down either the Americans or the English, because in 1797 they **needed** weapons, tools, flour, salted meat, and so much else from those gentlemen. But what's also true is that the trading Toussaint's government did with the English and Americans reinforced economic dependence. The government's economic policies were only expanding this dependence: instead of us being in one country's claws, there were several big hawks scoring points against us. What's more, after the War of the South, after the Spanish were overthrown, that policy got reinforced. On December 12, 1800, Toussaint issued a communiqué stating that the government would be collecting 20 percent of the value of all commodities that passed through Saint-Domingue's wharf, whether they be incoming (imports) or outgoing (exports). Twelve days later, **under pressure from the American consul**, Toussaint repealed the law and lowered the import tax to 10 percent. His December 31 communiqué referenced the American consul (Stevens) and publicly announced: Saint-Domingue's government was making this gesture as '**proof**' that it would '**maintain good business practices**' that it had always had with Americans.

'Good business practices' for whom? Not for Ti Piè and Lamèsi. When the government imposed lower taxes on imported goods, big traders overseas benefited most. Boatloads of Swedes, Danes, Englishmen, Jews, and especially Americans came to replace many of the French traders. They had the upper hand, along with the big warehouses **abroad** that controlled all the newcomers. The loss was Saint-Domingue's, because the government was levying higher taxes on outgoing commodity crops, commodity crops produced on the island. 'Good business practices' for whom? The capitalist countries' economic commissioners were selling their own countries' commodities at steep prices, and the government of Saint-Domingue was itself imposing taxes on Saint-Domingue's own goods! The 10 percent difference was a façade that enabled traders to buy less from Saint-Domingue and sell more of their own goods.

But big traders are greedy. If you let them get ahead, they'll rip out your very eyeballs. And so they kept pressuring Toussaint. On February 12, 1801, Toussaint lowered the taxes again on all commodity goods passing through wharfs on the Spanish side (10 percent export, 6 percent import!). In April 1801, he told the big traders they could carry debt with the State. In May, he loosened even more *kòd* [codes] for them. He lowered the import tax to 6 percent throughout the island **for all major commodities**: flour, salted meat and fish, tools, wood … He said that he made this decision 'under expert counsel'. My friends, both you and I well know who those 'experts' were: Edward Stevens and other commissioners from capitalist countries!

This meant: if a fool offers, only an idiot doesn't take. I don't know if that's true, but by golly, traders took. They took, and they gave to their bosses so the bosses could build factories in Europe and the United States. In 1801–02, there weren't just two or three officials in Cape Haitian, Môle Saint-Nicolas, Fort-Liberté, Port-au-Prince, Gonaïves, Jacmel, Les Cayes, Saint-Louis, and Anse-à-Veau. Ships from all the big capitalist countries were traveling back and forth to Saint-Domingue under the American flag. It's true, from 1776 on, when Stephen Coronio landed in Cape Haitian, Americans were playing patty-cake to get Saint-Domingue's business. During just the month of May and most of June 1782, sixty-four American ships arrived in Saint-Domingue (which was **thirty-two** ships per month!). So under Louverture's government, it was truly the land of milk and honey ... **In one single day** (February 4, 1802, the day Leclerc showed up in Cape Haitian), **there were thirty-five American ships at the wharf!** And the man controlling America's interests was a lofty commissioner: Tobias Lear,[70] former personal secretary to General George Washington!

the needle worked
the straight pin went to the ball

Some people claim (and they claim it a lot) that Toussaint's government maintained this trade because it needed weapons in case France came back to invade. **It's true, money from that trade allowed Toussaint to buy swords, revolvers, gunpowder, and 30,000 rifles and then some from the United States.** But Sister Lamèsi, who was a child at the time, told me that Louverture's officers bought more than a few mansions, fancy silverware, beautiful women, and pretty, faux gold necklaces through their own tricks in this trade. No one can make us believe that all those **German** musicians acting like divas at Toussaint's New Year's Eve parties were there to scare off the French in case of an invasion!

My friends, these words are clear. While Toussaint's organization solidly supported freedom for all, it never took a stand against economic dependence. And so, in 1797–98, as the organization was taking over the country's political apparatus, certain hawkish countries (especially England and America) got their claws on Saint-Domingue's production. When Toussaint reached the height of his power, he got trapped in the game of dependence by giving capitalist economic commissioners complete and total advantage. So even from that time onward, certain key leaders within the organization started distrusting their own government. Between 1799 and late 1801, most of the others were in bed with foreign traders. Saint-Domingue's workers became beasts of burden for the big bourgeois strutting around in Maine, New Hampshire, Massachusetts, Rhode Island, and Connecticut. Meanwhile, in Cape Haitian, Port-au-Prince, and Jacmel, wearing feathered hats on their heads, the strongmen danced at the ball with white women.

---

70 Tobias Lear (1762–1816) of New Hampshire worked for George Washington from 1784 to 1799.

when it rains
we'll plant beans
yes, we'll plant beans

Saint-Domingue's economic dependence was tied to another issue: the issue of Commodity crops. When one country's under the control of another, and when foreign commissioners control its production, that country produces what foreigners want it to produce. Most often, foreign countries need **commodity crops**, because they either can't produce them at home or because they cost too much to produce at home. In 1789, when Saint-Domingue shipped off more than 200,000 pounds of goods, they consisted of 143,000 pounds of **sugar**, 77,000 pounds of **coffee**, and 7,000 pounds of **cotton**. But this production mostly benefited political and economic commissioners, along with big plantation owners. There was a conflict between Commodity crops and the country's other products. This conflict was between the interests of plantation owners and French commissioners versus the interests of the slaves who were producing these commodities but never saw a five-cent copper coin from the profits.

Just as the organization refused to take a stand against economic dependence, it refused to take a stand against producing commodity crops. Dependence and commodity crops slept in the same bed. As the English often declared, 'the colony's prosperity lies in producing lots of commodity crops'. In 1801, Toussaint would take up the same slogan: 'A colony's trade comes down to one single thing: trading **commodity crops** and products from its territory …'.

It's true that under Toussaint, sugar lost ground. Coffee was booming. But any coffee worthy of the name is a **commodity**, just like sugar, just like cotton. Peasants planted coffee, but the coffee couldn't be eaten. Coffee accumulated within coastal warehouses of the bourgeoisie. Therefore, the conflict between Commodity crops and Food crops was firmly upheld under Louverture's government. And within this conflict, the government sided with the big coastal traders against the position of the people. Many foreigners (especially French) visited the plantations. Certain among them reported what they saw: 'We observed that all the fieldworkers had divided off a fairly large piece of land for their **own cultivation**; they devoted all their time to that piece of land, despite the threat posed by Toussaint Louverture's regulations specifically addressing this matter …'. 'They were only planting **food crops** …'. 'The whites grew such meager (food crops), poor devils, they had a hard time making ends meet'.

In reality, food plots were what interested the masses of Saint-Domingue. But Louverture's **government** did not hold that position. To the contrary: it favored commodity crops 100 percent. It favored **plantation commodity crops** over food crop farming, **commodity trade** over domestic trade within the country, and **commodity production** over the work of craftspeople.

On December 12, 1800, the government imposed a 20 percent tax on the value of all goods coming from small factories in Saint-Domingue: lime, bricks, leather, molasses, alcohol, etc. In January 1801, it set tax collectors loose. On February 8, Toussaint gave a speech in Santo-Domingo. He announced: 'The land awaits industrious arms that will make it yield prosperity for people who plant **crops that generate wealth**. On the other hand, people who keep planting **bananas, potatoes**, and **yams, products that are worthless to the colony**, they'll be in trouble'. Three days later, on February 11, 1801, he forbade people on the Spanish side to sell animals. A little while later, he imposed a tax on all animals crossing from one department to another (the law of March 7, 1801).

All those communiqués were like a single buckshot that Louverture's government fired against all other industries that might disturb production and the trading of **commodity goods** in Saint-Domingue. But those who took this shot in the chest were the masses of *nouveaux libres*, owners of food crop-farming plots, and sharecroppers, the same class that had defended freedom for all, and the same class that had supported the **organization** between 1793 and 1799. That buckshot hit them in the chest, and by late 1801, they couldn't just sleep things off and forget about them. As Sister Lamèsi likes to say, 'Throw it away to forget it, but pick it up to remember'.

I'll work night and day
so that when I return
I can buy a little bit of land
a little goat
a little cow
a little piglet

The position of Louverture's organization regarding the conflict between Big plantations and Food plots rode on the coattails of its position regarding Dependence and Commodity crops. But this position was

132   *Stirring the Pot of Haitian History*

especially obvious because of the transfer in social class that the leaders of *nouveaux libres* had undergone. As a matter of fact, those men had sought to become plantation owners in Saint-Domingue. Accordingly, from 1794 onward, Toussaint's policy geared itself to preserving plantations.

In July 1794, Lavaud had set out to divide up a few plantations to give to workers. Toussaint, who'd just crossed over to the French camp, advised him against this redistribution. At the same time, wherever the officers went, they broadcast the order: respect plantations. This order was upheld throughout the struggle to secure freedom. What's more, after Toussaint took over the political apparatus, he passed a ton of laws forcing peasants to work on plantations (May 18, 1798; August 3, 1798; November 15, 1798; March 4, 1799, etc.). On February 7, 1801, Toussaint decreed that Saint-Domingue's large plantations must remain fully intact. Peasants had teamed together to escape hardship. Two, three, or four of them would pool their money to purchase a field. Toussaint declared: Cut that out! He declared: To sell land in Saint-Domingue, the Town Council had to approve, the people buying the land had to explain to the authorities what they planned to do with it, and **the parcel had to exceed fifty *kawo*.**[71] On top of that, Louverture welcomed back former French plantation owners who'd run away. He told them: 'Children of Saint-Domingue, come home. We never intended to take away your property and plantations. The black people were **only asking for freedom**, the freedom God gave them. Children of Saint-Domingue, your house is wide open, and your lands are ready to welcome you'.

While Louverture was summoning the 'children of Saint-Domingue' who'd run away, its real children, those who hadn't tried to run away, who couldn't run away, stood salivating before the land. It's true, they'd yearned for Freedom, but this Freedom was inextricable from the land. The native culture that had developed in Saint-Domingue didn't distinguish freedom from fields! Since 1792 the position of the rebel slaves had shown that connection. If the masses had joined forces with Toussaint's organization, it was because the conflict between slavery and freedom was a banner conflict. But when they managed to seize that freedom, and when they'd secured it with their own physical strength, the conflict between plantations and food plots required resolution. Otherwise, **this freedom made no sense!**

---

71 A *kawo* is an amount of land approximately equivalent to three acres or 1.3 hectares (Freeman and Laguerre *Haitian Creole-English Dictionary* 358).

mosquito, watch out for zombies

Therefore, though Toussaint's organization may have started down the path with the people, it never took up the people's position on the issues of Dependence, Commodity crops, and Plantations. It stayed silent on dependence and commodity crops, and it favored big plantations. As the organization had taken complete control of the political apparatus, **those positions got reinforced**. The government unconditionally favored dependence, commodity crops, and plantations. The bond that had existed long ago between the people and the organization didn't exist between the people and **the government**. And so, to the extent that the government was getting established, and to the extent that fieldworkers were developing their positions on Dependence, Commodity crops, and Plantations, they also refused to march in step. They drew back, they obstructed things, and they started dissenting.

don't say that
don't say that
o, it's bragging

But despite this disagreement, Toussaint's government managed to keep Saint-Domingue on its feet. Business was thriving, and plantations were prospering. In 1801, Saint-Domingue exported nearly seventy-two **million** pounds of goods (71,830,612)! That was three times less than what it exported in 1789 (226 million and then some), but that also means it was **fifteen times** more than what its exports weighed in 1795.

This might well surprise you. You might well ask how Saint-Domingue got itself restarted despite these gnawing conflicts. Where did the country's stability come from? What kind of Gordian knot bound these conflicts together, especially the conflict between the masses and big traders and plantation owners? The people were free, many had rifles in their hands, many saw as clear as day that they were stuck in a rut, and many staked their lives on unattainable positions. What barrier blocked the path and kept the conflicts from taking off?

Do you give up? Well, my friends, it was the State.

I know some people will say that they already knew that. Which is to say, my challenge fell flat because they've always known the State's a pain in the neck that clamps down on ordinary people and messes things up. But it isn't that simple. Let's look for a moment at the state that showed its face when Louverture took over the political apparatus. Let's reflect some on the functions of the State in that society, the functions of the State in any dog-eat-dog society.

If you're feeling tired, and if sleep's about to overcome you, put a piece of ginger under your tongue, that's good for keeping your mind alert. As for me, I'll sip a little cinnamon tea to loosen up my vocal cords, because this conversation calls for alertness. Meanwhile, Vodou singer, please give us another song!

Jakomèl, you hold the authority
you hold the authority
Minister Azaka
O, there's no justice

Authority's not a social class. Small vendors often say: 'Big traders call the shots' and they're right in their own way. Market women often say: 'The tax collector calls the shots' and they're right in their own way. Peasants often say: 'The country sheriff deputy calls the shots' and they're right in their own way, too. Tenant-farmers say: 'Big landowners call the shots', and little kids say 'No, it's the Boogeyman'.[72] A barefooted beggar near the church bows his head and says: 'When the paddy wagon goes by, everybody toes the line'.

Traders, tax collectors, sheriffs, big landowners, and paddy wagon drivers aren't in the same social class. What's more, even if all together they represent authority (in their own way), authority's not the same thing as traders, tax collectors, sheriffs, or big landowners, much less paddy wagon drivers. Authority's not a social class. Authority's not a social category. Authority's not the government either. Governments rise and fall, but authority doesn't change just for that. In the United States, for example, the government changes about every eight years, and the authority, or the State stays firm. (If authority changed every eight years, society would collapse.)

[72] Charles-Oscar Étienne, or 'Chaloska', who commonly appears as a Carnaval figure, was chief of police during the term of Haitian President Vilbrun Guillaume Sam (February–July 1915). Étienne was responsible for the execution of 167 political prisoners. A crowd consisting of the victims' family members killed President Sam in the street outside the French consulate the next day. The story passed into legend and Chaloska became a boogeyman inspiring Carnaval costumes (Freeman 2004, 149).

From 1800–01, within the society of Saint-Domingue—like in any other society—the State was a referee at the center of a gigantic battle being fought within the society. But the State isn't just any referee. **It's a biased referee.** It's biased towards one class, then towards another; it favors one category, then another. But none of those biases look alike. None of those biases have the same slant as the others.

you'll lend me a chair
so I can sit down
so I can take a look
so I can look at them

In Saint-Domingue, each social force was struggling to achieve its own interests, and to pull the society in the direction of its own interests. The masses of former slaves and fieldworkers joined forces with other groups of *nouveaux libres*, especially Toussaint's officers, and they pulled the society towards their primary political interest: freedom. They seized that freedom and secured it by force, but what's more, they forced the rest of the society to recognize that freedom. And so we say, the camp of *nouveaux libres* had **political dominance** within the society.

But while *nouveaux libres* had political dominance within Saint-Domingue, it was the newcomers, the foreign commissioners, who were pulling the society in the direction of their own economic interests. Big plantation owners fed from the same trough. Therefore, we can say that foreign commissioners had **economic dominance**, and to shore up that dominance, they teamed up with big plantation owners.

Besides those political and economic battles, there was an ideological battle, too. We'll get back to **ideological dominance**, but from here on out you mustn't fall asleep and forget: class struggles were fought on three fronts. What's more, social forces with dominance on one of those fronts didn't necessarily have dominance on the other two.

That's not to say all those forces had equal standing. The standing of any one force is intertwined with the status of the economic terrain, political terrain, or ideological terrain within a specific situation and a specific society. Within Saint-Domingue's specific situation, from 1789 onward, the political terrain was most important. The battle being fought on that terrain, among all the social forces, acted unyieldingly upon both the economic and ideological terrains. Thus, we can say the **camp of nouveaux libres** had general dominance within the society.

But don't declare victory too soon like some *nouveaux libres* did, when freedom for all seemed to have become a sure thing. The dominance held by one social force didn't eliminate conflicts within the society, especially during a time of revolution. The general dominance on the part of *nouveaux libres* didn't eliminate other classes and categories: traders and plantation owners were clamping down within the economic terrain. Conflicts were stewing: Dependence versus Independence, Plantations versus Food plots, Commodity crops versus Food crops, White versus Black, Mulatto versus Black, Mulatto versus White, Catholic versus Vodou, French versus Creole … The State was the crossroads where all those conflicts converged.

within the crossroads of the *vèvè* that's where all the forces converge

The state's main function in a society is the **vèvè function**. The state pulls on all the conflicts in the society, it condenses them inside itself, it inscribes them with all their powers, and it traces their course like the *vèvè* inscribes the course of the *loua* [spirits] and the course of the ceremony. When we consider the central ideas of the State of Saint-Domingue (the 1801 Constitution), we discover the society's conflicts inscribed within the Constitution like the *loua* and ritual stations inscribed within the center of a *vèvè*. That's what leads wise people to say: 'The State is a catalog of conflicts within the society' and all its powers, are the society's *vèvè*.

For example, in 1801, the political dominance of *nouveaux libres* was inscribed within the Constitution. The Constitution stated: all people in Saint-Domingue are equal, regardless of their color. There cannot be any more slaves in Saint-Domingue, slavery is abolished forevermore, etc. (articles 3, 4, 5). All people have the right to manage their property as they wish (Article 13). The Constitution guarantees freedom to every single citizen. The government cannot arrest a citizen without reason, or it is considered abuse, and only a court can decide who is innocent or guilty (articles 12, 42, 43, 63, 64, 65, 66, 75). The Constitution acknowledged that a revolution occurred in Saint-Domingue (Article 28). When we place all those many articles alongside the articles of the *Kòd Noua* [Black Code], we see that Saint-Domingue's masses had a major impact on things, and we see just how far they forced Saint-Domingue's other classes to go. And the State's primary function, ten years after the cane fields were set ablaze, was to inscribe that dominance, or power.

But the power of the economic commissioners was also inscribed, just like the advantages the plantation owners had, just like the role of the government, just like the positions held by leaders of *nouveaux libres* within the government, just like the conflict between dependence and political independence, and a load of other conflicts that spread across the three terrains. Even the conflict between French and Creole was inscribed into the very language of the Constitution … Most officers in **the government** couldn't understand very much, even if a learned person read them all the French words that Borgella[73] and his other white French comrades wrote for the State.

Therefore, the state's main function was to gather these conflicts together under the same arbor. It inscribed the conflicts. We call that function of gathering/inscribing the *vèvè* **function**.

Mazaka Lakoua[74] brought *kòd* [cord]
to tie up the people of Bel Air
the people of Bel Air
wondered what they did

But the State didn't just inscribe the conflicts one at a time. It twisted those conflicts. It tied them up all together. This function is the **Gordian knot function** of the State.

When the Gordian knot ties together seven *kòd* [cords/codes], each individual *kòd* takes on more resistance. Which is to say, each *kòd* becomes more robust. But at the same time, when the *kòd* comes out of the knot (if it's able to come out), it comes out from a different direction, because all the other *kòd* are applying pressure on it. No *kòd* that comes out of the Gordian knot ever comes from the same direction that it went in.

---

73 General Jérôme-Maximilien Borgella (1773–1844) was a freedman who initially fought with French troops during Haiti's Revolution, and subsequently changed sides (Oriol 167).

74 Mazaka Lakoua (Mazaka Lakwa, i.e. 'Mazaka of the Cross') is a Vodou spirit in the Gede Rite, a tradition within the religion that focuses on sexuality and death.

By the same token, when the State binds the conflicts with all the society's particular powers, one type of power acts upon another, one conflict envelops another, and none of them ever comes out without the imprint of the Gordian knot. The 1801 Constitution inscribed freedom for all alongside political freedom (articles 3, 4, 5), and it reinforced them (articles 12, 14, 43–46, 63–66, etc.), but **at the same time** it tied that freedom to the table legs of big traders and plantation owners. Article 16 stated: fieldworkers had 'defects', which is to say they didn't like staying on plantations and their frequent attempts to escape were not in the colony's interest. And so the governor had the right to 'take any necessary **police** action that circumstances required' to stop fieldworkers.

For goodness sakes, when they tie a person to a chore, they don't let him budge, and they threaten to call the police if he acts like he might leave, that can't help but seem like slavery.

Was this freedom, as *nouveaux libres* understood it? No. Was this slavery, as many plantation owners daydreamed about? No. Was this an entanglement of both those interests? You bet! When the State restores a conflict within the society, it marks the cards of that conflict. The conflict bears the imprint of:

1. **its own power**: in the specific case of Article 16, plantation owners scored two points against fieldworkers.
2. **general power in the society**: however, workers had 'freedom', so for the State they were equal to plantation owners.
3. **the powers of all the other conflicts**: this political compromise was made on account of the economic dominance of foreign commissioners who controlled the trade of **commodity goods**.

At the same time as the State inscribes the conflicts with all their power, it also reroutes those conflicts. The conflicts are tied together, and no power that ever comes out is the same as when it started. There's not a single power that doesn't bear the scar of the State's function as Gordian knot.

Why? Because all the functions of the State join forces. While the *vèvè* function is tied to the Gordian knot function, both of those functions are tied to the third function of the State: the function of the counterweight.

in a bowlegged country all the healthy limp

The third function of the State is the function of **counterweight**. The State stands as a counterweight on the scales of society to strike a balance among the internal contradictions of that society.

From 1800–01, the State of Saint-Domingue was bowlegged. Freedom for all wasn't yet fully fledged, the war of the South had only just ended, predatory foreign countries were pressuring it on all sides, and plantation owners were sticking out their tongues. There were people on Louverture's own team who began distrusting the government. Balance was very hard to maintain within the State itself. Balance is always difficult for any revolution that's seeking to consolidate itself … Which is to say, the State was too heavy to hang onto its position, and its own weight was dragging it down.

But in truth, within Saint-Domingue the State wasn't only out of balance. The whole State itself was bent over. The State had to be bowlegged because its bowleggedness gave the society balance.

And so we shouldn't be surprised if we see the 1801 Constitution as chock-full of contradictions. It tied peasants to the table legs of plantation owners, yet it 'guaranteed freedom' to each citizen. It gave Catholic practitioners a greater voice than Vodou initiates (articles 6, 7, 8), yet it proclaimed that the law treats everyone the same way, without bias. It gave the governor the right to arrest any person under suspicion (Article 40), yet it also proclaimed that all citizens have the right to request which judge will judge them (Article 42).

In 1800–01, the third function of the State in Saint-Domingue was to stand as a counterweight on the scales of society to balance out the society's internal contradictions. To be sure, if you look at the State on its own, you'll see that it's too heavy for its own body. But when you weigh it alongside the society, **when you look at both plates of the scales within the society**, you see that the imbalance of the State is what gives society an aspect of balance. In a bowlegged country, all the healthy limp.

what a wild spirit
Badagri is

We've seen the three biggest functions of the State: the function of *vèvè*, the function of Gordian knot, and the function of counterweight. But we shouldn't forget that those functions aren't separate in the everyday life of the society. Those functions were born together, and they intertwine. If you understand that truth, you'll discover the fourth function of the State, the function that we'll call: the function of *chwal* [horse].

The conflicts in the society sit astride the State, and they lend it a mouth to speak. Quite often, the ideas aren't clear, that is, the words are like ritual language in Vodou ceremonies, because the State pressures each conflict and power that it appropriates from all the other conflicts. It plays this role to give society an appearance of balance. But let's suppose that one conflict speaks up so forcefully that it threatens that balance? This conflict (this force) appears as a *loua* [spirit] which refuses to follow the course of the *vèvè* and which appears before its time in the ceremony. This conflict appears as a wild *loua* that isn't inscribed in the *vèvè*, one that takes over a *chwal*. This *chwal* is the State, yes, it is!

It's true, this force can keep on saying whatever it wants. It's also true that **the government**, as the only master of ceremonies, might take some time pursuing that force, like the *laplas*, or chief assistant to a Vodou priest, demanding a *mazon* song to reject a wild *loua*. But as soon as the *mazon* is sung, we know that a wild *loua* threatens to spoil the party. We know the *chwal* is in a dire situation.

From the moment Louverture's government started acting like the only *laplas* in Saint-Domingue, there was one conflict that refused to play the balancing game: peasants were fleeing plantations, despite all the government's warnings. This conflict gripped the *chwal* so hard that Louverture's government started performing its *mazon* songs the way it knew best: with the army. Louverture's officers swung at fieldworkers with *boua-pini*, or prickly yellowwood sticks. It was this dreadful dance that certain learned people call: Louverture's authoritarian agrarian system.

a bull won't fit in a goatskin

Toussaint's authoritarian agrarian system was a badly calculated effort to make plantation workers wear army uniforms. Toussaint's organization was a military organization, and its strict discipline bore results in the political battle. And so Toussaint's government fused itself to that **political** outcome to give the impression that it was leading an **economic** battle. It made a badly calculated effort to organize fieldworkers like a military organization. It exploited the army to force workers to march in step with the State's desires.

In reality, from the moment Louverture took over the country's political apparatus, after Sonthonax's ouster, he unleashed the army's full force on the peasants' tails. The soldiers were supposed to keep the workers on plantations, whether they liked it or not. (Communiqués of May 18, 1798; November 15, 1798; March 4, 1799; and January 4, 1800). So, in a law that appeared on October 12, 1800, Toussaint made the authoritarian agrarian system crystal clear. The spirit of his statement went like this:

1. A soldier's chief responsibility is to obey his leader without complaint; that is how he defends his country's interests. As for managers, foremen, and fieldworkers, as well as officers, non-commissioned officers, and soldiers on plantations: their chief responsibility is to obey leaders without complaint.
2. When an officer, a non-commissioned officer, or a soldier disobeys, they put him in front of a military tribune, and the military tribune punishes him. Managers, foremen, and fieldworkers on plantations are subject to the same kind of punishment if they don't perform their duties.
3. A soldier has no right whatsoever to leave his regiment without permission from his supervisor. Fieldworkers may not leave plantations without permission from the authorities.

This position was grounded in two giant miscalculations: it made as though the economic battle had been carried out under the same conditions, and upon the same front, as the military battle. What's more, it resolutely refused the interests of the fieldworkers' social class on the economic front. Plantation workers had fought fiercely in the army of *nouveaux libres* because they saw their interests in: freedom for all. But they'd never march in step for the sake of an economic policy they didn't believe in. A bull won't fit in a goatskin!

o my mother sent me to weigh coffee
when I reached the entrance
a policeman arrested me on the spot

The first feature of Louverture's authoritarian agrarian system was his attempt to make fieldworkers fit into the skin of a military organization. But a live bull won't fit in a goat's skin. And so the second feature of the authoritarian system was his overuse of the army (the State's army) to force the bull to obey the rules. In the October 12 regulation, Toussaint stated straightforwardly: 'The Generals in charge of the departments will report directly to **me** about any slackness going on in the farming of their districts …' (Article 8). Toussaint kept an eye on the departments' commanders. Department commanders were controlling district commanders. District commanders were mistreating workers. The army didn't allow people to leave plantations. If a worker wanted to head into town, he had to obtain a permit. If he refused to work, or if they caught him wandering around, both he and anyone else who'd indulged him would pay a high price …

My friends, the fieldworkers didn't just suffer a little. Blabbermouths said that when high-ranking soldiers would discipline a worker, they'd make him walk naked between two lines of soldiers, and then with all the drums beating, the soldiers would shred the poor guy with mesquite branches! A white Frenchman told Charles Mackenzie[75] how Dessalines (who was inspector general of plantations) beat a pregnant woman near the city of Les Cayes. The woman suffered so many blows that she aborted on the spot … In fact, whenever Dessalines showed up, managers, workers, whites, mulattos, and black people shook like leaves in a Nor'easter. Christophe, Toussaint, and most commanders gave fieldworkers this same stinging treatment. But the authoritarian system wasn't enough to stop the slave masses. Toussaint Louverture didn't issue five communiqués in three years for no reason: the masses refused to obey! If freedom meant spending three years on the same plantation and working like a beast of burden from five in the morning to five at night, **this freedom made no sense!**

Towards the end of 1801, the raveled *kòd* [cord/code] binding the masses to the organization broke. A conflict between fieldworkers and

---

75 Charles Mackenzie (1788–1862) was the British consul in Haiti in 1826–27, an assignment about which he wrote in *Notes on Haiti* (1830) (Winston & Russwurm, 2010, p. 64).

7. Cousin that's not what you told me

government was emerging in Saint-Domingue, and this conflict would combine with the internal conflicts of Louverture's team. For both of them, in October 1801, the organization that had carried the banner of freedom in Saint-Domingue since 1793 was destroyed.

cousin
that's not what you told me
you told me that
if we moved in together,
you'd marry me

In October 1801, on a bunch of plantations near Limbé, the fieldworkers revolted. They killed the foremen and all the whites they could find, they started shouting, 'Long live General Moïse', and they prepared to knock heads with Toussaint Louverture. In the blink of an eye, fire covered the northern plains. Limbé, Dondon, Port-Margot, Marmelade, L'Acul, they were all on the hotplate. On the afternoon of October 29, the fire had just begun, and a French officer brought the news to Henri Christophe, who was commander of Cape Haitian. Immediately, Christophe and the commander Barada[76] (a white French officer) tore into the rebels. Toussaint and Dessalines rushed up to the North and thrashed everyone in their path. Certain experts said that 1,000 peasants died at the hands of those folks. A little while later, Maurepas arrested Moïse. On November 6, 1801, in the Great Fort of Port-de-Paix, a regiment of soldiers (under the command of Clervaux)[77] aimed their rifles at Moïse, following the order that Louverture gave. A little snitch reported that the men were scared to shoot. Moïse raised his head, looked at them, and exclaimed, 'Shoot already, for crying out loud, shoot already!'

A lot of experts have studied the colossal event they call the Moïse Affair. There are some who claim: Moïse wasn't smart, he really didn't see where Toussaint was headed. Others may claim that Moïse's ambition was what got him into trouble. As for me, I didn't come here to prove

---

76 Félix Barada was commander of the Place du Cap at the time Leclerc's troops landed in 1802. He was subsequently arrested and deported (Oriol 162).
77 Augustin Clervaux, an *ancien libre*, was a lieutenant and later a devoted general in Toussaint Louverture's army. In 1804 he was one of the signatories of the Acte d'indépendance d'Haïti and became one of Dessalines's most trusted generals (Madiou, 1989, vols. 1–3).

whether Moïse was 'smart' (Ti Piè's big toe couldn't care less!), and I wouldn't be one bit surprised if all the head honchos in Louverture's general staff were chock-full of ambition. I'm telling you straight up: if all those peasants marched behind Moïse, it wasn't just because they thought Moïse was **smart**. And if Toussaint killed a bunch of them, it wasn't just because of Moïse's personal **ambition**. (Unless all those peasants had the same ambition as Moïse!)

As for me, in my wandering search, I've heard the sound of many bells. But if we're gathered here today, it's because Sis' Lamèsi wanted to hold a gathering so you could understand what's happened to our family. And so, my friends, I'm telling you, the event they call the 'Moïse Affair' is one of the vast shudders of fever that's passed through the family. Besides all his personal traits, the young man they called Gilles Bréda (Moïse Louverture) stood out as the lone supporter of a specific political position within Louverture's organization. And to the extent that his organization was developing, Moïse Louverture started looking suspect in the eyes of his other comrades. All animals have biting instincts, right? In October 1801, Moïse's comrades bit him.

But then, as Lamèsi points out, in 1801, were they still his comrades?

fish bones aren't meant to be sucked

From the moment Louverture's organization showed up in Saint-Domingue, it had elements of nearly every social class within it. That didn't keep it from functioning as an organization of former slaves, because its political agenda was in the former slaves' interests, and it was led by a team of former slaves. However, from 1793, alongside Charles Belair,[78] Gilles Bréda, and all the other rebel slaves, there were *anciens libres* like Maurepas, and there were whites like Biret at the heart of the organization. And all was well. No social force can pull off a revolution if it doesn't have supporters in other classes within the society. While the

---

78 Charles Belair was a colonel and a general of a Haitian brigade. Encouraged by his wife, Sanité Belair, he rallied the population of the Artibonite to revolt against the arrival of the French expedition led by Leclerc. Dessalines and the other generals judged Belair's uprising to be premature. Considering him a rival, Dessalines, who at the time was working for Leclerc, had Belair captured and sent to Leclerc in Cape Haitian for judgment. Belair and his wife were executed on October 5, 1802, in Cape Haitian (Madiou 1989 2:361–69).

political battle is underway, the ideological battle doesn't end. **It must convince other sectors within the society that the ideas it's promoting will serve the entire society.** And so we have to applaud the political force of Toussaint's group, which didn't worry about stuffing whites, mulattos, plantation owners, and middle-class people into its pockets, as long as they agreed to support freedom for all people.

But every coin has two sides. The conflict within this open-armed movement was a hidden threat: elements from other classes could take the organization's wheel; they could exploit the organization to promote their own interests ... Between 1794 and 1801, a bunch of people from other classes joined Toussaint's team: plantation owners (whites as well as *anciens libres*), middle-class people ...

After the battle of Henri (1794), Toussaint recruited Blanc-Cassenave, Paul Lafrance, Morin, Savary, Chanlatte, and Chevalier.[79] When Toussaint crossed over to the French camp, he picked up a great number of black people, former slaves who were **already** in Lavaud's army (Pierre Michel, Léveillé,[80] etc.). At the same time, he recruited Henri Christophe, *anciens libres*, and former soldier Comte d'Estaing,[81] a man who'd long ago held his small fortune (hotel-restaurant) in the city of Cape Haitian. Further down the road, as the group was joining forces with the masses of *nouveaux libres*, it picked up people like Rodriguez and Vincent[82] (white commissioners), then people like O'Gorman and Saint-James[83]

---

79 Blanc-Cassenave, Paul Lafrance (a black colonel in the colonial army), Morin, lieutenant Cézaire Savary, Chanlatte jeune, and Chevalier were troops in Toussaint Louverture's army (see Madiou 1989, vol. 2).

80 Pierre Michel was a rebel leader, colonel and general. After Toussaint Louverture saved Lavaud's life from an angry mob in 1795, and Lavaud compensated Louverture by promoting him to the rank of lieutenant, Pierre Michel became one of Louverture's loyal generals. Baptiste Léveillé was a colonel who was loyal to Lavaud and Toussaint Louverture (Madiou 1989 1:303–06).

81 Charles Hector, Comte d'Estaing (1729–94), was the governor of Saint-Domingue from 1763–66. Because of his loyalty to the royal family, during the French Revolution he was executed by guillotine on April 28, 1794, in the Reign of Terror (Madiou 1989 1:36).

82 Colonel Vincent was sent from France to Saint-Domingue in 1800 in order to deliver messages to Toussaint Louverture from Napoleon Bonaparte (Madiou 1989 2:56–57). Details regarding Rodriguez were elusive.

83 Comte Arnold-Victoire-Martin O'Gorman (1743–1815), a noble sugar-plantation owner whose family first settled in Saint-Domingue in 1691, was one of the members of Toussaint Louverture's honor guard (Clarke de Dromantin 71). Once the French expedition invaded Saint-Domingue in 1802, he aligned

(plantation owners in the South who'd deserted to join the English, because they didn't agree with the revolution, and who returned when Toussaint and Rigaud had cleaned the English's clocks!).

And so from 1800–01, Louverture's team consisted of all kinds of people: Clervaux, Magny, Morisset, Monpoint, Vernet, Lamartinière (*anciens libres*); Agé,[84] Pascal, Borgella, Idlinger (colonists), and so many others. Supposedly, that last group (the colonists) was closer to the general-in-chief than anyone else. Agé was chief of general staff. Borgella was the government's main writer (he wrote the Constitution). Idlinger, a German lawyer and former businessman who'd gone bankrupt in Bordeaux (in France), was in finance. Vincent and Pascal were the only general advisors in charge. It's true, most officers were *nouveaux libres*. It's true, there was a division of black *nouveaux libres* (Dessalines), and a division of mulatto *anciens libres* (Clervaux). But despite that, I would submit this: to the extent that the organization was taking complete control over the political apparatus, **Louverture's own government was swallowing the organization.** The organization became fish mashed up in bouillon. The coalitions that he'd made along the way were now pains in the neck for him. Freedom for all was still around as an underlying political agenda, and the army of *nouveaux libres* was still around, but the other conflicts were on the move. And I also submit that there were

---

himself with the French general Leclerc (Madiou 1989 2:318). Saint-James was a noble officer in Toussaint Louverture's honor guard (Madiou 1989 2:88). Like O'Gorman, Saint-James abandoned Toussaint Louverture's cause after the French expedition landed (Madiou 1989 2:266).

84 Étienne Magny (1765–1807) was a black general. He remained loyal to Toussaint Louverture when the French expedition led by general Leclerc invaded Saint-Domingue in 1802. He resisted the French and lived to see the foundation of the Haitian state, remaining active for many years after the war (Oriol 222). Morisset commanded Toussaint Louverture's honor guard and participated in the battle of Crête-à-Pierrot (Oriol 227); Monpoint commanded the second squadron of Louverture's honor guard, which fought in the same battle (Oriol 225). Louis Daure Lamartinière (1771–1802) was an officer of color in the Haitian army and was the superior officer at the siege of Crête-à-Pierrot. He fought with Rigaud from 1793–98. When the French expedition led by Leclerc arrived in Saint-Domingue in 1802, Lamartinière fought honorably for Toussaint Louverture and for the cause of freedom. Lamartinière was killed in an ambush on November 2, 1802. The man who killed him, Jean-Charles Courjol, put his head on a pike (Madiou 1989, vol. 2). Toussaint promoted Pierre Agé (1756–1813) to the rank of brigade general in 1797, and simultaneously named Agé chief of staff of the army of Saint-Domingue (Oriol 154).

several groups of positions on those conflicts. I would even submit that Moïse Louverture was the only standard-bearer of the left's position, that is, the position closest to the people, and the position that demanded the greatest transformation within the society. I'd even hazard to say that there were other officers on that left side, even if they didn't share the same position as Moïse point-for-point, and even if they never conspired with Moïse. I salute these enlightened officers who died without acclaim. I salute Charles Belair! I salute Louis Daure Lamartinière!

three claps of thunder don't make rain …

There are people who could say that I'm taking chances with History, and I'm not holding back from telling you they're right. But History allows you to take chances if the chances are carefully calculated and if you're considerate enough to tell everyone that you're taking chances.

I don't claim to say that Moïse, Belair, and Lamartinière conspired together. I'm not even sure whether Moïse knew Lamartinière. But I'm tempting fate to say: there are plenty of events that would allow us to believe that several of the officers within Louverture's army weren't in complete agreement with the system, and they were to the left vis-à-vis the position that Toussaint maintained. At the same time, we can be sure that most of those officers had no political contact with one another (except for Moïse's fifth regiment); at the same time, too, we can allow ourselves to say: Moïse, Belair, and Lamartinière had so many things in common that **it could not have been 'chance' alone that was responsible**.

1) All three of those men were of the same generation, a generation that grew up together with the bonfire of revolution, the same generation as the fieldworkers that Toussaint had said were 'lazy' and 'misbehaving' because they hadn't suffered under slavery before, and they now refused to work on plantations. Moïse was born in 1772, and he was Toussaint's adopted nephew. Lamartinière was born in 1771. Both those men had just turned twenty when the slaves started setting fire to the Northern plains. Charles Belair himself entered the battle at the age of fifteen, in 1792, as Toussaint's personal guard. Which is to say, all three men came of age under the sound of a different bell.

2) None of those three men got caught in the trap of color prejudice. Toussaint ousted Moïse as commander of the War in the South (Dessalines

replaced him) because they found Moïse to be too soft on the mulattos. Lamartinière himself was so white that if you didn't know his grandfather, you'd have to assume he was French ... Nevertheless, when Leclerc landed, and when most *anciens libres* in the West were preparing to shout: 'Long live France!', Lamartinière joined forces with the *nouveaux libres*.

3) All three of those men disobeyed their military commanders to adopt the people's position against the French: Moïse during 'the Moïse Affair'; Belair, when he left Dessalines to enter the battle on the side of the maroon soldiers; and Lamartinière, when he went over Magny's head during the French disembarkation in Port-au-Prince.

4) The wives of all three of those officers went head-first into the battle to defend the cause of the people. It was Moïse's wife who sent the fifth regiment on Hédouville's tail. Sanité Belair butted horns in battle with both the French and Dessalines. Marie-Jeanne Lamartinière carried a rifle without complaint in the battle of La Crête-à-Pierrot!

three drops of water don't make a river ...

Those men took after each other in several ways, so to speak, even if they weren't connected enough for us to be able to say they formed a separate group. Which is to say, there was a series of officers in Louverture's own army that tended to adopt a position more to the left, a position closer to the people's interests than to the official position of the government. Because Moïse was higher up compared to the rest of that left wing, because Dondon's fifth regiment was closer to the fieldworkers than any other group of State-enlisted **soldiers** who ever set foot on Haitian soil, because of the personal relationship between Moïse and Louverture, and because of all the noise the 'Moïse Affair' made, Moïse's example stands out clearly. And so we'll take a chance and call it an **example**. An **excellent** example ...

In 1792, at twenty years of age, Moïse was an officer on the Spanish side under the command of Toussaint Louverture, and from that time up to the day his 'uncle' sent him to the firing squad, Moïse was always on the left wing in most battles of the revolution. In 1793, when the declaration proclaiming the organization's political agenda came out of camp Tourelle, Moïse was still there. In 1794, he crossed over with Toussaint to join the French. In 1796, after the Villatte Affair, Toussaint named him commander of the fifth regiment, where most of the soldiers were people from the North, especially Fort-Liberté and Dondon. Between 1796 and 1800, we find Moïse at the front of all the important **political** battles the organization led against the colonists. It's true, he was involved in military battles, too. For example, it was he who seized Las Cahobas from the English. He was the one Toussaint sent ahead at the start of the War of the South. It was he who took the lead in Santo-Domingo. But behind all that shooting, when we follow Moïse and the fifth regiment, we see a perfectly clear political **persuasion**: in the battle between *nouveaux libres* and *anciens libres*, Moïse kept a low profile; in the battle between *nouveaux libres* and colonists, Moïse was first in line. During the Villatte Affair, Moïse kept his calm. During the War of the South, Octavius[85] and a bunch of Rigaud's followers cornered Moïse in Fauché, and Moïse retreated. Louverture broke Moïse. Even so, when Colonel Vincent, a young French military engineer, and the **greatest advocate of leasing lands in the North**, returned from France, Moïse arrested him under the pretext that Vincent had orders to sow division among black people and mulattos. It was Toussaint who let the colonel go. It was Moïse who went after Roume before the invasion of the Spanish side. It was also Moïse whom Louverture sent to receive Hédouville, in his place. And again, it was Moïse and the fifth regiment (and Moïse's wife) who clashed with Hédouville. What's more, during both the Roume Affair and the Hédouville Affair, Moïse went into the countryside and **rallied the masses of fieldworkers to join the battle**. When Napoleon Bonaparte was planning Leclerc's invasion, Hédouville and other generals who'd spent time in Saint-Domingue named all the high-ranking officers whom they thought might serve as a fifth column among the *nouveaux libres*. They also called those people the 'stubborn' ones. Hédouville declared: the French needn't try and influence Moïse because he was 'difficult'. Leclerc had the order—if things went downhill—to kill Toussaint, Dessalines, and **Moïse**.

When Leclerc arrived in Saint-Domingue, and he realized that he couldn't locate Moïse, he wrote to the Minister of the Navy: Moïse had died, fortunately 'Toussaint got rid of him for us' (February 15, 1802 letter).

The American and English spies said similar things. While they could work Christophe in, and while they could accommodate Toussaint within their interests, they always had trouble with Moïse. Let's examine a letter that Edward Stevens sent to the American government, where he

---

85 Octavius was lieutenant colonel in Rigaud's army (Oriol 228).

identified the three generals' names: Toussaint, Christophe, and Moïse. Stevens stated:

'General Moïse replaced Christophe as commander in Cape Haitian. **I would have preferred that this change not be made** ... even if Moïse is a friendly man who easily makes decisions, and even though I have always had a very good relationship with him, I believe, in spite of that, he lacks the level-headedness and good sense the other has; and for **a long time**, I have **consistently** gotten **everything** that I wanted from Christophe. However, this change might not have such a bad outcome, as Toussaint intends to stay here until the war is over' (Stevens to Pickering, October 26, 1799).[86]

This letter was important, as were most of Stevens's letters. These weren't the words of a man writing a book for posterity. This wasn't even an official letter that could go public. It was a consul's letter to the government, a letter marked 'confidential' on the back like a spy letter. It was in the interest of the person who wrote that letter to describe the situation the way he saw it. The politics of his government hinged on that. The letter shows us that Christophe was a puppet in the commissioner's hands. We also see that Louverture was 'able' to continue providing them the advantages that Christophe regularly gave them (and there are other letters from Stevens' where he **guarantees** that he can make Toussaint change his mind on certain issues). So Stevens made sure to tell Pickering that if Moïse had his say, the Americans wouldn't have it this easy.

Were it up to Moïse, foreigners wouldn't have it this easy, because workers born in the country were meant to enjoy Saint-Domingue's assets. When Manigat (Hédouville's smarmy puppet) went to crush the fifth regiment, he declared that those men must be disarmed because they intended to seize the people's assets. In 1800, when the fieldworkers rose up against Roume (with Moïse's support), they demanded 'half of all large plantations', and they refused to work as 'mercenaries'. In 1800, the word was on the street: General Moïse opposed the abuses that the state

---

86 Edward Stevens' original letter: 'General Moïse supersedes *Christophe* in the Command of the Cape. I could rather have wished that this Change had not taken Place. 'Tho' the former is a Man of Energy and Decision, and I have always been upon the best Terms with him; yet I think he wants the Coolness and Good sense of the latter, from who I have been long accustomed to obtain every Thing I wished. This Alteration can, however, produce no ill Effect of the War'. Text from 'Letters of Toussaint Louverture and of Edward Stevens, 1798–1800'. *The American Historical Review*, vol. 16, no. 1, 1910, pp. 64–101. JSTOR, www.jstor.org/stable/1834309. Accessed March 16, 2020.

was committing against workers. Moïse was the only former slave who was expected to go along with all the bigwigs (especially white plantation owners) who were writing the Constitution. **He refused**. In 1801, the word got out: General Moïse opposed the government. He avoided the discussions of 'France' that remained on Louverture's lips. He told Louverture that he wouldn't turn cold and beat up black people like himself. In 1801, when people from Limbé, Dondon, Port-Margot, L'Acul, and Marmelade flew off the handle, they claimed: Toussaint, Dessalines, and Christophe teamed up with the French to put the people back in chains. They shouted: 'Long live Moïse', because they were certain Moïse was closest to them.

... but star dust makes dust

Which is to say, behind all the undertakings on the part of Gilles Bréda/Moïse Louverture within the Saint-Domingue revolution, a distinct tendency was fighting to take shape. We can quickly list its five features:

1) Avoid overly violent clashes with *anciens libres*
2) Defy French colonists in every possible way, and make things difficult for other foreign commissioners
3) Fight to change the plantation system
4) Rely on fieldworkers at all times for military strength
5) Make use of the mountains.

We can also quickly say that certain of those features—which were further to the left than the organization's official position—would resemble features of the original political agenda espoused by the Dessalines/Pétion organization during the war of independence. Certain others would remain features of the workers' movement well after independence.

Therefore, when all the high-ranking officers of Louverture's army joined together to crush Moïse, they were crushing a very distinct political persuasion: the far left. Toussaint appointed a military commission to judge Moïse: Christophe (black—*ancien libre*), Vernet (mulatto—*ancien libre*), and Pageot[87] (colonist/white soldier). Whether it was because they

---

[87] François Marie Sébastien Pageot was a colonist in Saint-Domingue who served in several positions as French military commander in the northern region; he presided over the court that condemned Moïse to death (Oriol 229).

didn't find enough proof that Moïse was involved in the conspiracy, or whether it was because they were terrified to harm the 'nephew' of the general-in-chief, they didn't inflict harm on Moïse. Toussaint redid the judgment, and he condemned Moïse to death! After that, he gave a speech (November 25, 1801) wherein he put every single officer on notice: the higher your rank, the more you must march in step down the path where Toussaint leads. Which is to say, Toussaint hastened to strike his left wing before that wing could really take flight, and also before officers and soldiers of the same persuasion could join up with the groups of maroon soldiers/rebel workers who'd never stopped agitating in the mountains, the groups rising up in Pandou (in 1796), in Cotereau (in September 1800), in Camp-Perrin (in October 1800), in Petite-Rivière, Saint Raphaël, Hinche, and Bánica in August 1801.

what will I say when I get home?

There's never smoke without fire. The Moïse Affair was like smoke rising over two major conflicts within the camp of *nouveaux libres*:

> 1) a hidden conflict within the Louverture organization (partner to a conflict between government/organization),
> 2) a conflict between the organization and the masses of workers (partner to a conflict between State/fieldworkers).

The Moïse Affair signals to us how those conflicts reached the entangled stage. Besides, when Toussaint attacked the small group that had borne the banner of the left within the army, he threatened other people who might have been of that persuasion, and together with Dessalines and Christophe, he wiped out a bunch of peasants just in case they got the wrong idea. But when Leclerc finally landed, Toussaint tried to lean on that same left wing, he tried to revive those same persuasions, and he tried to rally the same peasants.
  Too bad, it was too late: what the kitten's mother knows, the little rat's mother knows, too …

I'm not afraid of you, clown, You're a human

The Moïse Affair showed us that: the camp of *nouveaux libres* had its own conflicts, and as that camp was consolidating its power, the two social forces who'd converged to establish that dominance started going their own ways, according to their own interests. Conflicts between leaders of *nouveaux libres* and masses of *nouveaux libres* were entangled. Within the camp of *nouveaux libres*, the big soldiers were building up **their own dominance**. This dominance was intertwined with their social origins, their distinct social mobility, and their positions on the issues of dependency, commodity crops, and plantations, alongside their specific roles within the State of Saint-Domingue.

But the bundle of conflicts between leaders of *nouveaux libres* and masses of *nouveaux libres* couldn't appear too openly. Toussaint's general staff was rapidly abandoning the masses, it's true. But the very power of that general staff rested upon the masses' power. The threat of the masses kept the colonists from rebelling against the officers. So even though the *kòd* [cord/code] connecting them was broken, nobody was supposed to notice, because without it the party would be completely ruined. For balance to be maintained, in addition to the authoritarian agrarian system (**despite** the authoritarian agrarian system), it was essential that the masses not fully discover the bundle of conflicts that were heating up between them and Louverture's general staff. Those conflicts had to appear with a different face so that ordinary people wouldn't recognize them. **Those conflicts had to be disguised.**

In fact, within any dog-eat-dog society, the social force which seizes political power conceals such conflicts. But under Toussaint, given the specific conditions under which that power was developing, the function of that coverup had a unique importance. Louverture's team had to disguise the society such that the white plantation owners' and commissioners' economic dominance wouldn't be apparent, but above all so the masses of fieldworkers wouldn't be able to see the conflicts **within** their own freedom camp. The most important disguise was the disguise of conflicts **within the very camp of** *nouveaux libres*.

That specific disguise was the function of Louverture's Ideology. And this ideology did its job so very well, it keeps on repeating within the History of Haiti and it persists to this very day, even if its name has changed. If, for the period of revolution in Saint-Domingue, we assign to that ideology the name of Toussaint Louverture, we mustn't forget that certain of its branches reappear—with all the same vices but under different conditions—under Dessalines, under Christophe, under Salomon, under Éstimé, and before and after Christophe, Salomon and Éstimé. All the same vices but under different conditions, in Haiti as in Guadeloupe, in Martinique as in Africa: throughout the entire twentieth century, a branch of that ideology has donned the cloak of 'Indigenism'. All the same vices but under different conditions: there's another branch of that ideology that the bourgeoisie picked up so it could disguise its dominance over the people under the cloak of the 'Elite'.

Louverture's ideology didn't end with Louverture's government. It didn't start with that government either. I wouldn't want you to think that the government created the ideology, as though the general staff woke up one day, noticed the growing gap between itself and the masses, and decided to invent an ideology. No, ideology's a clever beast: it plays a sneaky game, and **the social force that the ideology serves** (the leaders of *nouveaux libres*, for example) **can get taken in by the disguise of their own ideology**. Especially if that ideology came from afar! Especially when its foundation spread across the various layers of society.

oh
life's strange sometimes
I often forget we're all brothers

The first disguise that Louverture's ideology put on to conceal the conflicts was the family disguise. Louverture's ideology claimed: instead of society being a bunch of **classes**, it is a single FAMILY. When Toussaint saw that workers refused to toil on plantations, he said to them: 'To the extent you used to sacrifice for former slave owners, you must now contribute to society, for the whole giant **family** we belong to'. On bona fide plantations, where regular people slogged away for big shots, the ideology gave them the family disguise (Constitution of 1801, Article 15). Each plantation was a '**family**' and 'each fieldworker, each laborer is a **member** of that **family**' (Article 16).

The family disguise didn't only exist within the society of Saint-Domingue. We also find it within the ideology of aristocrats and the European bourgeoisie. We find it in France, before, during, and after the 1789 Revolution. But in Saint-Domingue, as in all African countries or countries that have African descendants, the family disguise took hold even more strongly, because **it dovetailed with the** specific role that family and community played within those societies. So, Louverture's Ideology totally hummed along in that disguise. All problems within the society, any conflict between classes or categories of classes, appeared masked as problems 'within the family' that could be resolved 'within the family'. I wouldn't be surprised if Toussaint himself got taken in by this disguise. Gilles Bréda (Moïse Louverture) and Charles Belair passed for his 'little nephews'. (That didn't keep him from having Moïse shot, and it didn't keep Dessalines from arresting Belair as a traitor, but the 'nephew' concept helped keep the disguise firmly in place.) On that same pretext, Louverture played hardball to force his niece, a woman from the Chansi family (a black woman), to marry Colonel Vernet (a mulatto) in order to show how blacks and mulattos are all in the same family. Riding on the coattails of that same notion, Dessalines sought to marry off his own daughter, Célimène, to a young mulatto (Pétion). When the young girl refused, Dessalines arrested her boyfriend, a certain Colonel Chansi, a mulatto man from that very same Chansi family, who was Toussaint Louverture's own nephew … Which is to say, History is so comical that it brings tears to the eyes. Toussaint Louverture's own family would get caught in the trouble of this ideology of the family.

But, let's leave the nephew, and take up the uncle …

The family ideology is an extremely useful disguise for classes or groups in power; it's a disguise that covers any situation. It's a disguise that allows all kinds of people to be stuffed into the same sack, according to the political situation. The family might be all of humanity, for example: the enormous family of 'man' that religions like to tout, as if all people were brothers. The family might be all people who have a common ancestry: 'the indigenous family of Saint-Domingue'. The family might be all people of the same color: 'the great black family'. The family might be all people who come from the same Department: 'Brothers of the South'; all country people: 'Brothers of the back country'. In the history of Haiti, the family ideology is used above all to reinforce color prejudice. Beyond the economic and political bonds that joined them together, plantation owners and big mulatto merchants considered themselves to be one single family that had the right to do anything it wanted on Haitian soil. In the very same way, 'noiriste' opportunists (middle-class black people and plantation owners, especially) said: Hey, we're in the family, too. We have more rights than mulattos because the Haitian family's a family of black people, and so if we're mistreating the masses, it's basically just a big brother beating on a little brother!

For Toussaint Louverture himself, the family disguise covered any kind of group: sometimes *nouveaux libres*, sometimes *anciens libres*, and sometimes plantation owners. And so, within the particular political situation in Saint-Domingue, given the dominance that his own category was seeking to establish within the society, in the years 1798–1801, for Toussaint Louverture, the family was all 'people', all 'individuals' who set foot on Saint-Domingue's soil and who agreed with the principle of freedom for all.

All people, whatever their class, had to be in the family so that Toussaint could play his second game: the father game.

good father
willful child

The second disguise that Louverture's Ideology laid over the conflicts was the **father disguise**. That disguise dovetails with the first one. If the society is a whole family, and the government is the head of the family, then the head of the government is father to society, father to all the individuals within that society. 'Paternalism' (that is, posturing as father) is tied to greatness, because according to the prevailing beliefs within the society, the father is the most prominent person within the family. There were bunches of obsequious white colonists who said Toussaint was the Bonaparte of Saint-Domingue, that he was the one and only Hercules, the one and only Alexander the Great in the country. Toussaint himself told Colonel Vincent that Saint-Domingue's umbilical cord lay in his hands. On February 8, 1801, he said to the workers: 'I'm a good **father** who's talking with his **children**, who's showing them the road to happiness for themselves and all of their **family**'. He again said: 'I'm speaking to you as your **father**' (May 28, 1801). Three days later, he was talking with Dessalines about the *anciens libres*, and he said: 'I consider them my brothers, my **children**' (May 31, 1801). After the War of the South, while Toussaint was celebrating, a white woman came to sing for him. The song went like this:

> General (posturing as) our **father**
> all your **children** are friends
> Toussaint, Toussaint, hear our praises
> Thanks to you, everyone's **at peace**

in the name of the saints of heaven
in the name of the saints of the earth
in the name of the saints of the moon
in the name of the saints of the stars
here is a protective charm
for walking at night

To mask the conflicts, big shots in Europe as well as regional leaders in Africa commonly used the ploy of making political power appear to have supernatural origins. This ploy claimed that it was God who kept each person in her or his place, and it was God who gave the team in power dominance over the rest of society. To maintain that disguise, Toussaint drew on **both the Catholic religion and the Vodou religion**. Even while he was crushing Vodou (and we'll soon see why), the rumor ran through Saint-Domingue that Toussaint was a *makandal*.[88] As if to say, he was everywhere at once. There were many soldiers who believed that Toussaint could simply look them in the eye and know whether they were conspiring. After the 'Moïse Affair', Toussaint inspected the regiments, and he ran his eyes over the soldiers. Regular people were never more surprised than when they saw their fellows drop to their knees at Toussaint's feet to denounce themselves!

Also, at the same time, Toussaint propped himself up on the Catholic religion, with Te Deums here, and processions there. There was a Catholic priest, Father Lecun (a shameless, ill-mannered politician), who consistently treated Toussaint with as much honor and respect as the Holy Sacrament! He'd tell the people: 'God gave him to us, and God supports him!' The Catholic religion became a complete farce. In the middle of the war against the English, while Toussaint was in Gonaïves, each Sunday the parish priest of Marmelade came to say mass for the soldiers, and Toussaint used to force the officers to sing hymns. The 1801 Constitution recognized the Catholic religion as the only religion in Saint-Domingue (Article 6); it gave priests permission to enjoy their income on the workers' backs without fear of punishment, great or small (Article 7); it encouraged church marriages with pomp and circumstance (Article 9);

---

[88] François Makandal was a maroon Vodou priest who was skilled in producing poisons which he and his collaborators used to kill colonists and their livestock. He was captured and killed in 1758, his name passing into Haitian Creole as a term that designates a powerful spiritual being who can mysteriously inflict great harm (Dubois *et al.* (2020), 16–18).

and it outlawed divorce (Article 10). To be sure, those pretensions had different purposes. But it's also true that they helped display to workers that Toussaint was the one and only black Spartacus that the Catholic priests had predicted, a rugged male whom God had sent with a special blessing that bestowed upon him all kinds of powers.

I believe in God
yes, Santa Maria
Santa Maria who comes from Africa
I believe in God
yes, Santa Maria

Those words seem like magic, and some people hasten to say that the Vodou religion allows more leeway for magic than does the Catholic religion. As if to say, why didn't Toussaint make use of Vodou in order to assume this supernatural posture? The answer to that question is embedded within the political power that Vodou had while Louverture's *nouveaux riches* were establishing their dominance within the camp of *nouveaux libres*. Toussaint leaned on Vodou, but he couldn't lean too far because Vodou organizations were the only other organization within the camp of *nouveaux libres* that was opposite Louverture's general staff. Whereas the Catholic clergy wouldn't allow another Spartacus to compete with Toussaint, any other knowledgeable person who displayed strong ability might be another Makandal, another Boukman Dutty, or another Romaine-la-Prophétesse. Whereas the Catholic game was obvious to Toussaint's team, the Vodou game surpassed him. If the team of *nouveaux riches* had been able to control Catholic organizations since 1798, they had no control over Vodou organizations. The 1801 Constitution stated: the Government of the colony gives each Catholic priest a territorial limit within which to practice the religion, and those priests may **never form a single team** within the country, for whatever reason they might want to give (Article 8). In 1801, Toussaint wouldn't have allowed himself to give a Vodou priest territorial limits for his or her practice. Just as Vodou organizations had spread disrespect for the former system and former 'leaders', they also refused to bow their heads before Louverture's regime. And so, Louverture stated: I want that broken up. On January 4, 1800, Toussaint outlawed Vodou dances as well as songs, because, he claimed: 'the leaders of those dances only want to spread chaos and laziness'. From the way Toussaint twisted his mouth to speak this warning, we can see what made him fearful: he said **leaders**, he said **chaos**, and he said **laziness**. Why? Because leaders of Vodou organizations were spreading the rumor that plantation workers should stop working. They were denouncing a system that was nourishing Louverture's general staff. Thus, the government outlawed 'any dance, any nighttime gathering, whether in the city, in towns, on plantations, on mountains or on the plains'. (That article and a section of the *Kòd Noua* were like two peas in a pod!)

When Louverture's army captured a group of Vodou initiates, it was a massacre of innocent angels. They beat *oungan*, *manbo*, choir leaders, and choir members. After that, they arrested everyone. In April 1801, Dessalines led a raid on a Vodou group: he made the soldiers load bayonets onto their rifles, and he wiped out fifty initiates on the spot!

And so Louverture's general staff attacked Vodou groups because those groups threatened their political power. But Louverture's Ideology propped itself up on religion (both Christian and Vodou) to disguise that political power as a magical power, a special power that supernatural forces (either God or the spirits) gave the uncle so he could run the country.

Louverture's Ideology took up a bunch of other beliefs, a bunch of other manners, and a bunch of other affectations from the ideological domain of aristocrats. Soldiers in Toussaint's personal guard dolled themselves up like English officers. The musicians who played violin at Louverture's receptions hailed from Germany. He had wreaths of flowers over here, chandeliers over there, white tablecloths on the tables, and white women on the couches. On those occasions Toussaint used to sneer at black officers and tell them: 'As for yourselves, black people, go figure out how to acquire these manners, and learn to look proper in public. This is absolutely the way things are when a man is raised in France! My children are going to be like that'. (Toussaint's children were being raised in France.)

he's black, eats sweet potatoes
she's black, eats plantains
whites eat bread
whites work

But Louverture's Ideology wasn't an aristocratic ideology. He took a piece of it from the aristocrats' ideology, the piece that he needed to support the dominance of *nouveaux libres* leaders, the piece that the particular entanglement of social forces in Saint-Domingue allowed him to pick up. But a big part of Louverture's ideology was rooted in the beliefs, the manners, and the pretensions of the European bourgeoisie.

The first ploy that Louverture's Ideology appropriated from the bourgeois ideological domain was a ploy claiming that 'work brings satisfaction'. Those words conceal the exploitation that there was within the work, along with all the other conflicts that existed between the classes that were bound up with the society's primary industry. In one of Toussaint's speeches (February 8, 1801), he stated: 'I want (fieldworkers) to work more than they did in the past'. The October 1800 regulation stated: Each person must carry out useful work for the society because that is the only way to secure freedom, the freedom which brings peace and joy to the whole society. The ploy was well framed, but you shouldn't fall for it. It's true that all individuals need to work for the good of 'the society', but not all work is useful to all 'the society'. In a dog-eat-dog society, the work is 'useful' to the class with economic dominance in the society. The cart-pusher's peace doesn't lie in pushing the cart. The fieldworker's joy doesn't lie in planting food crops.

disrobe, disrobe
O mercy, O Mary, mercy

The second big ploy that Louverture's Ideology appropriated from the bourgeois domain was the ploy of **respecting property**. When Saint-Domingue's revolution exploded, the slaves' first mission was to burn plantations. Toussaint suddenly changed course and joined the French in May 1794, at the same time the French bourgeoisie was undercutting its own revolution. In July 1794, the bourgeoisie broke off the revolution. It said to the masses of workers: what you previously knew is no more. There will be no more rampages to destroy property. Property (and all the rest of society) is actually changing only in terms of ownership. Therefore, **respect property**.

During that same July of 1794, Toussaint assured Lavaud that his army would respect property. That respect meant: don't seize assets. But it also meant: don't **divide up** assets. In 1794, Toussaint opposed redistributing land to peasants. In that same year, 1794, Lozeau (a French deputy) stated that the French government could not divide up properties in France. If it made the mistake of doing that, the country would collapse. In 1795, Boissy d'Anglas,[89] another French politician, announced to the government in France: 'We must secure the assets of all the rich people'. In 1797, the French bourgeoisie killed Baboeuf, who had demanded **economic** equality alongside political equality. In 1801, Toussaint executed Moïse who'd refused to accept the economic system that the government had set up.

The ploy of 'respecting property' is tied to the bourgeoisie's ploy of 'Equality'. You remember that Toussaint had alleged to the exiled plantation owners, 'Freedom is all that the black people were asking for', the right for them to be equal to all people before the law, or political equality. But he hastened to tell the *nouveaux libres* that they'd never sought to seize the assets of Saint-Domingue's colonists, especially the plantations. Which is to say that they had no need for redistribution of wealth, they didn't need **economic equality**.

Toussaint's discourse sounded exactly like what was said by Boissy D'Anglas, a French politician who was fighting to establish total dominance for the bourgeoisie in France. Boissy d'Anglas stated: 'Civil equality, that is all a reasonable person can demand. Total equality is a daydream' (June 23, 1795). The bourgeoisie also stated: 'Equality means that laws are the same for all people'.

That ploy concealed a fundamental problem within the society: differences between classes. It's true that laws must be the same for all people, but that isn't complete equality. Equality means that all people have equal opportunities, and that all classes are on level footing. Equality means economic equality, too.

---

89 François-Antoine Boissy d'Anglas (1756–1828) was an author, attorney, and politician during the French Revolution and Empire. During the Revolution he was elected to the National Convention, sitting in the political *centre*. He supported Robespierre at the start of the Reign of Terror (Anchel 155).

little boy don't touch my hair
you're making me look uncouth

The last big ploy that Louverture's Ideology took from the domain of the French bourgeoisie was the 'elite' ploy, the ploy of 'capable people'. That ploy went like this: neither social class nor social category maintains the various forms of dominance in the society; rather, it's a team of 'respectable people', an 'ideal' team, 'the cream' of society, the 'finest jewels' of society, and they're in that position because they're able to do the best job.

That ploy came unequivocally from the bourgeois domain in France. It was again Boissy d'Anglas who stated: 'It's the best among us who should govern …'. Under Louverture's government, those words served as an excuse to put an 'elite' of commissioners and plantation owners at the head of Saint-Domingue. Most civilians within the government came from those two classes. Blabbermouths recounted Toussaint's injustice to a young black man who was seeking a job as a judge. Toussaint asked the man if he could speak Latin. The man said: No. Toussaint mumbled two inside-out Latin words and told the man he wasn't competent to judge people if he didn't know how to speak Latin. Which is to say, it was the small white elite that could speak Latin (and was Latin!), who was capable of running the country. The mistake Toussaint made was in not taking the time needed to inquire about the interests of which class they were 'capable' of leading. It's true, given the conditions that slaves had lived in before the revolution, there was a lot of knowledge that wasn't accessible to them. It's true, there were many skills the *nouveaux libres* masses didn't have. But it's also true (according to what science says) that no class of people is created more capable than another. And the history of our country shows us that capable people were never lacking in Haiti. Before, as well as after, Toussaint, 'capable people' were always in charge, but from the first day they started carrying the banner, the group hasn't gone forward one step.

Yet the ideology of capable people persists in the country of Haiti. Long after Toussaint, an organization of big shots (they were called the Liberal Party) decreed: 'Power is for people who are most capable'. To this day there are people who say: mulattos are most capable of doing business, intellectuals are most capable of leading, and foreigners are most capable of finding solutions for the country. Which is to say, workers are most capable of suffering!

Boissy d'Anglas, who often threw rocks, but wasn't very good at hiding his hands, said straightforwardly that the 'capable men' he was talking about were people who owned property. Which meant: the way the society started was, the people with assets were always the capable people.

Therefore, my friends, the Ideology of Louverture appropriated its various branches from both aristocrats and the European bourgeoisie, from the supporters of those two classes who waltzed into the community of Saint-Domingue. And we've seen how it blended those various ingredients into its own sauce, according to the dominance of different social forces in Saint-Domingue. This combination was neither aristocratic ideology nor European bourgeois ideology. Depending on the situation, it was closer to either one or the other. Depending on the situation, it assumed its own distinct air.

Papa Gede's a handsome man
Gede Nibo's a handsome man
he's dressed all in white
so he can climb up to the palace

One of the particular pretensions of Louverture's Ideology was the **indigenist** ploy. The recipe for that ploy is easy: 'one dose of the field-workers' ideology, one dose of the middle classes' ideology, one dose of bourgeois ideology, and one dose of feudal ideology (that is, the landowning aristocrats' ideology). Stir with a wooden spoon, and place over a fire. Wait for the broth to start simmering'.

When it began to simmer, the indigenist discourse went like this:

'THE RACE' is an entire family (feudal ideology), and this family isn't only exploited, they also **denigrate** it (slave/fieldworker ideology).

Therefore, '**better elements**' of the race (bourgeois ideology), '**big brothers**' who are the wisest members of the family (feudal ideology), must fight for '**political equality**' (bourgeois ideology) and family '**honor and respectability**' (feudal ideology).

The political equality of the race comes about when capable people within the family take control of the '**government**' (middle-class ideology).

Respectability for the family comes about when big brothers in the family attain a higher 'position' than that attained by people who used to denigrate the race (feudal ideology + middle-class ideology).

That ideology didn't suddenly pop into the heads of Louverture's general staff, that's for sure. But when we trace the path of that general staff from 1793 to 1802, when we take up its beliefs, its manners, and its pretensions, both before and after Toussaint's takeover, we'll see how he appeared within the community of Saint-Domingue as a colossal black Spartacus who'd come to avenge all the injustices committed against the race. He assumed his posture of father before the masses, and all his team members were like big brothers to the *nouveaux libres*, who were carrying the banner of political equality. And so, for most of them, equality had been achieved, because they themselves had taken over the political apparatus. In the end, supposedly for the honor and respectability of the family, they assumed the affectations of aristocrats.

when he's dressed all in white
he looks like a deputy

When Toussaint was collecting white women and German musicians, when he was pointing out aristocrats to say, 'My children will be like that, too', when most of the general staff were imitating French officers, and when the general-in-chief himself was obsessed with 'France! France!' the indigenist ideology reached the end of its path … Likewise, it would run its course when Henri Christophe (who'd also sent his own child to learn manners among whites) assumed the affectations of an English aristocrat within the country of Haiti, with 'barons' here, 'counts' there, 'Sirs' of this, 'Sirs' of that, and castles and carriages all around. And it wasn't for nothing that people who called themselves 'indigenists' during the twentieth century sang those two men's praises, without asking any questions.

when he's dressed all in black
he looks like a senator

One of the main differences between Toussaint and twentieth-century indigenists is that Toussaint prevailed more quickly. At the end of the day, during this twentieth century, if you go take on aristocratic airs, everybody will fall over laughing at you—that's out of style. Thus, the indigenists today assume the posture of great intellectuals because that category has the greatest appeal today among people who are 'denigrating' the race. All the same vices, but under different conditions, the discourse hasn't changed much.

Except, between 1791 and 1804, there was a bona fide revolution spreading through Saint-Domingue, a revolution that charted its own path despite the indigenist *nouveau libre* general staff, regardless of that indigenist general staff. And that revolution wouldn't backtrack before it had gotten hold of the society's foundations, before it had established political Freedom. Truly. Completely.

Thus, when we retrace the course of either Ideology, of Louverture's organization, or the State of Saint-Domingue, we must never forget that **that Ideology, that organization, and that State, despite all their weaknesses, had a massive *potomitan* [centerpost] that traversed them: FREEDOM FOR ALL**, a freedom tied to the rights of all field-workers who were equal before the law and before anyone else in Saint-Domingue.

the clever goat
grazes at the foot of the mountain

True, it was essentially an organizational weakness that made Leclerc fail to put chains on people's feet. The government was bowlegged. When the invasion took place, **plantation owners and French commissioners betrayed Toussaint**. Despite all the efforts of Magny and especially Lamartinière, Agé, Dalban, Lacombe and father Lecun[90] did everything they possibly could to open the doors of Port-au-Prince to Boudet.[91] **American commissioners stuck a dagger in Toussaint's back**. In Cape Haitian, Tobias Lear requested Christophe's permission for himself and a certain Captain Rogers to help Americans escape with their own assets, along with **all other whites who wanted to flee the island**. What's more, Tobias Lear boarded a fast boat and went off to join Villaret de Joyeuse,[92] and he gave the French commander information about Christophe's

---

90 Agé (general), Dalban (leader of a brigade), Lacombe (director of the arsenal), and Father Lecun were prominent Europeans living in Port-Républicain (i.e. Port-au-Prince) when the boats of the French expedition of 1802 were spotted from the shore. They were all devoted to France and French interests and recommended welcoming the French forces (Madiou 1989 2: 180–82).

91 Boudet was a French general who arrived in Saint-Domingue with Leclerc during the expedition of 1802. He was sent to secure Port-Républicain and he succeeded in doing so with 6,000 troops, 400 of whom he lost in the fighting required to push out the Haitian troops led by Lamartinière. The arrival of the French had led to the retaliatory killing of many members of the white community and the discovery of their cadavers cast a pall over his initial victory (Madiou 1989 2:180–87).

92 Louis Thomas, Comte de Villaret de Joyeuse (1748–1812), directed the fleet that brought Leclerc's expedition to Saint-Domingue (Oriol 248).

regiments, plus advice about where and when French soldiers should attack Cape Haitian.

Many *anciens libres* [mulattos in the South, especially] **also ran to the French side before one shot was fired**. Nérette, in Saint Louis, ran away. In Les Cayes and Jérémie, mulattos took to the streets **declaring that they were French**; they made Laplume and Dommage bow their heads before Bonaparte's troops. **The black *anciens libres* retreated too.** In the North, the magistrate Télémaque[93] (a black *ancien libre* who was born in Martinique) ordered the city to welcome Leclerc.

And so, the organization's two biggest weak spots, which appeared during the war, were ideological weaknesses. Toussaint failed to get the masses to rise up. Toussaint still believed in the French talk of France. True, the masses didn't take themselves for French. To the contrary, several small groups of maroon workers and maroon soldiers agitated throughout the country, and **most of them refused to collaborate with the organization**. When Toussaint started losing, Sila, Makaya, Ti Nouèl Priyè, and Sansousi ... entered the guerrilla war, the kind of war that they knew best.

But at the same moment that the guerrillas were helping reinforce the *nouveau libre* camp, Toussaint threw in the towel.

what you have in your hands is yours

Some learned people say that it was taking chances, not surrendering. Which is to say that Toussaint was catching his breath so that he could strike again. It's true, Toussaint's army was exhausted, but Leclerc's army was more exhausted, and Toussaint knew that. **Toussaint didn't need to take chances.** When Toussaint sent Leclerc a communiqué stating that he'd surrender, Leclerc didn't believe it. Leclerc wrote to his boss in France to say: 'Toussaint sent word to me that we should come to an agreement and stop the war. **I don't believe a word of it** ... I have over

---

93 César Télémaque was the mayor of Cape Haitian when the boats of the French expedition of 1802, led by Leclerc, moored near the town. He invested considerable effort in trying to convince Henri Christophe and other leaders in the city to welcome the French troops. He also begged Christophe not to set the town on fire, a request that Christophe didn't heed when he saw the French disembarking. Christophe's troops were stationed throughout Cape Haitian and quickly set the town's wooden structures alight (Madiou 1989 2:170–77).

1,200 soldiers in the hospital ... I have neither food nor money ... The government must send supplies, soldiers and money, **that is the only way we can save Saint-Domingue'** (letter dated February 15, 1802).

It was while Leclerc was crying for help that Toussaint surrendered. Why?

Because Toussaint assumed that France wouldn't go back on its word. Toussaint assumed that France wouldn't deceive him. Toussaint believed in the 'respectability' of the French bourgeoisie and aristocrats. Bonaparte, Leclerc, Boudet, they all theoretically agreed to guarantee freedom if the people put down their weapons. Toussaint believed: a promise is a debt. In the hustle and bustle of political reality, people who sell on credit end up in the red: exploiters must never be exploited. A promise is not a debt! Toussaint Louverture's debt was the revolution, and his collateral was the army and the masses. He threw away that promise for the 'word of honor' of a bunch of French officers who had neither honor nor respect. As Roger Dorsainville[94] said: 'Toussaint let them capture him in an ambush ... He didn't give up on freedom, but he gave up on independence, **the only guarantee of this freedom**'. He knew where he wanted to go, but he got lost on the way. Yet ...

before I started walking
mountains were mountains
and rivers were rivers

the whole time I was on the road
mountains weren't mountains
and rivers weren't rivers

when I got to the end of the road
mountains were mountains
and rivers were rivers

But the principle of Freedom for All, Toussaint's central principle since 1793, is a principle we should respect. It's the underlying principle of Saint-Domingue's revolution. That principle is what set the masses' movement

---

94 Roger Dorsainville (1911–92) was a Haitian historian, diplomat, and writer. He wrote several works about Haitian history and Toussaint Louverture, including *Toussaint Louverture, ou, La vocation de la liberté* (1965 [1987]).

onto a path of no return. That principle destroyed Jean-François's and Biassou's groups. That principle dismantled Vilatte and all his stubborn men. That principle incinerated the English, and it blew off Hédouville's top hat. That principle overthrew the color aristocracy that André Rigaud set up in the South. That principle led the Spanish to keep an eye on what was happening in their backyard.

If we're denouncing the organization, the State, and Toussaint's ideology, it's not to denigrate their specific functions within the Revolution of Saint-Domingue. We're seeking to identify the illness that's passed through the family. We're seeking to identify where that illness came from. Lamèsi's gathering, it's a gathering of intelligent people; it's a gathering of mouthy children. This gathering wasn't meant to denigrate Toussaint, Dessalines, Christophe, or Pétion. But those men must come down onto the grass so the people can learn a few things, because ever since they've sat up on their high horses, Champs-de-Mars hasn't changed its face.

Therefore, we won't gloss over the weak spots in Louverture's ideology, the weak spots in his organization, or the weak spots within his government. We won't fail to mention that most of those weak spots are still devastating the health of Haiti's children to this very day. And we won't fail to mention this, either: even in 1802 the strength of this ideology, and the strength of this organization, were more important than its weak spots. At the same time as Leclerc's invasion crushed Toussaint personally, it forced all the roots that Toussaint was able to dig up to reappear reinvigorated.

In 1802, it was the *potomitan* of Louverture's Ideology that made maroons refuse to give up. It was Louverture's tactics that made *nouveaux libres* generals join forces with maroon soldiers and fieldworkers. The experience within Louverture's camp was what allowed them to team up with *anciens libres* who agreed with the political agenda. It was Louverture's government that provided them the contacts to purchase weapons from the Americans and the English. It was Louverture's State that revealed, like it or not, that Freedom made no sense without political Independence. And I don't hesitate to tell you, if the events that came about after Louverture went into exile came about, it was because Louverture opened the gate. There's something for us to respect. There's something in him for us to appreciate. There's something for us to admire in the efforts of most of the people who signed their names at the bottom of the 1804 declaration of independence. They went to the right school. They were able to unite with a willful people, the very first people who allowed themselves to say, 'Enough is enough!' with sufficient courage to chase out the biggest army Europe had ever seen at that time.

But to fully take in these ideas, which spring from a trustworthy source, your eyes must be well scrubbed so you can recognize the illness each time it reappears. I see that you're heavy-eyed, and I, too, am about to nod off: I'm not leaving today. And so, if Lamèsi wants, I'll give the floor to another singer. I'll take up this conversation again tomorrow night ... The children need some sleep. Grinn Prominnin is taking his rest ...

But look, Lamèsi, look!

Up in the sky, stars are challenging the moon ... But, close by, near the fence, seven lightning bugs are denouncing the hardship ...

Brooklyn
September 1975–May 1977

JULY 15 1977

LAKANSIEL COLLECTION

NEW YORK

Bibliography
(1977 Original Text)

Book titles, authors' names, and places of publication appear below in their original language, format, and spellings.

ADAMS, Henry: *Napoleon I and San Domingo* in *Historical Essays* (New York, 1891).

American Historical Review: 'Documents: Letters of Toussaint Louverture and Edward Stevens' (#26, 1910).

ARDOUIN, Beaubrun: *Études sur l'Histoire d'Haïti* (Port-au-Prince, 1958) original: 1853–60.

BACON-TACON, Pierre Jean-Jacques: *Mémoire ou Réponse de PJJBT aux dénonciations de Sonthonax Père, marchand à Oyonax et Sonthonax Fils ex-commissaire du Directoire à Saint-Domingue* (Paris, 1802).

BEARD, John R.: *Life of Toussaint Louverture* (London, 1853).

BESSON, Maurice: *Vieux Papiers du Temps des Iles* (Paris, 1925).

BOISSONNADE, Prosper Marie: *Saint-Domingue à la veille de la Révolution et la question de la Représentation Coloniale aux États-Généraux* (Paris, 1906).

BOISROND-TONNERRE, Félix: *Mémoires pour servir à l'Histoire d'Haïti* (Paris, 1851).

BRUTUS, Timoléon C.: *La Rançon du Génie* (Port-au-Prince, 1945).

CARTEAUX, Félix: *Soirées Bermudiennes* (Bordeaux, 1802).

Cercle Jacques Roumain: 'Résumé critique d'Histoire d'Haïti' (#1) typed.

CHARLEVOIX, Pierre François Xavier de: *Histoire de l'isle espagnole ou de Saint-Domingue* (Paris, 1730–31).

CHAZOTTE, Pierre Étienne: *The Black Rebellion in Haïti* (Philadelphia, 1927).

CLAUSSON, L.J.: *Précis Historique de la Révolution de Saint-Domingue* (Paris, 1819).

COLE, Hubert: *Christophe King of Haïti* (New York, 1967).

CORVINGTON, Georges: *Port-au-Prince au Cours des Ans* (Port-au-Prince, 1972).

COTTEREL, François Frédéric: *Esquisse Historique de l'Incendie du Cap à l'Expulsion de Sonthonax*

COUSIN D'AVALLON: *Histoire de Toussaint Louverture* (Paris, 1802).

DALMAS, M.: *Histoire de la Révolution de Saint-Domingue* (Paris, 1814).

DEBIEN, Gabriel: *Les Esclaves aux Antilles Françaises* (Basse-Terre, 1974).'

DESCOURTILS, Michel Étienne: *Voyage d'un Naturaliste en Haïti* (Paris, 1935) original: 1809.

DORSINVILLE, Roger: *Toussaint Louverture ou La Vocation de la Liberté* (Paris, 1965).

DUBROCAS, Louis: *The Life of Toussaint Louverture* (London, 1802).

EDWARDS, Bryan: *A Historical Survey of the French Colony of San Domingo* (London, 1797).

FOUCHARD, Jean: *Les Marrons de la Liberté* (Paris, 1972).

Plaisirs de Saint-Domingue (Port-au-Prince, 1965).

FROSTIN, Charles: *Les révoltes blanches à Saint-Domingue aux XVIIe et XVIIIe siècles* (Paris, 1975).

GERSHOY, Leo: *The Era of the French Revolution* (Princeton, 1957).

GRAGNON LACOSTE, Thomas Prosper: *Toussaint Louverture* (Bordeaux, 1877).

HECTOR, Michel and MOISE, Claude: *Le Régime Colonial Français à Saint-Domingue* (Port-au-Prince, 1962) typed.

INGINAC, Joseph Balthazar: *Mémoires depuis 1797 jusqu'à 1843* (Kingston, 1843).

JAMES, C.L.R.: *The Black Jacobins* (New York, 1963) 2nd edition.

JEAN-BAPTISTE, Saint-Victor: *Haïti, sa lutte pour l'émancipation* (Paris, 1957).

LACROIX, François-Joseph Pamphile, baron de: *Mémoires pour servir à l'Histoire de la Révolution de Saint-Domingue* (Paris, 1819).

LAUJON, A.P.M.: *Précis Historique de la Dernière Expédition de Saint-Domingue* (Paris, 1805).

LAURENT, Gérard M.: *Coup d'oeil sur la politique de Toussaint Louverture* (Port-au-Prince, 1949).

LAURENT, Mentor: *Erreurs et Vérités dans l'Histoire d'Haïti* (Port-au-Prince, 1945).

LECLERC, Victor-Emmanuel: *Lettres de Saint-Domingue* (Ed: Roussier, Paris, 1937).

LOGAN, Rayford W.: *The Diplomatic Relations of the United States with Haïti 1776-1891* (Chapel Hill, 1941).

MACKENZIE, Charles: *Notes on Haïti* (London, 1830).

MADIOU, Thomas: *Histoire d'Haïti* (Port-au-Prince, 1847-48).

MALENFANT: *Des Colonies, et Particulièrement de celle de Saint-Domingue* (Paris, 1814).

METRAL, Antoine-Marie-Thérèse: *Histoire de l'Insurrection des Esclaves dans le Nord de Saint-Domingue* (Paris, 1818).

MICHEL, Antoine: *La Mission du Général Hédouville à Saint-Domingue* (Port-au-Prince, 1929).

MOREAU DE SAINT-MERY, Médéric-Louis-Elie: *Description Topographique de la Patrie Française de Saint-Domingue* (Philadelphia, 1797-98).

Loiset Constitutions des Colonies Françaises (Paris, 1784).

OTT, Thomas: *The Haitian Revolution* (Memphis, 1973).

PRICE-MARS, Jean: *Le Phénomène et le Sentiment religieux chez les nègres de Saint-Domingue* in *Une étape de l'évolution Haïtienne* (Port-au-Prince, undated).

RAMEAU, Mario and AMBROISE, J.J.D.: *La Révolution de Saint-Domingue* (Port-au-Prince, 1963) typed.

Revue de la Société Haïtienne d'Histoire et de Géographie: 'Assemblées nocturnes d'esclaves à Saint-Domingue' (#116, 1972).

SAINT-REMY des Cayes, Joseph: (Ed.) *Mémoires du general Toussaint Louverture écrits par lui-même* (Paris, 1853).

SANNON, H-Pauléus: *Histoire de Toussaint Louverture* (Port-au-Prince, 1920-33).

SCHOELCHER, Victor: *Conférence sur Toussaint Louverture* (Port-au-Prince, 1966) original: ?

SCIOUT, Ludovic: *La Révolution à Saint-Domingue: Les Commissaires Sonthonax et Pòlvérèl*, in *Revue des Questions Historiques* (#20).

SOBOUL, Albert: *Précis d'Histoire de la Révolution Française* (Paris, 1962).

STODDARD T. Lothrop: *The French Revolution in San Domingo* (Boston, 1914).

SYDENHAM, M.J.: *The French Revolution* (New York, 1965).

TROUILLOT, Ernst: *Prospections d'Histoire* (Port-au-Prince, 1961).

TROUILLOT, Hénock: *Économies et Finances de Saint-Domingue* (Port-au-Prince, 1965).

TYSON, George F.: (Ed.) *Toussaint Louverture* (Englewood Cliffs, 1973).

VASTEY, Pompée Valentin, baron de: *Essai sur les causes de la révolution et des guerres civiles d'Hayiti* (Sans-Souci, 1819).

Le système colonial dévoilé (Cap Henry, 1814).

WIMPFFEN, François Alexandre Stanislas, baron de: *A Voyage to Santo Domingo* (London, 1797).

For the Trouillots: An Afterword to the English Translation of *Ti difé boulé sou istoua Ayiti*

by Jean Jonassaint

Nothing more rewarding in an academic life than seeing a project inspired by one of our courses, seminars, or lectures leading to a publication by a third party. This feeling of mission accomplished is even greater when said publication is important and historically significant. What else to say about the English translation of Michel-Rolph Trouillot's capital work, *Ti difé boulé sou istoua Ayiti* (1977), and its publication by Liverpool University Press than that they are irreversibly major milestones in the recognition of the Haitian language, both as a language of culture and of knowledge: culture of a people, knowledge of a people, that of Haiti, today, often disparaged or misunderstood.

The same comments may apply to Asselin Charles' English translation of Franketienne's *Dézafi* published by the University of Virginia Press in 2018. Regardless of the value or the acuity of these passages into English, their mere existence as academic works marks a decisive stage in the radiancy of the Haitian language, more generally known under the questionable label of Haitian Creole or Creole.[1] This comparison

---

1 In my opinion, drawing from Nanie Piou's arguments in her seminal article, 'Linguistique et idéologie: ces langues appelées *créoles*' (1979), the terms 'Creole', 'Creole language', and 'Haitian Creole' are not scientifically valid concepts to name the language spoken by Haitians. Therefore, I prefer the terms 'Haitian language' (*langue haïtienne*) and 'Haitian' (*haïtien*), which are in line with the way we name languages in French or English. Indeed, even when one can think that the language of the Haitians is not a 'langue de civilisation ou de culture', or cannot or will not access such status, as Pierre

between these two works is even unavoidable, for *Dézafi* was a source of inspiration or challenge for Michel-Rolph Trouillot,[2] who, under the pseudonym of L. Raymond, commented on this novel in *Lakansièl* 4 (1976),[3] a left-wing review of the Haitian diaspora from New York that he co-edited and published with, among others, Jean Coulanges from Montreal. It was at Coulanges' house that I really got to know MRT, thanks to the late Haitian novelist, Émile Ollivier (1940–2002), *l'ami Milo*, our friend Milo, as we used to call him, at the very moment when he was tackling (or was preparing to tackle) the gigantic task of producing a first scholarly and popular history of the Haitian Revolution. According to Lyonel Trouillot, it is in this same issue of *Lakansièl* that he published a first draft of *Ti difé boulé*, 'Lindépandans dévan-dèyè', also signed L. Raymond.[4] But the transtextual relationships between these two authors and books extend further.

Ti difé boulé sou istoua Ayiti: Its Roots and Beyond

Not only does MRT quote and paraphrase *Dézafi* in this seminal book ('Min, zonbi gouté sèl Bouanèf changé figi'),[5] but also, like Frankétienne, he uses a mythical popular Haitian figure, Grinn Prominnin, as one of the main characters of his history of Haiti. In *Dézafi*, this same character is portrayed with the features of the duo Kamélo and Filojèn, who are described as tougher than 'grinn-pronminnin'.[6] Moreover, echoing the unusual paratextual closing note of *Dézafi*, 'Frankétienne kòmansé ékri roman DÉZAFI an janvié 1975; li fini an jiyè 1975',[7] MRT, at the very end of his book, similarly gives the places and dates of the production of his text, 'broukli-n / septanm 1975 / mé 1977'.

> Perrego suggests in his article 'Les Créoles', where, after several detours and deep thinking, he has to shift from 'créole' to 'haïtien' (p. 617) to name the language of the Haitian people.
> 2 Subsequently in the text, MRT or Trouillot.
> 3 See L. Raymond 'Dézafi' 30–32.
> 4 See L. Raymond 'Lindépandans dévan-dèyè' 46–50.
> 5 Michel-Rolph Trouillot *Ti difé boulé sou istoua Ayiti* 41; see above, *Stirring the Pot of Haitian History*, p. 29.
> 6 Frankétienne *Dézafi* 28; in Asselin Charles' translation: 'Kamélo and Filojèn are worse than wandering seeds' (13).
> 7 'Frankétienne started writing the novel *Dézafi* in January 1975; he completed it in July 1975' (translation mine). This note is absent from Asselin Charles' English translation.

Based upon these clues and the author's own statements to Richard Brisson in a 1977 interview on Radio Haïti-Inter,[8] we can say that MRT started to write this first book after the release of *Dézafi* in August 1975. However, we must also emphasize that the differential typography common to both works is by no means a borrowing from Franketienne. Indeed, such a textual layout in the Haitian language, in even more complex form, can be found in the very first issue of *Lakansièl*, most likely published in January 1975, or at least the first quarter of that year. For example, this issue contains a full page of an untitled text bearing an atypical typography, signed 'atélié tanbou libeté',[9] a cultural animation group of which MRT, according to Lyonel Trouillot, was one of the founding and most productive members. Moreover, MRT was in charge of the typographic composition of the group's publications, the one shaping the layout of *Lakansièl*, therefore was well positioned to develop an awareness of the capital role of typography in the readability of texts.

Aware of the importance of working on forms for effective communication, although exploring a sphere other than the poetic or the fictional, Trouillot, plunging into the sources of the national history, borrows from the popular narrative traditions of the country the adequate forms (*lodyans*,[10] folk tales, songs, proverbs, riddles, mythical characters)[11] to shape his writing. In doing so, he goes one step further in the exploration of the Haitian language and its discursive features initiated by two illustrious predecessors, Franketienne, and more notably Georges Castera, author of the collection of poems *Konbèlann* (1976), a good part of which had circulated in the Haitian leftist circles of New York since 1970–71. Indeed, MRT finds the right everyday Haitian phrases for this scholarly historical analysis illuminating the

---

8 See Michel-Rolph Trouillot's interview with Richard Brisson.
9 See *Lakansièl*, 4, 1976, p. 15.
10 For Haitians, *lodyans* is a very distinctive Haitian form of pleasant and instructive narrative (an account of the social or sociopolitical life of the community, an everyday inventive oral performance linked to the genius of the narrator/performer in dialogue with his audience), which differs from the *kont* (folk tales rooted in old traditions of fixed forms), the *tripotay* (a negative account of specific individuals, gossip), or the *télédyòl* (usually a political account, a rumor intended to provoke political change or at least some social turmoil).
11 For more concrete and specific examples of the use of Haitian traditional forms in TDB, see Jocelyne Trouillot-Lévy 'Ti dife boule sou istwa Ayiti, yon klasik pami klasik' 172–77.

class struggles which led to the revolution of 1804, such that it could be accessible to Haitians of all origins. Thus, he follows one of the fundamental lessons of Mao Zedong's thought, which inspired him, at least in part (consciously or not). I am not sure that MRT was strictly speaking a Maoist, although the cover page of *Lakansièl* displays the 'Hundred Flowers Campaign' slogan: 'Let a hundred flowers bloom, let a hundred schools of thought contend', but he was Marxist. His book, to a certain extent, results from the cultural and political turmoil of this period in the history of Haitians abroad—notably the diaspora of North America in the 1970s, known as *Action patriotique* ('Patriotic Action')[12]—, wherein it was necessary *to speak the language of the people*, as prescribed by the Great Helmsman, Chairman Mao. On this matter, to the best of our knowledge, more than any of us, scholars or intellectuals inside or outside of Haiti, MRT was able to make the bridge between scholarly and popular traditions, and simultaneously to offer a first expanded attempt to rigorously think about the national real in Haitian within a 200-page volume, whose bibliography comprising both Haitian and foreign sources offers a very first proof of its rigorousness.

This work does not come from nowhere. We can trace its roots to articles signed L. Raymond dating back to the first half of 1975, 'Pou drésé kozman' in *Lakansièl* 2, and especially 'Ki mò ki touyé lanpérè' in *Lakansièl* 3. This latter essay opens like a series of riddles, some authentic (1, 2, 4), the others entirely or partially forged, playing on the sidelines of the historical and the playful (the history and the story). Clearly, Trouillot echoes both paradigms: first, the death of Emperor Jean-Jacques Dessalines as told by one of the most famous names of Haitian official historiography, Beaubrun Ardouin, reproduced alongside the first page of his article; second, the play by the experimental theater group, Kouidor, with the same title, but in French, *Quel mort tua l'empereur?*, premiered at the beginning of 1975. Indeed, I do think, it is partly from this famous performance that MRT borrows the Brechtian distancing effect of *Ti difé boulé*, which echoes the question-and-answer dialectic that is profoundly anchored in the Haitian space within popular forms such as riddles, *lodyans*, or daily talk.

It is not without consequences that MRT's first attempt to publish in Haitian on Haiti's history is inspired by the Brechtian approach of

12 On this period of the Haitian diaspora's history in the USA, see Carolle Charles 152–59.

Kouidor, at least he borrows its title from their famous play, *Quel mort tua l'empereur?* ('Which Bad Spirit Killed the Emperor?').[13] This is even more relevant, since he announced this same title for the second part of his history of Haiti that, to the best of my knowledge, he never completed. That said, the emergence of popular voices in *Ti difé boulé sou istoua Ayiti* is a crucial source of distancing effect to remind the reader that it is History, but also a story that acquires meaning by his or her active deciphering as a subject being challenged on almost every page through popular figures (Lamèsi, Tipiè, Sédènié, Janpétro, Zòt ...) or, more ironically, Haitian luminaries (the director, the judge, or the pastor ...), whom Trouillot stages to tell, contextualize, question, and analyze this narrative, taking it out of the mythical to transform it into an object of reflection and action.

Unfortunately, to date, this capital contribution has not been appreciated at its fair value. A single example might suffice: the silence of Jean Durosier Desrivières on this founding text in his 'Brief exploration of literature in the Creole language in Haiti, from its beginnings to its affirmation', dated December 2, 2011,[14] recalling the near silence of the Haitian press in general on the book. Indeed, we retrace very few mentions of *Ti difé boulé sou istoua Ayiti* in the Haitian press either inside or outside the country beyond Trouillot's 1977 radio interview with Richard Brisson, and an article by Jean Dominique with the luminous title, 'L'Istoua d'Ayiti? Youn tiré kont, youn chèché kont' (1977),[15] which highlights two main features of this publication: to tell stories (to amuse) / to stir up contradictions (to instruct). But the statistics on its dissemination are even more significant: the number of publications on this work is very limited, its impact marginal, especially compared to MRT's

---

13 The title of this groundbreaking Haitian play is a word-for-word translation of a colloquial phrase, *ki mò ki touye lanperè*, usually translated into English by 'What's going on/What happened/Find out?'—see '*mò*' in Freeman and Laguerre *Haitian Creole-English Dictionary* 533; Targète and Urciolo 131. However, the English translation we offer here, following Kouidor Archive site (https://kouidor.com/plays/quel-mort-tua-lempereur/), reflects the explicit political and mythical stance by Kouidor in revisiting our history and society through the metaphor of the assassination of Emperor Dessalines, and the Haitian Vodou concept of the dead as spirit, more obvious when using the word *lèmò* (the dead, not death, *lamò*, *lanmò*).
14 See Jean Durosier Desrivières.
15 Please note that I was unable to locate a copy of this article; my citation follows its entry in the critical bibliography on MRT's works established by Drexel G. Woodson in 'Byen Pre Pa Lakay'.

Silencing the Past (1995). A simple search in the ProQuest database on January 25, 2020 shows 2,945 occurrences for *Silencing the Past* versus thirty-six for *Ti difé boulé*. Regarding the presence of titles in higher education's libraries, here again the differences are disproportionate. According to WorldCat, the first edition alone of *Silencing the Past* is held by no fewer than 728 libraries worldwide, compared to twenty for *Ti difé boulé*. We can thus see the critical importance of this English translation, which will certainly promote a wider dissemination of the work, and a broader impact.

The Connection with Past

After these detours on the genesis and the reception of MRT's first book, let us return to the relationships between its English translation, co-translator Mariana Past, and myself, author of this afterword.

The gratification, for us, is double when of this object (whatever its format or its nature), we are asked to make a presentation or a comment to accompany its opening or closing. How to express my joy, the feeling of a certain *plenitude* when former student Mariana Past, now esteemed colleague, asked me for an afterword to her co-translation, with Benjamin Hebblethwaite,[16] of Michel-Rolph Trouillot's great book, which, one day in the autumn of 2002, I had put on the program of an independent study that I supervised at Duke University, at her express request. According to the syllabus, 'this independent study [...] will focus on Haitian language and culture; all readings'—among them, may I add today, three of the most important Haitian books of all time: 'Frankétienne's *Dézafi* (Port-au-Prince, 1975), Georges Castera's *Konbelann* (Montréal, 1976), and Michel-Rolph Trouillot's *Ti difé boulé sou istoua Ayiti* (Brooklyn, New York, 1977)—'and discussions will be conducted in Haitian Creole'.

This seed was planted, by chance of an encounter, with little certainty or conviction, at a time when I had a strange feeling that some dark forces were plotting against my professional future, which should have pushed

---

16 Associate Professor at the University of Florida, in the Department of Languages, Literatures, and Cultures, Hebblethwaite is not a newcomer to the Haitian linguistic universe. Indeed, he was among the editorial assistants of Albert Valdman's *Haitian Creole-English Bilingual Dictionary* (2007), a reference tool that I occasionally use to enlighten my explorations of my mother tongue.

me to reject this additional task, but the fruits were going to exceed all expectations.

My link with Past is not limited to the student/professor/colleague relationship; it is also rooted in the similarities of our respective births. Mariana was born American in the English-speaking Caribbean, Barbados, a country that claims to be the very first producer of rum in the world in 1703—Mount Gay, a rum that I was introduced to by Mariana, and that has since become one of my favorites. I was born Haitian to a mother of North American origin by virtue of her great-grandfather Aristide Gabriel Sylvain.[17] This dual attachment to North America and the Caribbean may explain our shared interest in the Americas and the need to explore its shores. Past completed a dissertation, under my co-supervision, at Duke University, *Reclaiming the Haitian Revolution: Race, Politics and History in Twentieth-Century Caribbean Literature* (2006), which 'examines how the trope of the Haitian revolution (1791–1804) is reactivated by the fiction of Caribbean writers at a crucial moment in history: the era of the Cuban Revolution, African Independence movements, and the Duvaliers' regime'.[18] Since then, she has continued to analyze this wide corpus of texts, so close and so different, as instructor-researcher, and as translator.

Translators, we are all on the fence, cultural couriers, facilitators engaged in a difficult task, especially when handling an innovative text or one of an emerging language with very few reference instruments, and a rather limited written corpus. Trouillot's text puts us in front of all these challenges, starting with 'ti difé boulé sou', the first part of the title. To some extent, the phrase echoes both a very common expression during confrontations between young and old folks, 'pousé difé' ('fan the fire') and the Duvalierist propaganda which used the song 'Min difé, difé nan kay la o' ('There is fire, fire in the house') on the radio to alert the population of imminent dangers such as invasions or internal or external attempted coups against the regime. For myself and the

---

17 The same Sylvain's ancestor is the grandfather to Georges Sylvain who published *Cric? Crac! Les fables de La Fontaine racontées par un montagnard haïtien et transcrites en vers créoles* (1901), and his daughter, Suzanne Sylvain, better known by her married name, Suzanne Comhaire-Sylvain, who wrote the first dissertation on 'Haitian Creole', *Le Créole haïtien* (1936), and also the very first study on the tales of Haitian folklore, *Les Contes haïtiens: 1ère partie Maman d'leau* (1937) and *Les Contes haïtiens: 2ème partie conjoint animal ou démon déguisé* (1937).
18 See Past iv.

Haitian colleagues I consulted, including Dr. Asselin Charles and Dr. Jean Norgaisse, this phrase appears to be an expression created by MRT; while for a few others, such as the linguist Dr. Jean-Robert Cadely or the historian Pierre Buteau, it is an authentically Haitian expression, although each of them ascribes it a different meaning. However, all of us largely agree that Trouillot's phrase suggests a process of clarification or confrontation that I would tend to translate by 'Spotlight on', or 'Light on', and Trouillot's translators render beautifully as 'Stirring the Pot', thanks to Evelyne Trouillot. Whatever the case, I cannot settle this debate here. Likewise, I cannot assess MRT's text, much less its English translation, given my entanglement within a network of common or overlapping stories. To a certain extent, I am judge and party of both ventures: the paratextual (my afterword) and the metatextual (the English translation by Past and Hebblethwaite), as Gérard Genette defines these terms,[19] and this brings me back to my relationships with the Trouillots in Haiti—on the one hand, a series of encounters dating back to my high school years and, on the other, my first years in Montreal.

The Relationship to the Trouillots, Father, Son, and Consorts

How can I depart from this web of acquaintances without going through the biographical, the autobiographical, trying as far as possible to say from where I am speaking? Namely, MRT was an acquaintance, and I became a friend of his brother Lyonel (the well-known writer, journalist, and educator), one of the best friends of one of my great friends, the historian Pierre Buteau, who was more than instrumental in the efforts to bring the Trouillots to agree to various stages of this long process of translation and publication.[20] I am a former student of his father, Ernst, and his

---

19 See Genette chs. I and II.
20 I take this opportunity to warmly thank Pierrot, and to recall that he, like the Trouillots and Ollivier, grew up in the Saint-Antoine district that Lyonel Trouillot wonderfully evokes in his first novel, *Les Fous de Saint-Antoine* (1989), as well as Franck Étienne, in his first novel, *Mûr à crever*, subtitled 'genre total' (1968). A neighborhood particularly interesting at the time for housing both a little bourgeoisie more or less rich or impoverished, on the edge of a hill alongside John Brown Avenue, better known as Lalue, where one finds the posh girls' school of the Sisters of Saint Joseph of Cluny, Sainte Rose de Lima, caught between the popular Poste Marchand, and ruelle Nazon (today, Martin Luther King Avenue), the location of the Catts Pressoir College of a certain emerging bourgeoisie.

uncle, Hénock, of whom I think MRT was more or less a spitting image: shy, hardworking, versatile. Indeed, unlike his flamboyant father who lectured with remarkable ease, almost without notes, if memory serves, he reminded me rather of his uncle who, head down, in a monotone voice, read his lecture notes, always dense and well-documented, almost word for word from large notebooks, often notes or drafts of books to come, it seems to me today. A hard-working and prolific writer, from the 1940s to the 1980s, Hénock Trouillot published some twenty books of differing lengths in various genres: novel, historical, ethnographic or sociological essays, theater, literary history, and criticism.[21]

MRT—himself a poet, singer-songwriter, literary critic, historian and anthropologist, editor and amateur typographer—left us a less profuse literary or scholarly legacy, but his contribution to Haitian thought is remarkable whether or not one shares his perspectives.[22] Inhabited by an incredible desire to explore Haitian realities from different angles, his work *Ti difé boulé sou istoua Ayiti*, which presents itself as a puzzle through its differential typography, is an obvious trace of the various hats he wore. But even more remarkable is the unique contribution of this volume to a properly Haitian historiography (or *essayistics*) in the Haitian language, and, at the same time, to world historiography. Indeed, as MRT reminded Richard Brisson, this burst of traditional popular discourse within a scholarly text was unprecedented in historical studies at the time, although it could be found in anthropological studies—rather in the form of quotations, I would specify, not as discursive or narrative models of the very process of writing as in his book.

A very relevant example to illustrate this point is the opening of the chapter devoted to the Code Noir, the second of the book, '**Kòd noua / pou maré / ti kochon**', pp. [18–19].

---

21 See among others: *Chair, Sang et Trahison* 1947); (with Catts Pressoir and Ernst Trouillot) *Historiographie d'Haïti* (1953); *La République de Pétion et le peuple haïtien* (1960); *Lumumba, cette lumière (tragédie africaine)* (1971); *Les Origines sociales de la littérature haïtienne* (1962); *L'Itinéraire d'Aimé Césaire* (1968); *Les Limites du créole dans notre enseignement* (1980); and *Introduction à une histoire du vaudou* (1983).

22 On this point, see *supra* Lyonel Trouillot's preface to this volume, which lays out a brief and emotional intellectual story of his older brother; and Woodson and Williams. For a greater understanding of the exceptional place of MRT's work in contemporary Haitian Literatures, and the challenges it represents for Caribbean Studies at large, see my articles, 'Haitian Literature in the United States, 1948–1986' (2002), and 'Transnationalism, Multilingualism and Literature: the Challenge of Caribbean Studies' (2007).

2. Kòd noua pou maré ti kochon

Ay ay (1)[23]
Janpétro (2)
chinn (3)
ki chinn (4)
li kasé (5)
ki diré kòd. (6)

1 Lékòl gin régléman-l, travay gin régléman-l, léta gin régléman-l. Labib gin lè 10 kòmandman.

2 Trafik gin régléman-l, lagè gin régléman-l, lapè gin régléman-l, simitiè gin régléman-l: mò rèd, lévé do-ou! Sé nan simitiè k-gin plas...

3 Latin gin régléman-l, anglé gin régléman-l, kréyòl gin régléman-l. Travay latè gin régléman-l, ékri diskou gin régléman-l. Bal ki bal gin régléman-l: si ou pa gin kravat ou pa la.

4 Kòm ki diré, lò n-lévé jé-n, nou ouè sièl la plin régléman. Zòt ba yo tout kalité non. Gin kòmandman, gin régléman, gin kòd. (Sé pa kòd ou maré kochon an non, min pito sé té sa.) Gin dékrè, gin dékrè-loua, gin laloua. (Sé pa laloua k-anmè yo fè rinmèd la non, min pito sé té sa.)

5 Kòm koua tout régléman sa yo ta la pou ryin? Non diréktè! Kòm ki diré yo ta inosan? Non jij! Kòm koua sé lavi-a sa? Otan, pastè, otan!

6 An n-fouyé zo nan kalalou...

---

23 The numberings are mine for the purpose of analysis. For an English translation of these two pages, see *supra*, *Stirring the Pot of Haitian History*, pp. 9–10.

On these two pages, like a snapshot of the differential typography within the work, spreads a *mise en abyme*[24] of the analysis of history which is a criticism of Haitian historiography and its teaching through dialogues between various social actors including, among others, Janpétro, 'dirèktè', 'jij', and 'pastè'. This approach coincides with the Marxist criticism of family, school, justice, and religion. Moreover, as shown below, it dovetails with a family tradition: a concern for a rigorous analysis of the sources, towards a certain epistemology of Haitian historiography dating back to 1953 with *Historiographie d'Haïti* by Catts Pressoir and Ernst and Hénock Trouillot. In *Ti difé boulé*, this questioning of the discourse on history and these dialogues with peers are not expressed in a clear academic manner as in the long bio-bibliographical notices by the elder Trouillots, father and uncle, in *Historiographie d'Haïti*, but rather in an enigmatic, ironic, even enjoyable form as shown in the series of questions and answers in paragraph 4 of our example. Specifically, here, the dominated resorts to slyness in saying 'no' to the agents of power: pretending to reaffirm the latter's authority, he mischievously designates him by his title or position within state apparatuses: schools (director), courts (judge), churches (pastor). Another example is this false riddle of paragraph 3, 'Bal ki bal gin regléman-l: si ou pa gin kravat ou pa la', which, with a touch of humor, refers to the protocol of city attire (suit and tie) for Haitian dance evenings of yesteryear. A rather ridiculous requirement, now more or less obsolete, in a country where average daily temperatures vary between 70° to 80° F, 'except in the hilly regions, where averages are about 10 degrees cooler'.[25] Such a discursive strategy recalls the series of riddles opening MRT's first historical essay in Haitian, the aforementioned 'Ki mò ki touyé lanpéré?' (1975).

Finally, across these two pages, the *mise en abyme* of a criticism of Haitian historiography is even more evident at all three levels by the words 'kòd' and 'kochon' (or their synonyms 'chinn', 'régléman', 'Janpétro', 'Nou'), which repeat and answer one another within the chapter title, itself composed of three lines in bold script, six lines of an italicized epigraph, and six paragraphs of an introduction in Roman font, particularly paragraphs 4 and 5. These references to the Black Code and to the equally black pig, sacred animal—that of the Bois Caïman ceremony—but also profane, a source of daily food for the Haitian (*grès kochon kuit kochon*) and a metaphor for this same subject

---

24 On this concept, see Dällenbach 15–18, 51–52, 82–83.
25 See Crawford-Adiletta n. pag.

(*ti kochon mandé manman l, poukisa dyòl ou long konsa, manman kochon reponn, tan ou a ouè*), generate a wordplay on *kòd*, 'code' and 'rope', that only the Haitian language allows. The same word, deeply rooted in national history and Haitian daily life, refers to two orders of constraints—socio-historical or legal, on the one hand, and physical on the other—but also a certain enjoyment in deciphering our oral code rendered in the writing. I, a Haitian reader, find a similar pleasure in reading in paragraph 6, 'An n-fouyé zo nan kalalou', rather than a banal 'An n-chèché konnin' or 'An n-chèché konprann'—calque of European or North American academic formulas—to remind us of the difficulty, if not the impossibility, of calling into question the official or traditional history well anchored in the minds of educated Haitians. This reference to 'kalalou' (French, *gombo*; English, 'okra'), a vegetable or dish based on this fruit with or without meat or fish, is a way of saying in a very Haitian way, 'let us turn over every stone in the search of truth, even if the task is decried, if not prohibited': a dual break with the empty speeches or talking points, better said in the French *langue de bois* of the Academy, of Marxist ideologues as much as those of the official or traditional Haitian history.

Towards a Conclusion: The Link to *Ti difé boulé sou istoua Ayiti*

This volume combining the staging of history and the *mise en abyme* of its analysis, modeled on popular Haitian language forms, creates a set of mirrors that brings a certain enjoyment to the Haitian reader, which may be rather difficult, if not impossible, to convey in another language or to another audience. Indeed, this enjoyment is linked to the intimate and the unexpected experience of a return to the depths of the mother tongue spreading black on white in visible signs resonating in the deepest recesses of memory, recreating the pleasures of a typically Haitian lost childhood or adolescence. We can therefore say that MRT is first of all a *writer* in the sense given to the term by Roland Barthes,[26] and his text, while intentionally didactic, is in the order of the *scriptible* rather than the *readable*.[27] Moreover, at the same

---

26 See Barthes *Le Plaisir du texte* 81; Barthes 'Écrivains et Écrivants' 147–54.
27 Jean-Michel Rabaté defines the two concepts in his article, 'Barthes, Roland', as 'texts that merely obey a logic of passive consumption ["readerly" *(lisible)* texts] and texts that stimulate the reader's active participation ["writerly" *(scriptible)*]'. See Barthes *S/Z* 9–12, 161–62, 187–88.

time, MRT breaks with the historiographic illusion of an established truth unrelated to its instances of production and reception, which finds echo here in a dual staging of personal stories: first, that of our author in his acknowledgments ('youn grap mèsi bay tout fanmi, tout zanmi-kamarad …'), and subsequently my own in this afterword. This ultimate recourse to the biographical and the autobiographical here deliberately underscores the close relationships between the various actors within Haitian socio-literary or sociopolitical life, making an objective reading of our writings or stories very difficult, as well as any real totalitarian drift.

Whatever the righteous may say, within the land of the Tomas of Ayiti, as the proverb goes, 'tout moun gen yon grenn zanno kay ofèv' ('everyone has an earring at the goldsmith's'). In other words, we of the more or less educated middle and upper classes, we are all connected by the top or the bottom to the power and the opposition in a big family from the coast, the plains, or the hills, both bourgeois and working-class, rich or poor, urban and rural, mulatto or black … Thus, MRT and his uncle, like his father, occupy two extremes of the Haitian politico-ideological spectrum, Marxism and *Noirisme* (a Haitian version of Indigenism which, according to some scholars, led to Duvalierism).[28] However, to some degree, they share the same conception or practice of history that is a counter-history, another history tending towards an epistemology of the discipline, of which perhaps the most obvious example in Hénock Trouillot's work is *Le Drapeau bleu et rouge: une mystification historique* (1958). Not only did he dedicate the text to 'Son Excellence le Dr. François DUVALIER', but besides the proper address to the same ('Mr. President of the Republic'),[29] he underlines his presence at the closing of the text (note 6, p. 34), along with that of his spouse and his General Staff at the lecture reproduced in this brochure.

Without definition or explanation of this filiation, MRT implicitly recognizes this kinship in his aforementioned 1977 interview with Brisson; but he does so explicitly at the opening of *Silencing the Past* (1995).[30]

---

28 See among others: Hurbon 81–117; Michel-Rolph Trouillot, *Les Racines historiques de l'état duvaliérien* 205–38, or the updated English version of this latter book, *Haiti, State against Nation: The Origins and Legacy of Duvalierism* (1990).
29 Hénock Trouillot, *Le Drapeau bleu et rouge* 13 (my translation).
30 On this point, in *Silencing the Past*, MRT writes: 'Ernst and Hénock Trouillot influenced this project both during their lifetime and from beyond the grave

The book's subtitle, 'Power and the Production of History', is an epistemological twist echoing the uncle's critique of certain 'classical Haitian historians' and their sources:

> To be properly understood, first, a historical narrative must be placed within the framework of the doctrinal thought of its author. We know Céligny Ardouin, Beaubrun Ardouin, and St.-Rémy as dedicated apologists of Alexandre Pétion. They never hid it. Witness their successive writings. It was natural for them to tend to attribute to him, rightly or wrongly, the largest role within the events in which this historical figure participated. Historians placed in a situation where doubt is cast on the narration of events they relate, should quote documents, duly appropriate documents.
>
> Where might we find this letter from General Alexandre Pétion to General Jean-Jacques Dessalines? Since it must be asked, if the letter is not apocryphal or rather imaginary, what is its content? Why do historians who refer to it, not quote it?[31]

Here we are, Ladies and Gentlemen, at the end of our exploration of a fundamental book by a son of a long-standing Haitian family of historians and writers, for whom all the 'Praise immediately swells in our throats', to quote Francis Ponge.[32] And, you, informed readers, or merely attentive ones, you have probably already understood that the hybrid nature of *Ti difé boulé sou istoua Ayiti* demands a hybrid reading as well. That is what I endeavored to do from Las Terrenas, in the land of Haiti on the other side of the border, where I wrote the first lines of this afterword, to Syracuse, where I work, passing through Paris and New York, between the last days of December 2019 and May 2020, in memory of my father and mother, Japhet Jonassaint and Yvette Sylvain, and for my children,

---

in ways that are both transparent and intricate. I cannot date my interest in the production of history, but my first conscious marker is my perusal of the work they coauthored with Catts Pressoir, the first historiography book I read' (xi). It is interesting to note that the first chapter of *Silencing the Past*, 'The Power in the Story', except for the biographical notes, like his very first reading of history, *Historiographie d'Haïti* (1953), is mostly a review of the literature assessing historical research, an evaluation of the production of historical narratives.

31 Hénock Trouillot, *Le Drapeau bleu et rouge* 20–21 (my translation).
32 Ponge, *Le Pré* n. pag.

Pierre Alexandre and Anne Isabel, who, one day, may be able to enjoy their multiple legacies.[33]

Jean Jonassaint, Syracuse University

---

[33] From one filiation to another, like a *coda*, let's thank friends or colleagues (former or current) who, knowingly or not, helped me shape this piece on Michel-Rolph Trouillot's exceptional book, *Ti difé boulé sou istoua Ayiti*: Michel Adam, Ginette Adamson, Catherine Benoit, Pierre-Marc de Biasi, Bruno Blache, Miryam Bar, Andrée Fortin, Gail Bulman, Jean-Robert Cadely, Dominique Fisher, Lise Gauvin, Asselin Charles, Gregson Davis, Claude Dauphin, Marlene Daut, Daniel Delas, Franck Étienne, Marie Andrée Étienne, Kathy Everly, Dieudonné Fardin, Robert Fatton, Karla FC Holloway, Hérard Jadotte, Jacques Jonassaint, Samuel Jubé, Jaklin Kornfilt, Lélia Lebon, Gaétan Lévesque, Claudine Michel, Walter Mignolo, Cathryn R. Newton, Jean Norgaisse, Linda Orr, Leslie Péan, Nicoletta Pireddu, Claire Riffard, Alicia Rios, Ghislain Ripault, Françoise Rubellin, Amina Saïd, Francine Saillant, Pierre Saint-Amand, Silvio Torres-Saillant, Marie-Denise Shelton, Mireille Sylvain, Évelyne Trouillot, Lyonel Trouillot, Chenet Veillard, Claude Veillard, André Vanasse, Frantz Voltaire, and some great former students and former professors (living or deceased).

Appendix

Pages 194–97

    'ki mò ki touyé lanpérè'
    ('What bad spirit killed the emperor')
    by L. Raymond, pseudonym of M-R. Trouillot
    (*Lakansièl* 3, 1975, pp. 37–39)

Pages 198–202

    'lindépandans dévan-dèyè: dapiyanp sou révolision'
    ('Independence Upside-Down: Seizing Revolution')
    by L. Raymond (*Lakansièl*, Spécial nouvelle année, 1976, pp. 46–50)

1806 — LAKANSIEL SOULIGNE — LA MORT DE

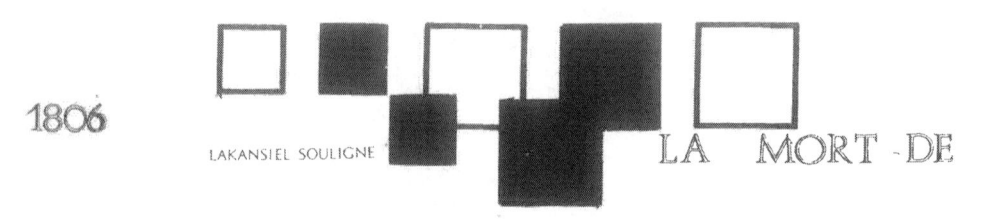

...En approchant du *Pont-Rouge* le malheureux empereur y vit l'officier qui remplaçait Gédéon, vêtu comme lui, et arriva en cet endroit dans la plus grande sécurité. Mais *l'embuscade se prolongeait au-delà* du Pont-Rouge: il était donc au milieu des troupes qui la formaient. Dans le grand chemin, il y en avait pour représenter la 3 eme. le colonel Léger, son aide de camp, qui avait servi dans le Sud sous Geffrad et Gérin, reconnut des militaires de la 15eme et de la 16 eme; il lui dit: "Mais ce sont les troupes du Sud! - Non, répondit l'empereur, cela ne peut être; comment pourraient-elles se trouver ici?"

Les généraux Gérin, Yayou et Vaval étaient dans l'embuscade. En cet instant, Gérin cria d'une voix forte: "Halte! Formez le cercle! "

A ce commandement, les troupes qui étaient dans le bois, derrière l'empereur, en sortirent tumultueusement pour lui barrer le chemin au cas qu'il voulût retourner sur ses pas, tandis que celles qui étaient sur les côtés et en avant vers la ville, sortirent aussi. On peut juger de l'effroi qu'officiers et soldats éprouvaient en présence d'un chef comme Dessalines!

Mais lui, en les voyant obéir à ce commandement militaire, reconnut le piège qui lui avait été tendu et devint furieux: animé de ce courage qui le distinguait à la guerre, il saisit sa canne et en frappa les soldats auxquels les officiers criaient vainement: feu! feu! *Je suis trahi! dit-il*: ôtant un pistolet de ses fontes, *il tua un militaire*. Mais, se voyant trop cerné par les troupes, il tournait son cheval pour rebrousser sur la route, quand un jeune soldat de la 15eme, nommé Garat, sur l'ordre d'un sous-officier, lâcha son coup de fusil, dont la balle atteignit *le cheval* qui s'abattit. C'est alors que Dessalines cria: "*A mon secours Charlotin!* "pour l'aider à se dégager sous le cheval: probablement ce colonel se trouvait le plus près de lui en ce moment, ou bien il comptait plus sur son dévouement. A ce cri de détresse du chef qu'il aimait, tout en déplorant ses défauts, Charlotin, *héros de la fidélité*, se précipita de son propre cheval et vint pour le relever. ce fut en cet instant que les soldats, reprenant leur aplomb, firent une décharge sous laquelle périrent Dessalines et Charlotin.

Les diverses circonstances de cette sanglante catastrophe avaient exigé moins de temps que nous n'en avons mis à les relater.

Dessalines, le fier et intrépide *Dessalines*, tombant mort par les balles de ces troupes haïtiennes avec lesquelles il avait conquis l'indépendance de son pays, on devait s'arrêter à cet épouvantable attentat. On s'assura à cette époque que plusieurs officiers supérieurs tracèrent le funeste exemple d'une fureur impardonnable, sur le cadavre du chef qu'ils avaient tant redouté; que le général Yayou et le chef de bataillon Hilaire Martin de la 16 eme, lui portèrent plusieurs coups de poignard; que le général Vaval voulut décharger sur lui ses deux pistolets, qui ratèrent; et que le chef d'escadron Delaunay fendit la tête de Charlotin d'un coup de sabre, peut-être en ne voulant que frapper aussi le cadavre de l'empereur.

Comment les soldats eussent-ils respecté le corps de Dessalines, après cette fureur des chefs? Ils lui coupèrent les doigts pour prendre ses bagues de prix; ils le dépouillèrent de ses vêtements, ne lui laissant que sa chemise et son caleçon; ses armes, ses pistolets, sabre, poignard, devinrent la proie des pillards. Le général Yayou ordonna aux soldats d'emporter le cadavre en ville, sur la place d'armes, en face du palais du Gouvernement. dans ce trajet d'une demi-lieue, ce cadavre fut incessamment jeté comme une pâture à la foule qui accourait de tous côtés; et chaque fois qu'il en fut ainsi, on lui portait des coups de sabre, on lui jetait des pierres.

Ce corps inanimé, mutilé, percé de tant de coups, à la tête surtout, était à peine reconnaissable: il resta exposé sur cette place d'armes jusque dans l'après-midi, où une femme noire, nommée *Défilée*, qui était folle depuis longtemps, rendue à un moment lucide, ou plutôt mû par un sentiment de compassion, gémissait seule auprès des restes du Fondateur de l'indépendance, lorsque des militaires, *envoyés par ordre du général Pétion*, vinrent les enlever et les porter au cimetière intérieur de la ville, où ils furent inhumés. *Défilée* les y accompagna et assista à cette opération; longtemps après ce jour de triste souvenir, elle continua d'aller au cimetière, jetant des fleurs sur cette fosse qui recouvrait les restes de Dessalines. Quelques années ensuite, Madame Inginac y fit élever une modeste tombe sur laquelle on lit cette épitaphe: *Ci-git* DESSALINES, MORT A 4 8 ANS.

192   *Stirring the Pot of Haitian History*

DESSALINES

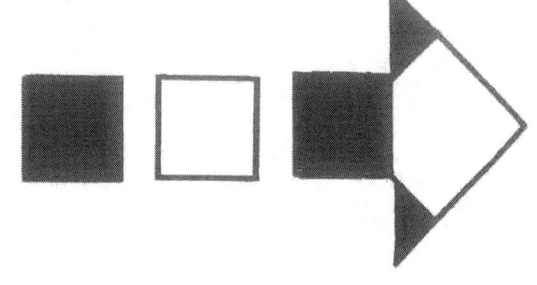

ki mò ki touyé lanpérè?

1975

Lanpérè mouri, nou minm nou vivan. Min sé té vouazinay vié grann. Lò kouji-n vouazinay boulé fò ou chaché konnin kilakòz pasé lakay pa-ou pa trò louin.

Ki manti zòt ba nou sou lanmò lanpérè?

GIN MECHAN PASE MECHAN

Défin mouché Beaubrun Ardouin ak tout you digdal konpayèl k-ap fè propagann anba chal pou boujoua ak gro péyi blan, vlé fè konprann Jean Jacques mouri jan li mouri-a pasé li té trò méchan. Mézanmi, ala dé lafrans! Sa-a sé pa istoua d-Ayiti, sé istoua pou fè moun dòmi...Istoua pou lè péti zanfan, "fanfan a bien su sa leçon". Méchansté pou ki lakòz? Méchansté ak ki moun? Méchansté pou défann mamit mayi Gro Jan? Osnon méchansté pou défann souè ak san Tisè ak Zaka? Osnon ankò [sa fèt toutan] méchansté nan kont mal tayé Gro jan ak Goldinberg ap réglé sou do abitan?

Diakout méchansté sa-a vi-n avèk diòl li tou maré. Nou pap pran matou nan makout. Yo pa janm rivé espliké-n kilakièl dé sèt méchansté. Yo vépa di-n dé ki prévyin.

NEG RICH SE MILAT

Gin you lòt pòsion moun ki di sé lagè nèg nouè ak milat ki lakòz lanmò Dessalines. Nou di: otan! Mové laron!

-tim tim?
-boua chèch
-kaptinn dèyè pòt?
-balé!
-kaptinn anba kabann?
-potchanm
-m-viré, m-viré, m-viré?
-pèp
-dlo kouché?
-mélon dlo
-dlo désann?
-libèté!
-sa k-manman bourik?
-bourik!
-sa k-travay manjé mal?
-Sò Yèt!
-min ki mò ki touyé lanpérè?
- !

Kòm koua sa nèg konnin sé pou lagaléri. Kòm ki diré pouason nan dlo pa konn koté sous koumansé. 171 zan, moua pou moua, san rétiré. san méte, Jean Jacques Dessalines, nèg vanyan, gason kanson dévan gason, tonbé nan pouinn fè pa nan bariè Pòtoprins. Kòm ki diré ti nèg bliyé? Kòm ki diré ti nèg bouké chaché konprann ki lakièl de "attendu que" ki fè lanpérè té tonbé. Zòt di: nanpouin sonn, nanpouin maladi. Atò mouin konnin: lè pa gin sonn, malad mouri...

Appendix 193

Eské nou janm tandé nèg nouè ak nèg po klè goumin pou plézi akrochay? Milat avèk nèg nouè pa goumin nan Bòdmè, yo pa goumin Delmas, é dépi ti konkonm té jouinn ak béréjinn milat ak nèg nouè mét ansanm lò lajan métè yo ansanm. Yo pa fou, yo pa anrajé. Ki lakièl dé rézon ki ta fè yo lévé you jou lindi matin épi tonbé tiré fizi adouat agòch, dévan dèyè, san pa gin viv nan galata?

Défin Jean Jacques, gason kanson, ki pat minm non ak Dessalines, min papa-l té siyin Acau, défin Jean Jacques Acau té di: milat pòv sé nèg, nèg rich sé milat! E défin Jean Jacques Acau sé nèg ki té manyin fizi. Li té konnin, pasé ni rou ni mouin, nèg pa goumin pou grémési.

Kidonk, lè nou sonjé Jean Jacques [kit Acau-kit Dessalines] n-ap di nèg ti zòrèy: otan! Nan pouin gòl amin k-ap pasé.

GEDE ZARIYIN

Gin kèk lòt nèg ki di yo gin lizaj listoua, ki vlé fè nou konprann Dessalines chiré pit pasé li t-ap défann lamas. Nan lidé nèg sa yo Dessalines té fè akrochay ak tout gro zotobré ki t-ap pran tè péyi d-Ayiti pou yo ak fanmi yo sèlman. Alòs, jénéral ak majò mét ansanm, fè konplo touyé lanpérè. Eské sé vré? Eské lan-pouin lòt rézon? Ki mò ki touyé lanpérè?

Zouézo pa fè nich you sèl jou, min sé ti branch kolé ki fè kabann toutrèl. An nou kolé ti branch, jou va jou vyin, nich lan va fèt.

TET ANSANM

Lò Saint Domingue té anba pat Lafrans té gin 3 klas sosial ki t-ap kouazé kouto. Klas kolon blan manman yo, ak klas nèg lib yo. Nèg lib sa yo, sé té milat [piti kolon] ak nèg nouè nan k-té jouinn libèté tankou Tous-saint Dessalines ak Christophe. Pou Ayiti indépandan, sé klas nèg lib ak neg esklav ki té kolé tèt yo ansanm. Lè sa, fizi tiré, boukan flanbé 3 foua pa jou nan jadin péyi Saint Doming. Nèg nouè, milat, gason kou fanm, timoun kou granmoun lonjé douèt nan figi linjistis. Blan fransé rété diòl louvri...

CHYIN MANJE CHYIN

Min lò lindépandans parèt, jouèt chyin manjé chyin koumansé. Chak òm soti pou fé rout pa-l.

a[Ansyin lib yo té goumin fè lindé-pandans ak lèzòt yo pasé yo té bouké ouè blan fransé sèl mèt latè ak konmès Saint-Domingue. Lindépandans-lan pou yo, sa té vlé di: ansyin lib t-ap pran plas blan fransé. Kòm pifò yo sé té milat indépandans pou ansyin lib sé té milat sèl mèt péyi d-Ayiti. Kidonk sé you kèsion lajan k t-ap réglé. Pasé ansyin lib yo pat ouè you ti milat zonzon, san tè san léritaj vi-n manjé nan manjé lèzòt ki té fè rot zétid an france!

a[Nouvo lib yo, yo minm, té fè lindé-pandans pasé yo té sispèk nan afè blan fransé sa-a, you jou ti krik ti krak yo té ka rétounin esklav, kidonk yo t-ap pédi ni lajan ni pouvoua, ni sak ni krab. Min zonbi té déja gouté sèl. Nèg yo té koumansé gin tè, yo té gro jénéral nan lamé Louverture. Christophe té gin palè déja. E sé pa poutèt nou di sa ké li pa

Stirring the Pot of Haitian History

Christophe ankò. Min nou di sa pou fè konprann lò lindépandans fi-n fèt intérè Christophe ak DESSALINES ak tout lòt jénéral nèg nouè ki té nan lamé Louverture pat fouti égal égo ak intérè nèg boua ki pat janm gin anyin. Kidonk, nouvo lib yo, apré lindépandans, t-ap séyè séparé pouvoua ak plantasion égal égo ak ansyin lib.

c[Sa fè 2 sot nan 3. E jé rétyin zin. Jé rétyin zin-an, sé esklav. Poukisa esklav yo té fè lindépandans?

Esklav yo té fann nan dingon blan fransé pasé yo pat soti pou janmin, gran janmin, ankò travay pou choual sa galonnin. Yo té vlé tè yo t-ap travay la rélé yo chè mèt chè métrès.

DESSALINES té di minm bagay. E sé sètin Dessalines mandé anrajé dèyè tout ansyin lib ki t-ap vòlè tè yo. Min Dessalines t-ap chaché fè tè sa yo rét nan min léta, you léta abitan té koumansé sispèk pasé abitan té santi sé jénéral [nouè kou milat] ki t-ap poté Sin Sakréman nan posésion fèt Dié sila-a.

Abitan tonbé fè ròklò. Yo désann lavil, yo vépa travay tè. Dessalines fòsé yo tounin. [Zòdonans 25 oktòb 1804], li mandé kat didantité [7 désanm 1804]. Abitan fè ròklò pi rèd. Yo maron nan boua. Liv istoua pou lagaléri pa rinmin palé sou sa. Trè Chè Frè "L'Instruction Chrétienne" [ki pou koumansé pat gin doua fouré bouch nan késion konsa] pa fi-n rinmin nèg sa yo tròp. Min sa sé zafè pa Lafrans!

Tou sa pou di, ti nèg nan mòn pat kontan. Mouché Germain té lévé pran lèzam ak you kolonn abitan pasé yo pat dakò ak gouvènman sila-a [Madiou Tòm 3, p. 2L7 - Ardouin Tòm 6 p. 48]

DESSALINES MOURI POUKONT LI

Kidonk you diakout moun nan péyi-a té gin problèm ak gouvènman Dessalines-lan

Ansyin lib yo pat kontan poutèt Dessalines pat kité yo vòlè tè.

Abitan, nan mòn ak laplinn pat kontan pasé DESSALINES t-ap fòsé yo travay minm jan ak anvan lindépandans.

E si gin nouvo lib ki pat faché, yo pat fi-n trò kontan non plis, pasé DESSALINES pat ba yo pi fò tè li té pran nan min ansyin lib yo.

Nan lagè klas sosial yo té koumansé dépi prémié janvié 1804-la, DESSALINES té poukont li. Li pat nan intérè mas yo, sé sa k-fè mas yo pat soutni-l. Léta li t-ap séyè fè pap é abit péyi d-Ayiti-a, mas yo té ouè, klè kou dlo kòk, sé chèf yo ki ta pral dirijé-l, you kolonn birokrat tankou Inginac ak Boisrond Tonnerre.

Si you nonm ap chaché léson nan lanmò Dessalines-la, l-ap jouinn anpil, pasé sé soukous ou pran yè ki fè démin vansé pi bèl.

1[Tout moun jouinn jodi-a ap di sé linion tout ayisyin ki pou fè péyi-a vansé.

Lanmò dessalinesmoutré nou minm si gro jan dakò pou linion nan diòl, lò jou rivé li mété pié ak tout kouray sou tèt Ti Jan ak Ti Fifi.

2] Nou konnin jouinn jodi-a you gouvènman koté Léta ap kontrolé mouvman klas yo pa you rèv ni you tonton nouèl. Min nou konnin tou [sa DESSALINES pat konnin] sé lamas é lamas sèl ki pou dirijé you gouvènman konsa. Nan roulib sa-a, you nonm ta ka chaché ouè ki jan nan 20 èm sièk la you gouvènman tankou Allende [Chili] pa fè sètin érè ki sanblé -nan jan pa yo- ak érè Dessalines yo.

3] You lòt gro léson pou nou pran, lò nou fi-n réfléchi sou véritab rézon pou lakièl Jean jacques mouri, sé aprann pou nou tout aprann you vérité ki tris anpil. Istoua d-Ayiti tout bon-an, Istoua yo rélé Istoua-a, Istoua ki rantré nan mouèl événman yo avèk you digdal poukisa-a, Istoua lagè Gro jan ak Tijan, Pétion avèk Goman, Geffrard avèk Picot, Boyer ak Acau. Istoua ti poul sou granchimin avèk malfini sou do tòl, Istoua d-Ayiti sa-a ponko ékri.

L. RAYMOND

Espésial:
prémié fèt nasional ané-a

lindépandans dévan-dèyè

dapiyanp sou révolision

Vouala, le premier Janvier 1804, sous linstigasion du général Dessalines, par devant chef de la keksion, tout chef yo le signant, **L'Acte de l'Indépendance de l'Etat d'Haïti**

Mézanmi nou konprann? Si nou kouè nou konprann sé méyè pou La France. Si nou sispèk nou pa konprann, miyò pou péyi d-Ayiti. Pasé paròl yo palé la-a, yo pa palé-l pou nou konprann. E pou ki tout bri? Koté mistè sila-a kouché? Pou ki tout palé fransé sa-a sou lindépandans nou-an? Ki sa k-té fèt jounin sila-a, zòt pa ta rinmin nou konnin? Pasé nou tout konnin, dépi ti zòrèy mét lévit, rozèt nan kou pou tédéròm, sé pasé l-gin kozé pou l-di li pa vlé nèg Ginin konprann...

Kidonk, chimin jinnin. E dépi chimin an jinnin sé pozé pou n-pozé késion. Sé pa gro késion konpliké, késion nèg fò yo, non. Késion nèg sòt, késion k-sanblé la dous ki vyin. Pasé kouè-m si nou vlé mézanmi, késion k-pi fasil yo, sé yo minm pou nou pi pè. Pasé sé ladan yo zòt paré nas pou makonnin-n. 9 é 1, 10. Tout moun konn sa. Min g-on "jé rétyin zin" ladan. "Jé rétyin zin" sa-a, si n-bliyé-l, nou san lè rét ak Zéro. Kidonk, fò nou chaché sa zòt ban nou ak sa l-kinbé.

Zòt di nou, lé prémié janvié 1804, jénéral noua ak milat ki té goumin kont blan fransé yo réyini sou plas Gonayiv... Yo di atandi ké yo kalé Rochambeau, blan fransé bijé bésé tèt, Ayiti vi-n indépandan.

Trè byin, tonton. Min koté jénéral sa yo té sòti? Koté yo té aprann goumin? Epi, pa gin jénéral san lamé. Ki lès lamé yo té ginyin? Koté lamé sa- té sòti? ...E jé rétyin zin...

Gin you disètasion yo rinmin bay élèv klas bakaloréya. "Eské Toussaint té vlé lindépandans? Diskité..."

Mézanmi ala dé lapinn. Sa ki gin la-a pou diskité? Ki mélé zòtèy Ti Piè sa Toussaint té vlé, sa l-pat vlé! Listoua sé pa sa nèg té vlé, sé sa li té fè. An jouèt konsa, malè pa mal, sa ou té vlé-a sé pa li ou fè...

Sa pa vlé di poutan Toussaint pa gin anyin pou ouè ak késion lindépandans lan. Lò ou ap joué domino sé you bout ki minnin you lòt. Dékabès la pa fèt lò ou frapé min-ou sou tab la. Kidonk fò nou chanjé késion an. Ki sa gouvènman Toussaint an té fè ki gin rapò dirèk-dirèk ak lindépandans Ayiti?

Lò Toussaint monté opouvoua kòm gouvènè Sin-doming g-on oun latriyé nèg nouè ki t-ap goumin avèk mousié ki vi-n gro zotobré nan lamé fransé-a. Nèg sila yo vi-n gin tè, ak abitan ki t-ap bouriké pou tè sila yo ka fléri. Nou kapab di gin you klas sosial tou nèf ki pran chè nèt al kolé: nouvo lib yo.

Si n-kontinié palé présé -pasé sé pa bout sa-a k-intérésé-n nan kozé-a- nou kapab di toujou, klas sa-a pat gin minm intérè ak ni abitan san tè yo ni afranchi ki té gin tè dépi lontan. Gin pliziè dokiman ki moutré sa. 7 févriyé 1801 Toussaint pran you loua pou anpéché moun achté bitasion pi piti pasé 50 karo. Sé té you fason pou anpéché ti abitan sou prèl yo achté tè. You fason pou yo bijé travay sou tè gran plantè: "Min abitan yo pat vlé travay pou moun ankò, kit nouè, kit blan. Yo mété yo an 7 pou achté tè ansanm pou travay ansanm pou tèt pa yo! [Madiou, Tòm 2, p.88] Chak loua gouvènman-an pran, yo pasé sou li. Toussaint bijé voyé Dessalines al pété fièl you group vodou nan laplinn Cul-de-Sac. Lamour Dérance pran chinn nan mòn Bahoruco. Toussaint bijé pran loua pou maspinin kiltivatè ki t-ap "insandié, piyé, vòlè". [Loua 10 out 1801, loua 11 out 1801] Dessalines ki té gin 32 bitasion sou kont li [oui fout!] té konn antéré réfraktè yo tou vivan, dapré sa Mackenzie di. Kit sé vré, kit sé pa vré, sa pou nou sonjé, sé lagè pèpétièl [é san sékou] ki té gin ant nouvo rich yo ak abitan yo. E pi bèl égzanp lan sé istoua Moïse Louverture. Lò Toussaint ouè névé-l mété kò-l nan kan patizan pèp la pou rélé sou linjistis, li fiziè-l! Sé dépi sou doub 6 yo chita dékabès...

Késion-an sé pa dénigré ni Toussaint ni Christophe ni Dessalines ni Pétion. Késion-an sé fè yo désann sou gazon an, pou pèp la ka konprann ti kras, pasé dépi dat yo chita sou choual yo anlè-a, Channmas pa janm chanjé figi...

Lè Leclerc débaké ak lamé fransé, batay maré, nèg nouè pèdi, lè Toussaint Dessalines Christophe al pou siyin lapè, gin you pakèt abitan ki di yo pap mèt ba lèzam. Yo di lagè pa yo-a poko fini. Leçlerc fè anbaké Toussaint brid sou kou. Lòt jénéral yo rété nan lamé fransé-a. Lè sa-a, gin you bagay ki rivé Histoire d'Haïti a rozèt yo kouri pasé sou li. Jénéral nouè yo tonbé tiré sou rébèl nouè ki té réfizé fè lapè, ki t-ap fè gériya nan mòn nan. Pandan Leclerc al an vakans La Tortue [!], Dessalines, Chrsitophe, Pétion, Clerveau, Jean Louis Louverture al chasé nèg maron nan boua.

Poukisa sé yo blan fransé yo té voyé? Poukisa yo té aksépté? E sitou poukisa yo pa rivé kalé gériya yo?

Blan fransé té bézouin fè abitan olèmin. Leclerc té pran you loua pou tout abitan vi-n dépozé zam yo. Min jénéral fransé yo té konnin yo pa t-ap kapab rivé mouté sou do pèp la si yo pat gin indijèn k-ap ridé yo. Pou you gro péyi kalé you ti pèp, fò l-gin 5kièm kolòn li nan ti pèp la. Pandan lokipasiòn, mérikin té bijé fè La Garde d'Haïti. Sé pou minm rézon sa-a blan fransé pat kouri ak jénéral indijèn yo.

Anpil moun di Leclerc té gin lidé pran nèg sa yo apré. Sé trè posib. Min sa pa fèt. Sa pa fèt pasé li té bézouin yo pou fè pèp la olèmin pou li. Abitan yo pat ap goumin kankou lamé Toussaint an. Sé gériya yo t-ap fè. Pou kalé you gériya, fò gin moun ki konn péyi-a.

Poukisa Dessalines, Christophe, Pétion, Clerveau té aksépté goumin kont nèg nouè kanmarad yo pou lamé fransé-a? Gin nèg ki di sé konbèlann yo t-ap bay Leclerc, sé fint yo t-ap fè, asavoua ké yo té gin lidé chanjé kan dépi lè sa-a. Sé byin posib, min lidé yo pa intérésé nou. Listoua di nou yo t-al goumin.

Appendix 197

Gin nèg ki ta ka di sé pasé yo té méchan! Yo pap sis! Dessalines méchan ak pèp la épi Dessalines méchan ak Rochambeau, sé 2 grinn zanno dépaman.

Ki véritab rézon pou lakièl ansyin ak nouvo lib yo té goumin kont abitan yo?

Lè nouvo lib yo mét ba lèzam, yo rantré tou angran nan lamé Leclerc-a. Yo kinbé grad yo, yo kinbé zam yo, yo kinbé bitasion yo. Yo pa pèdi okinn nan privilèj yo t-ap joui yo. Min pou yo té kontinié bouè poua-a, fò yo té péyé réstoran.

Ansyin lib yo fè parèy. Nèg tankou Pétion ki té sot an France ak Leclerc vi-n chaché byin papa-l, annik kontinié fè sa li t-ap fè anvan an, obéyi chèf li. Kidonk, problèm nan sé you problèm klas sosial. Ansyin lib ak nouvo lib t-al goumin kont abitan pasé li té nan intérè **klas sosial pa yo. Yo té gin abitan ki t-ap truay pou yo, yo té vlé abitan sa yo kontinié bouriké. Yo apiyé sou kolon ak gouvènman fransé ki té déja vlé krazé nèg mòn yo. Yo pral fè alians ak klas abitan yo lè yo ouè avèk blan fansé lèspri yo pa t-ap janm pozé.** Yo vi-n ouè si yo pa kolé tèt ak pèp la yo pap sis! Min sé zam pèp la ki fè yo chjanjé lidé.

Pasé, sé pani 2 ni 3 nèg ki té réfizé lapè Leclerc-a. Té gin pliziè group ki t-ap minnin gériya sa-a. Sanglarou, Janvier Thomas, Auguste, Samedi Smith, Goman, Jean Panier, Lamour Dérance, Lafortune, Sanite Bélair, Charles Bélair, Sans Souci, Jacques Tellier, Macaya, Marougou, Macaque, V-a Malheureux, Noel Prieur, Mathieu Fourmis, Gilles Bambora, tou sa sé té chèf gériya, é té gin lòt ankò nèg bliyé.

E sé pa ni youn ni 2 koté non plis gériya sa yo t-ap fèt. Pandan Sans Souci ak nèg Congo yo té Dondon, té gin lòt chèf nan Nò-a: Macaya, V-a Malheureux etc. Janvier Thomas té Barradères, Auguste té Saint-Louis du Sud, Samedi Smith té nan Torbeck, Lamour Dérance té nan La Selle. Gériya té kouvri lakay tankou foumi rouj nan Kenscoff, tankou ti pouin ti koua nan kayé matématik.

Bon. An nou fè you pozé pou nou ouè sa n-aprann.

N-aprann you pakèt bagay. Nou sètin koulié-a, abitan ki t-ap planté tè, ki t-ap goumin dépi Boukmann pat janm mété ba lèzam. E lè nou réfléchi sou sa n-ap ouè kouman zòt anrajé. Zòt dékoupé "L'Histoire d'Haïti" an ti moso: périòd sési, périòd séla. Kòm ki diré gro Istoua d-Ayiti-a sé you pakèt "histoires" ki séparé. Zòt ta vlé fè n-konprann lò Leclerc kouri ak Toussaint, lapè vi-n fèt, lagè sispann. Epi kèk tan aprè, lagè lindépandans pran chè avèk Dessalines ak Pétion.

Nou minm nou di non. Périòd yo bon pou fè élèv lékòl sonjé dat ak non, pou yo pa mélanjé Geffrard Ainé ak Fabre Geffrard, La Crête à Pierrot kazèn, ak La Crête à Pierrot bato. Min périòd yo maské you pakèt vérité. Pasé lagè abitan saklé béché t-ap fè ak Boukmann ak Jean François ak Toussaint-an, sé li minm yo kontinié fè kont Toussaint, kont Leclerc, kont Dessalines, kont Pétion ak Rochambeau. Sé li minm Goman, Acau ak Péralte t-ap kontinié. Périòd aprè périòd, dépi la trèt pou jis jounin jodi, abitan pa janm chanjé kan. Sa ki pa vlé konprann, sé mèyè...pou LA FRANCE ak Etazini. Min nou tout ka ouè koulié-a, pou ki sa zòt déchiré kèk paj Istoua d-Ayiti-a pou fè lagè Lindépandans koumansé ak Dessalines. Si tout non dròl sa yo sité, sèt istoua dé Ti Nouèl Priyè, Va maléré, Makak, Jil Banmbora ak Sanglarou [you kolonn non sispèk] gin anpil lòt paròl k-ap obliyé palé... Sé rézon pou lakièl zòt pran stati chèf yo, li mété sou néchèl, li fè Place des Héros. Elèv lékòl di "des zéros" min sa-a, s-on lòt paròl krochi...Sa nou aprann pou n-pa bliyé: si pa gin PÈP, pa gin "héros".

198 *Stirring the Pot of Haitian History*

Gin you lòt késion yo rinmin diskité ak élèv bakaloréya [podiab!] asavoua dépi ki lè Dessalines ak Pétion té gin lidé goumin pou lindépandans. Ki mélé zòtèy Ti Piè! Listoua sé pa lidé you nonm ginyin. An jouèt konsa, malè pa mal, lidé ou ginyin sé pa sa ou fè...

Listoua aprann nou lò blan fransé gadé yo ouè goumin goumin, abitan pa mét ba lèzam, yo ouè sòlda nouè kou milat janbé nan kan rébèl tankou sa sot fèt Viétnam, yo nèvé, ponpé, piafé. Alòs jénéral nouè ki té nan lamé blan fransé yo vi-n gin 2 pié nan you grinn soulié. Yo vi-n nan pozision jinnin tankou manba avèk kréson nan mitan 2 kasav rouayal. Chak foua yo tounin sot batay, gériya fi-n kalé yo, blan an gadé yo you jan sispèk. Kòm koua: ki konfiolo ou gin ak nèg nouè kanmarad ou yo ki fè ou pa kalé yo?

Lò bab kanmarad ou pran difé, ou mété bab pa ou a la tranp. Jénéral yo té konnin kouman blan té fè dappiyanp sou Toussaint pasé yo té sispèk li. Yo koumansé sové grinn pa grinn janbé nan lopozision.

Charles Bélair, Larose ak François Capois La Mort té déja nan kan abtan yo. Capois té òganizé nèg nan Nò yo sériézman. agè-a té pran figi. Sitirasion an té vi-n difisil nèt pou ansyin ak nouvo lib yo. Pétion ki té rantré ak blan fransé yo pou krazé nèg nouè kouri chanjé kan. Magloire Ambroise pran chinn. Clerveau ak Christophe lévé kanpé. Fransé yo paré you pèlin pou Dessalines. Mouché pa pran, li sové, é malgré li t-ap konspiré dépi anvan, sé lè sa-a li rantré nan goumin tout bon vré, zam alamin.

Kidonk, é sé you vérité ki inpòtan anpil, sé gériya abitan yo ki fòsé 3/4 jénéral yo janbé nan kan pèp la. [Si pa gin pèp pa gin éro!] Abitan yo goumin pou fè lindépandans pou minm rézon yo té konmansé goumin nan Bois-Caïman, pou yo sispann travay pou choual k-ap galonnin!

Min éské sé konsa sa pasé?

Kouman fè non Makak, Sanglarou, Goman ak Banmbora pa anba papié lindépandans lan? Lò m-li Acte de l'Indépendance de l'Etat d'Haïti, mouin ouè you kolonn non byinnélvé ki sonnin kankou non fransé...Eské chèf yo té chanjé non?

Osnon, eské révolision an té chanjé chèf?

Pou mété blan fransé yo dèyò, sé tout nèg nouè yo ki té goumin bò kot abitan yo. Lamé ki fè dinniè batay pou lindépandans Ayiti-a sé you kokinn chinn tèt kolé, sé alians pliziè klas sosial: ansyin lib yo [Pétion etc.], nouvo lib yo [Dessalines etc.] ak ABITAN YO. Min nou sot ouè sé pa konsa ansyin ak nouvo lib yo vi-n jouinn mas yo. Sé sitirasion-an ki té fòsé yo. Kidonk, nan dinniè kout kat la, tou lé 3 klas yo té dakò pou lindépandans. Yo té di:an nou mété ansanmm pou nou fout blan yo dèyò. Min yo pat di ki jan kat-la t-ap bat lò lagè-a fini.

Yo pat di, min jénéral ki té fi-n pran gou bonbon yo, té koumansé ranjé kabann yo byin bonnè, pou lè lannouit rivé yo té gin koté pou dòmi.

Atout sé pa yo ki té koumansé batay-la, atout sé pa yo ki té minnin plis moun ladan, pasé yo té gin linstrisksion -kit militè, kit litèrè-, pasé yo té gin ekspérians ansyin "politichyin" yo, ansyin ak nouvo lib yo éliminé youn apré lòt tout chèf ki té kolé ak pèp-la.

Lò Dessalines pran Charles Bélair, li di Leclerc: "Sé pa ti kras faché mouin faché kont tout moun ki suiv Charles Bélair nan révòlt kriminèl li-a... Sé pou nou konsidéré Charles kankou you chèf brigan épi pou nou pini-l kankou yo pini brigan" [Lèt Dessalines bay Leclerc, 23 Fruktidò] E lò lagè-a pran chè, lò Dessalines ak Pétion janbé vi-n jouinn pèp-la, ansyin

Appendix 199

chèf sa yo pa sispann konsidéré abitan yo kòm "brigan". Gin nèg ki di yo té gin "intansion sékrèt". Kouman yo fè konnin E ki gadé zòtèy Ti Piè. Listoua pa fèt sou intansion piblik alé ouè intansion sékrèt. An jouèt konsa, malè pa mal, intansion sékrèt ou chanjé...

An nou gadé sa k-té pasé... Lò Pétion kité lamé fransé yo, li kontré ak Petit Noel Prieur, angiz li fè alians avè li, li bouè soup sou tèt Ti Noel. Li lobé Prieur, épi li nonnmin Clerveaux jénéral troup gériya mouché-a. Ki fè, Prieur pèdi fil, Clerveaux monté, Pétion monté pi ro. Lò Pétion ak Clerveaux sènnin Okap, Christophe al jouinn yo. Li pasé sou tèt Prieur, li té déja tou pat vlé ouè. Konsa, grinn pa grinn, nouvo lib ak ansyin lib yo fouré kò yo nan lamé-a, kankou Tonton Nouèl nan lachéminé. Sé anro yon pasé.

Lò Dessalines janbé nan lagè-a, li sènnin Saint-Marc, li rélé Larose vi-n édé-l. Larose di gériya-l yo pap fè you pa pou u ni ridé nèg ki té vann Charles Bélair bay Leclerc-la. Boisrond Tonnerre ki té rinmin Jean Jacques kou 2 grinn jé-l, di: lò Larose kuipé mouché, Dessalines fè ranmasé tout travayè yo té ka jouinn, fizié yo si yo pa vini. An 8 jou, tout moun konn tiré, Dessalines vi-n gin lamé pa-l, li vag Larose.

Sé sètin, konésans ansyin ak nouvo lib yo té nésésè an pil pou lagè lindépandans lan. Pétion té konn tiré kannon. Dessalines sitou té you michan militè, ansyin élèv Toussaint Louverture. Nou pa kapab di lindépandans t-ap pasé pi byin SI nèg sa yo pat rantré. SI yo pat antré, li té ka pa fèt ditou. Epi, sitou, Listoua pa gin si. Listoua sé eksplikasion sa ki rivé. E sa ki té rivé-a klè. Pasé yo té gin konésans politik ak konésans militè, ansyin ak nouvo lib yo pran kontròl lagè-a. E kòm kontròl militè lagè-a chita pouvoua yo, yo pran kontròl politik la tou. Yo fouré min, lévé kokin. Yo fè you koudéta nan lopzision, DAPIYANP SOU RÉVOLISION.

Paròl la lou, pa vré? Pandan m-ap ékri sa-a, kòm ki diré m-ouè sa m-ap di. Kòm ki diré m-ouè konsékans sa gin pou yè matin, sa gin pou démin soua. Kòm ki diré m-konprann pouki Goman té goumin kont Rochambeau, pouki minm Goman sa-a té goumin kont Pétion... Kòm ki diré m-konprann pouki apré lindépandans gin nèg ki pa mèt ba lèzam.

1804 sé you viktoua, sé vré. Sé you viktoua sou kolon yo, sou La France, ak tout lòt péyi ki té konprann tè indyin yo té mouri kité-a t-ap tounin gad manjé yo. Sé you viktoua PÈP AYISYIN, pasé li té gin okazion fè Léta pa-l nan péyi pa-l. Sé trè byin si nou répété nou sé prémié ti pèp nan l-Amérik la ki té rélé: "Yanki no home" dèyè prémié yanki, dépi nan tan lontan. Sé trè byin, min sa pa rèt la. Prémié Janvié sila-a, Dessalines palé ak pèp-la an kréyòl, min kòm li pat li papié, nou pa konnin sa li té di. Poutan, Boisrond Tonnerre té li diskou fransé Dessalines nan pou yo. Li té di yo: aba La France. Li té di yo: nèg ki rélé nèg tout bon fèt pou goumin pou yo pa pèdi libèté yo. Li té di yo: Indépandance ou la Mort . Min li té di yo tou, an bon fransé, pasé Boisrond Tonnerre té konn ékri fransé:

[Pèp,] si janmin ou réjété, osnon si janmin ou babié sou règlèman loua k-ap protéjé avni-ou la dépozé nan tèt mouin pou pròp bonnè-ou, oua mérité sò tout pèp ingra"

22 Oktòb 1804, 9 moua apré lindépandans, Dessalines pran you loua pou fizié abitan ki t-ap kouri sové al an egzil. 25 Oktòb 1804, li déklaré abitan ki réfizé travay nan mòn, ki vi-n kaché lavil sé éléman danjré, soua k-ap chaché sové, soua ki vi-n mèt dézòd. An Janvié 1807, Goman, nèg boua, ansyin maron, gason kanson, nèg ki t-ap goumin pou abitan dépi sou tan Louverture ak Leclerc, viré gériya li-a sou Pétion. Alòs?

Mézanmi, kòm ki diré mouin tris. Kòm ki diré m-kontan épi m-tris an minm tan. Kòm ki diré m-konprann pouki g-on pakèt paj ti zòrèy déchiré nan Istoua d-Ayiti nou-an. You pakèt paj. You diakout chapit. Ginyin li boulé. Gin lòt li viré dévan dèyè. Gin lòt li séré pou jé nou pa kontré. Kòm ki diré m-konprann valè manti k-pati nan pa konprann ak fèt éspré...

Jan n;-ouè sa-a yé la, ginlè fò n-chanjé profésè, oui...

L. RAYMOND

200   *Stirring the Pot of Haitian History*

Bibliography for English Translation, Translators' Note, and Afterword (2020)

Anchel, Robert. 'Boissy d'Anglas, François Antoine de'. *Encyclopædia Britannica*, edited by Hugh Chisholm, vol. 4, 11th ed. Cambridge University Press, 1911, p. 155.

Barthes, Roland. 'Écrivains et Écrivants'. *Essais critiques*. Paris, Seuil, 1964.

——. *S/Z*. Paris: Seuil, 1970.

——. *Le Plaisir du texte*. Paris, Seuil, 1973.

Beauvoir, Max. *Le grand recueil sacré, ou, Répertoire des chansons du vodou haïtien*. Port-au-Prince, Edisyon Près Nasyonal d'Ayiti, 2008.

Beauvoir, Rachel, and Didier Dominique. *Savalou E*. Montreal, Les Éditions du CIDIHCA, 2003.

Blackburn, Robin. *The Overthrow of Colonial Slavery, 1776–1848*. London, Verso, 1988.

Bonilla, Yarimar. 'Burning Questions: The Life and Work of Michel-Rolf Trouillot', 1949–2012. *NACLA Report on the Americas*, vol. 46, no. 1, 2013, pp. 82–84.

Casimir, Jean. *Pa bliye 1804/Souviens-toi de 1804*. Port-au-Prince, Communication Plus, 2004.

——. 'From Saint-Domingue to Haiti: To Live Again or to Live at Last!' Prologue to *The World of the Haitian Revolution*, edited by David Patrick Geggus and Norman Fiering. Bloomington, Indiana University Press, 2009, pp. xi–xviii.

Castera, Georges. *Konbèlann*. Montreal, Éditions Nouvelle optique, 1976.

Charles, Carolle. *The Haitian Americans: Transnationalism in the Construct of Haitian Migrants' Racial Categories of Identity in New York City*. New Haven, Human Relations Area Files, 1998.

——. 'New York 1967–71, Prelude to "Ti Difé Boulé"', *Journal of Haitian Studies*, vol. 19, no. 2, 2013, pp. 152–59.

Clarfield, Gerard H. *Timothy Pickering and American Diplomacy, 1795–1800*. Columbia, University of Missouri Press, 1969.

Clarke de Dromantin, Patrick. *Les réfugiés jacobites dans la France du XVIIIè siècle: l'exode de toute une noblesse pour cause de religion*. Presses Universitaires de Bordeaux, 2005.

Comhaire-Sylvain, Suzanne. 'Haitian Creole'. *Le Créole haïtien*. Wetteren, Imprimerie De Meester; Port-au-Prince, Chez l'auteur, 1936.

———. *Les Contes haïtiens: 1ère partie Maman d'leau*. Wetteren, Imprimerie De Meester, 1937.

———. *Les Contes haïtiens: 2ème partie conjoint animal ou démon déguisé*. Wetteren, Imprimerie De Meester, 1937.

Crawford-Adiletta, Laura. 'Weather and Climate in Haiti'. *traveltips.usatoday*, www.traveltips.usatoday.com/weather-climate-haiti-12394.html. Accessed June 3, 2020.

Dällenbach, Lucien. *Le Récit spéculaire. Essai sur la mise en abyme*. Paris, Seuil, 1977.

Daut, Marlene. *Tropics of Haiti: Race and the Literary History of the Haitian Revolution in the Atlantic World, 1789–1865*. Liverpool University Press, 2015.

DeGraff, Michel. 'Linguistic Equality Is a Precondition for Political and Economic Equity'. *Boston Review*, May 9, 2016.

Dejean, Yves. *Yon lekòl tèt anba nan yon peyi tèt anba*. Port-au-Prince, FOKAL, 2006.

De Lacroix, Pamphile. *Mémoires pour servir à l'Histoire de la Révolution de St-Domingue*. Paris, Pillet aîné, 1819.

Desrivières, Jean Durosier. 'Brève exploration de la littérature en langue créole en Haïti, de ses balbutiements à son affirmation', June 6, 2019, www.berrouet-oriol.com/litterature/breve-exploration-de-la-litterature-en-langue-creole-en-haiti-de-ses-balbutiements-a-son-affirmation/. Accessed April 19, 2020.

Dominique, Jean. 'L'Istoua d'Ayiti? Youn tiré kont, youn chèché kont', 1977, cited in Woodson, Drexel G. 'Byen Pre Pa Lakay', *Journal of Haitian Studies*, vol. 19, no. 2, 2013, pp. 183–202.

Dorsainville, Roger. *Toussaint Louverture, ou, La vocation de la liberté*. 1965. Montreal, Éditions du CIDIHCA, 1987.

Dubois, Laurent, and John D. Garrigus. *Slave Revolution in the Caribbean, 1789–1804: A Brief History with Documents*. New York, Bedford/St. Martin's, 2017.

Dubois, Laurent, Kaiama L. Glover, Nadève Ménard, Millery Polyné, and Chantalle Verna, eds. *The Haiti Reader: History, Culture, Politics*. Durham, NC, Duke University Press, 2020.

Dupuy, Alex. *Rethinking the Haitian Revolution: Slavery, Independence, and the Struggle for Recognition*. Foreword by Robert Fatton. Rowman & Littlefield, 2019.

Farmer, Paul. *AIDS and Accusation: Haiti and the Geography of Blame*. Berkeley, University of California Press, 1992.

Fatton, Robert. *Roots of Haitian Despotism*. Lynne Rienner, 2007.
Fick, Carolyn. 'Emancipation in Haiti: From Plantation Labour to Peasant Proprietorship'. *After Slavery: Emancipation and Its Discontents*, edited by Howard Temperley. London, Frank Cass, 2000, pp. 11–40.
Franketienne [Franck Étienne]. *Mûr à crever*. Port-au-Prince, Presses Port-au-Princiennes, 1968.
——. *Dézafi: roman*. Port-au-Prince, Fardin, 1975.
——. *Dézafi*. Translated by Asselin Charles. Charlottesville, University of Virginia Press, 2018.
Freeman, Bryant, and Jowel Laguerre. *Haitian Creole-English Dictionary*. Lawrence, Institute of Haitian Studies University of Kansas, 1996–2004.
——. *English-Haitian Creole Dictionary*. Lawrence, Institute of Haitian Studies University of Kansas, 2010.
Genette, Gérard. *Palimpsestes: la littérature au second degré*. Paris, Seuil, 1982.
——. *Palimpsests: Literature in the Second Degree*. Translated by Channa Newman and Claude Doubinsky, Lincoln, University of Nebraska Press, 1997.
Gilbert, Myrtha. 'Mizè, Pwodiksyon agrikòl ak Pwojè gwo pisans nan peyi d'Ayiti'. *Le Nouvelliste*, March 3, 2016.
Hebblethwaite, Benjamin. 'French and Underdevelopment, Haitian Creole and Development: Language Policy Problems and Solutions in Haiti'. *Journal of Pidgin and Creole Languages*, vol. 27, no. 2, 2012, pp. 255–302.
Hurbon, Laennec. *Culture et dictature en Haïti*. Paris, L'Harmattan, 1979.
'Jean-Baptiste Chavannes'. *The Louverture Project*, www.thelouvertureproject.org/index.php?title=Jean_Baptiste_Chavannes. Accessed July 24, 2019.
Johnson, Ronald. *Diplomacy in Black and White: John Adams, Toussaint Louverture, and Their Atlantic World Alliance*. Athens, University of Georgia Press, 2014.
Mackenzie, Charles. *Notes on Haiti, made during a residence in that republic*. London, H. Colburn and R. Bentley, 1830.
Madiou, Thomas. *Histoire d'Haïti*. Port-au-Prince, Henri Deschamps, 1987–89 [1848].
Nicholls, David. *From Dessalines to Duvalier: Race, Colour and National Independence in Haiti*. New Brunswick, Rutgers University Press, 1996.
Oriol, Michèle. *Histoire et dictionnaire de la révolution et de l'indépendance d'Haïti: 1789–1804*. Port-au-Prince, Fondation pour la recherche iconographique et documentaire, 2002.
Past, Mariana. *Reclaiming the Haitian Revolution: Race, Politics and History in Twentieth-Century Caribbean Literature*. Ph.D. dissertation, Duke University, 2006.
Past, Mariana, and Benjamin Hebblethwaite. 'Ti difé boulé sou istoua Ayiti: Considering the Stakes of Trouillot's Earliest Work'. *Cultural Dynamics*, vol. 26, no. 2, 2014, pp. 149–61.

Perrego, Pierre. 'Les Créoles'. *Le Langage*, edited by André Martinet. Paris, Encyclopédie de la Pléiade, Gallimard, 1968.
Piarroux, Renaud *et al.* 'Understanding the Cholera Epidemic, Haiti'. *Emerging infectious diseases*, vol. 17, no. 7, 2011, pp. 1161–68. doi:10.3201/eid1707.110059.
Pierre, Jacques. *Kite Kè M Pale*. Durham, Torchflame Books, 2016.
Piou, Nanie. 'Linguistique et idéologie: ces langues appelées *créoles*'. *Dérives*, vol. 16, 1979, pp. 13–30.
Ponge, Francis. 'Le Pré'. *La Fabrique du Pré*. Geneva, Skira, 1971, n. pag.
Pressoir, Catts, Ernst Trouillot, and Hénock Trouillot. *Historiographie d'Haïti*. Mexico City, Instituto Panamericano de Geografía e Historia, 1953.
Rabaté, Jean-Michel. 'Barthes, Roland'. *The Johns Hopkins Guide to Literary Theory and Criticism*, edited by Michael Groden *et al.*, Baltimore, Johns Hopkins University Press, 2005–12. www.litguide.press.jhu.edu.
Raymond, L. (Michel-Rolph Trouillot). 'Pou drésé kozman'. *Lakansièl*, vol. 2, 1975, pp. 39–40.
———. 'Ki mò ki touyé lanpérè'. *Lakansièl*, vol. 3, 1975, pp. 37–39.
———. 'Dézafi'. *Lakansièl*, vol. 4, 1976, pp. 30–32.
———. 'Lindépandans dévan-dèyè: dapiyanp sou révolision'. *Lakansièl*, vol. 4, 1976, pp. 46–50.
Roc, François. *Dictionnaire de la Révolution haïtienne: 1789–1804: dictionnaire des événements, des emblèmes et devises, des institutions et actes, des lieux et des personnages*. Port-au-Prince, Éditions Guildives, 2006.
Ros, Martin. *Night of Fire: The Black Napoleon and the Battle for Haiti*. New York, Sarpedon, 1994.
Schuller, Mark. *Humanitarian Aftershocks in Haiti*. New Brunswick, Rutgers University Press, 2016.
Sylvain, Georges. *Cric? Crac! Les fables de La Fontaine racontées par un montagnard haïtien et transcrites en vers créoles*. Paris, Ateliers haïtiens, 1901.
Taber, Rob. *The Issue of Their Union: Family, Law, and Politics in Western Saint-Domingue, 1777–1789*. Ph.D. dissertation, University of Florida, 2015.
Targète, Jean, and Raphael G. Urciolo. *Haitian Creole-English Dictionary with Basic English-Haitian Creole Appendix*. Kensington, MD, Dunwoody Press, 1993.
Tarter, Andrew. 'Haiti Is Covered with Trees'. *Enviro Society*, May 19, 2016, www.envirosociety.org/2016/05/haiti-is-covered-with-trees/. Accessed April 24, 2020.
Temperley, Howard. *After Slavery: Emancipation and Its Discontents*. London, Frank Cass, 2000.
Trouillot, Hénock. *Chair, Sang et Trahison*. Port-au-Prince, Imprimerie Pierre-Noël, 1947.
———. *Le Drapeau bleu et rouge: une mystification historique*. Port-au-Prince, Imprimerie N.A. Théodore, collection 'Haitiana', 1958.

———. *La République de Pétion et le peuple haïtien*. Port-au-Prince, Société haïtienne d'histoire, de géographie et de géologie, 1960.
———. *L'Itinéraire d'Aimé Césaire*. Port-au-Prince, Imprimerie des Antilles, 1968.
———. *Lumumba, cette lumière (tragédie africaine)*. Port-au-Prince, Imprimerie des Antilles, 1971.
———. *Les Limites du créole dans notre enseignement*. Port-au-Prince, Imprimerie des Antilles, 1980.
———. *Introduction à une histoire du vaudou*. Port-au-Prince, Éditions Fardin, 1983.
———. *Les Origines sociales de la littérature haïtienne*. Port-au-Prince, Imprimerie N.A. Théodore, 1986 [1962].
Trouillot, Lyonel. *Les Fous de Saint-Antoine*. Port-au-Prince, Deschamps, 1989.
———. *Agase lesperans*. Port-au-Prince, Atelier Jeudi Soir, 2017.
Trouillot, Michel-Rolph. Interview about *Ti difé boulé sou istoua Ayiti* with Richard Brisson. *Radio Haiti-Inter*, July 1977, Radio Haiti Archive, www.repository.duke.edu/dc/radiohaiti/RL10059-RR-0094_01.
———. *Ti difé boulé sou istoua Ayiti*. Brooklyn, Edisyon Lakansièl, 1977.
———. *Haiti, State against Nation: The Origins and Legacy of Duvalierism*. New York, Monthly Review Press, 1990.
———. *Silencing the Past: Power and the Production of History*. Boston, Beacon Press, 1995.
———. *Ti dife boule sou istwa Ayiti*. Port-au-Prince, Edisyon KIK, 2012.
Trouillot-Lévy, Jocelyne. '*Ti dife boule sou istwa Ayiti*, yon klasik pami klasik', *Journal of Haitian Studies*, vol. 19, no. 2, 2013, pp. 172–77.
Ulysse, Gina A., Nadève Ménard, and Evelyne Trouillot. *Why Haiti Needs New Narratives [= Sa k fè Ayiti bezwen istwa tou nèf = Pourquoi Haïti a besoin de nouveaux discours: a post-quake chronicle]*. Middletown, Wesleyan University Press, 2015.
Valdman, Albert, Iskra Iskrova, Jacques Pierre, Nicolas André, Benjamin Hebblethwaite *et al*. *Haitian Creole-English Bilingual Dictionary*. Bloomington, Indiana, Creole Institute, 2007.
Winston, James, and John Brown Russwurm. *The Struggles of John Brown Russwurm: The Life and Writings of a Pan-Africanist Pioneer, 1799–1851*. New York University Press, 2010.
Woodson, Drexel G. 'Byen Pre Pa Lakay'. *Journal of Haitian Studies*, vol. 19, no. 2, 2013, pp. 183–202.
Woodson, Drexel G. and Brackette F. Williams, 'In Memoriam Dr. Michel-Rolph Trouillot (1949–2012)'. *Caribbean Studies*, vol. 40, no. 1, 2012, pp. 153–62.
Zéphir, Flore. *The Haitian Americans*. Westport: Greenwood Press, 2004.

Index

Adams, John 104, 128
Africa 17
Agé, Pierre (General) 106, 117, 147, 166
Ago 39
agrarian society 54
Akao 54
America 17
  see also United States
American, Americans 40, 92, 100, 103
  American capitalists 104–105
  American consul 104, 129
  commissioners betraying Toussaint Louverture 166
  Louverture purchasing weapons from 169
  Louverture's collusion with 107
  Moïse's attitude toward 151
  ships at Cape Haitian wharf 130
  ships patrolling outside Jacmel
  Stevens' letter to government 150
  trading with Toussaint Louverture 128
ancien libre, anciens libres 17–18, 22
  allied with French camp 114
  as a clique 107
  as enemies of the French government (in 1796) 93
  blockaded in South by English 103
  collaboration with Toussaint Louverture's organization 145–47, 169
  control of land 86
  defeat in War of the South 115
  Dessalines' recruitment of 113
  differences with nouveaux libres 87
  fighting against Toussaint Louverture (in 1799) 110
  fighting nouveaux libres 89, 96, 150
  fleeing Jacmel (in 1800) 112
  impact of Villatte Affair on 92
  Jacmel as stronghold of 110
  joining nouveaux libres 87
  Louverture's relationship with 94
  mistakes of 90
  problems of 87
  relationship with Sonthonax 94
  Republican position of 101
  returning to French camp 149, 167
  Rigaud's leadership of 100
  role in military commission judging Moïse 152
  seizure of fleeing colonists' property 88, 98
  wealth of 86
Angola 24
Anse-à-Veau 129
Artibonite Valley 83
Aséfi 6
authoritarian agrarian system (caporalisme agraire) 142–43
  masses' refusal to obey 143
Ayiti Toma 52, 88, 106, 120

Badagri, Ogou (Vodou loua) 141
Bainet 112
Balaguer (Joaquín)
  killing Haitians 23
Balcarres (Earl), Alexander Lindsay (governor of Jamaica) 103
Bánica 153

baptism of slaves 17
Barada, Félix 144
Basel (Switzerland) 116
Bauvais, Louis-Jacques 107, 110, 113
Bel Air (neighborhood) 138
Belair, Charles 145, 148–49, 156
Belair, Sanité 149
Besse, Marcial 80
bezique (cards) 25
Biassou (rebel leader), 72
   as Viceroy of Occupied Territories 125
   guerrilla leader 56
   selling slaves 126
   Vodou priest 56
Bible, the 10
   contradictions within 17
   submission within 17
black Spartacus (description of Toussaint Louverture) 159, 165
Blanc-Cassenave 146
blood 23, 108–109, 115
   hereditary (psychological) illness of Haitians xxx, 7, 43, 51, 109, 115
   oath taken at Bois Caïman 57
Bois-Neuf (reference to Frankétienne's *Dézafi*) 29
Bois-Pin 59
Bonaparte, Napoleon 115, 120, 122, 150, 167, 168
Bonaventure 80
Bonn 34
Boogeyman (Charles Oscar Étienne, 'Chaloska') 135
Bordeaux 34–35, 38, 147
Borel 69
Borgella, General Jérôme-Maximilien 138, 147
Boston xxxii
Bouanèf 176
   see also Bois-Neuf
Bouapiro ('Tallest Tree') 82
Boudet, Jean 166
Boukman (Boukman Dutty) 159
   guerrilla leader 56
   Vodou priest 56

bourgeois, bourgeoisie
   French controlling Saint-Domingue 26
   social class (general) 14
   see also French
Boyer, General and President Jean-Pierre 7
   in Cape Haitian 1820 7
   in Jérémie 8
   in Santo Domingo 1822 7
   making Dominican blood flow 23
Brazil
   as prototype for sugarcane plantations 25
   exploitation of laborers within 25
Bréda, Gilles see Moïse
buccaneers 11, 23
Buteau, Pierre (historian) 182
Bwa Kayiman (Bois Caïman), Ceremony of
   as blood oath 57
   as mystical ceremony 57
   as political oath 57
   as strategy meeting 57

Caco leader 54
Les Cahiers du vendredi ix, x, xv, xvii, xviii, xxii
calinda rhythm, dance, and ceremony 55
   as cultural celebration, Vodou celebration, and political 'meeting' 57
   role in hatching plots 60
de Cambefort, Joseph-Paul-Augustin (Colonel) 51
Camp-Perrin 153
candelabra cactus thicket 6
Caonabo 23
Cape Haitian (city) 7, 24, 27, 38, 46, 48, 51, 62, 70–71, 77, 85–86, 88–89, 92, 103, 107, 122, 125, 129–30, 144–46, 151, 166–67
   setting fire to (in 1802) 120
capitalist
   countries (general category) 129
   economic commissioners of 129, 130

208   *Stirring the Pot of Haitian History*

Caradeux 13
Carlo 107
cart-pusher 161
Casimir, Jean xxix
Castera, Georges xiii, xxi, 177, 180
Cathéart (English spy) 127
Catholic Church 137, 140, 158
  blessing slavery 17
  Constitution of 1801 gives territorial limits to Catholic priests 159
  farcical aspects of 158
  influence on Haitian politics 69n37
  priests' prediction of Louverture's arrival 159
Cavaillon 112
Central Plateau 83
Champs-de-Mars 109, 169
Chavannes, Jean-Baptiste 47–48
  coalition sought with slaves 47
Chanlatte, Antoine 117, 146
Chansi (Colonel) 156
Chaplèt 59
Christophe, Henri 40, 106, 114, 143–44, 155, 165–67, 169
  1820 death posited as end of Haitian Revolution 40n19
  American manipulation of (Edward Stevens' letter to Pickering) 150–53
  attack on Cape Haitian 167n93
  defeat by Leclerc 120
  order to burn Cape Haitian 120
  personal wealth 127
  recruitment by Louverture 146
  role in siege of Jacmel 110–112
chwal ('horse', person possessed by a *loua*) 141
  chwal function of the State 141
city person (description of Grinn Prominnin) 6
class (social) 14, 22, 28, 32, 44, 65, 66, 73, 80, 108, 142
  as coalitions 67
  as social force 98–99, 105, 155, 161
  class interests controlling France 34

class struggle 136
  diversity within Toussaint Louverture's organization 145
  how it seized power 51
  interests of 123
  living out primary conflict 26
  Louverture disguising 163
  relationship to authority 135
  role in controlling country 25
  situation after revolution 126
  transfer in 133
Clément, Mister (metaphor for thieving politician) 126
  as social climber 126
Clément (plantation) 40
Clervaux, Augustin 80, 107, 108, 110, 120, 144, 147
coalitions 40–41, 69
  definition of 68
  formed by French bourgeoisie 44
  of big colonists 42
  of free people 42–43
  of French commissioners and freedmen 62–63, 68, 70–72, 83
  of Hédouville and Rigaud 99
  of Toussaint Louverture and slave masses 72, 81, 90, 147
  of whites 43
  sought by *petits blancs* (which failed) 68–69
  split of 44–49
cock fighting
  metaphor for Saint-Domingue 76, 96, 100
code *see kòd*
Code noir see kòd
coffee xxxv, 6, 24, 130
  as booming commodity crop (in 1789) 131
  big traders selling to France 35
  connection to slavery 27
  destined for foreigners (unlike food crops) 25
  planting sugarcane instead of 24
colonists *see* French, Spanish, Dutch, Americans

color (race)
    color prejudice benefiting colonists 43–44
    color problem 43, 107
    during War of the South 108
    ideological interests of *petits blancs* 98
    manipulation 107–108
    prejudice 105–106, 148
    prejudice in the South 106
    prejudice of Hédouville 105
    prejudice reinforced by family ideology 156
    prejudice within Rigaud's camp 107
Columbus, Christopher 22
commissioners (French) 26, 62, 68, 77
    alliance of Louverture's group with 81, 82, 92
    American 166
    and color prejudice 44, 47
    and exploitation 42
    and free coalition 42
    and plantation owners 37–38, 43–44, 46, 48
    aristocrats' political commissioners 66
    conflicts with big landowners 45
    consequences of ending slavery for 81
    control of production 131
    declining dominance of (after 1789) 98–99
    economic 34–35, 129
    economic dominance of 136, 139
    failures of their army 72
    fighting northern plantation owners 48
    Louverture's use of 163
    loyalty of mulattos to 73
    loyalty of the army to 46
    Moïse's defiance of 152
    not owning plantations 45
    offering freedom to slaves (on June 21, 1793) 71–72
    offering property to slave leaders 72
    pitting *anciens libres* against *nouveaux libres* 96
    political 34
    power of 49, 138
    recruitment into Louverture's army 146
    role of coalitions for 62, 63, 67, 70
    serving France 34
    special commissioners (of June 1800) 112
    The Second Civil Commission 64
    The Third Civil Commission 93, 96, 116
    threats posed (after 1800) 116
    trying to save Saint-Domingue for France 72
    versus aristocrats 71
    versus slaves 123
    waning power after Galbaud Affair 124
    with *nouveaux libres* controlling Saint-Domingue, 94
    withdrawing support for *anciens libres* (1794) 87
commodity crops
    controlled by commissioner classes 37, 139
    higher taxes on outgoing under Toussaint Louverture 129
    Louverture's government's preference for 132
    opposition to food crops 25, 123, 124–25, 137
    relationship to dominance 154
    relationship to economic dependence 131–32, 134
    selling under Louverture 114
    sold to France 34, 37
conflict, conflicts 123–24, 141
    banner conflict 123, 133
    disguising of 154
    entangled stage 13, 50, 153
    growing stage 13
    ideological 53
    in camp of *nouveaux libres*
    sitting astride the state 141

210   *Stirring the Pot of Haitian History*

slave versus owner 13
unbound stage 13, 49, 53, 72
see also contradiction
Congo 24
Connecticut 130
Constitution of 1801
abolishment of slavery 137
acknowledgement of Saint-Domingue revolution 137
authoritarian agrarian system 143
bias towards big traders and plantation owners 139
bias towards *nouveaux libres* 137
exclusive recognition of Catholic religion 140, 158
guarantee freedom 137
limitations of fieldworkers' freedoms 139
maintenance of conflict between French and Creole 138
outlawing divorce 159
protection of property owners 137
reflecting the counterweight function 140
reflecting the Gordian knot function 138–39
reflecting the *vèvè* function 137–39
contradiction, contradictions xxx, 82, 179
between Slavery and Freedom 123
internal to society 140
within Bible 17
within Constitution 140
within Haitian society and its structures xiii, xxii
within middle class 32
within superior position of domestic slaves, urban slaves, and overseers 30
see also conflict
copper 89, 131
Corail Affair 106
cord *see kòd*
Coronio, Stephen 129
Cotereau 153
cotton 24, 131

counterweight 139–40
coup (d'état) 8
metaphor for the State's function in balancing society's contradictions 140
craftspeople
abandonment of by French bourgeoisie 95
commodity production valued over 132
dependence of French bourgeoisie on 64
Creole (Haitian Creole) language 16, 179, 183
'Creole corner' approach within Haitian diasporic publications xxi
'Creole' (*Kreyòl*) as questionable label 175
as rules-based 10
as tool of resistance 56
conflict with the French language in Constitution of 1801 138
creating form and meaning with xxiii
developing institutions that prioritize xxxiii
feature of native-born culture 53
Haitian Creolists xxvi
limits on potential xxxii
linguistic equality as a precondition for political and economic equity xxxi
progress of xxi
status of in Haiti xxxii
the choice to write in xxxii

Dahomey 24
oath ceremony 57
spirits 57
Dalban 166
Danes 129
d'Anglas, François-Antoine Boissy 162–63
Daugy 69
De Lacroix, Pamphile 127
Delva 91, 110

dependence 25, 36
  and class that serves foreigners 99
  and commissioner class 98
  as fundamental Haitian problem 105
  economic and political dependence 127–28, 130–31
  feature of primary industry 37, 123
  Hédouville's goal of 101
  relationship to commodity crops 131
  relationship to food plots 132
  Rigaud's position on 104
  Toussaint Louverture's ignoring of 134
  versus independence 38, 124, 125, 137–38
Dérance, Lamour 56
d'Esparbès 64, 70
Desrouleaux, Louis 80
Desruisseaux, Renaud 91
Dessalines, Célimène 156
Dessalines, Jean-Jacques
  abuse of fieldworkers 143
  among leaders of *nouveaux libres* 85–86, 90, 106, 147, 153, 155, 157, 169
  attack on Jacmel (1799) 110–12
  attack on the North with Louverture (1801) 144
  attempt to marry his daughter to Alexandre Pétion 156
  capture of Belair 145n78
  conflict with Belair 149, 156
  death (in 1806) 88, 110n62, 178, 179n13
  declaration of independence from France 28n13, 40n19, 53n26
  enters Les Cayes aside Louverture (1800) 112
  joins Louverture's capitulation to Leclerc (1802) 122
  Leclerc's order to execute 150
  massacre of Vodou group 160
  mistrust of by workers 152
  ousting of Hédouville 102
  overthrow of André Rigaud's army 115
  participation in Louverture's army 80
  personal wealth 126
  political alliance with Alexandre Pétion 152, 188
  recruitment for Louverture's army 113, 115
  replaces Moïse as commander of War in the South 148–49
  seizure of Bainet (1799) 112
d'Estaing (Comte), Charles Hector 101, 146
dog-eat-dog society 31, 40, 51, 52, 97, 135, 154, 161
dominance 92, 98, 99, 104, 154, 155, 157, 158, 163, 164
  bourgeois 162
  foreign commissioners' economic 139
  general 137
  inscribing with *vèvè* function 138
  of capitalist traders 104, 105, 136
  of *nouveaux riches* 159, 161
  political 137
Dominican Republic 22, 121 (map)
  Dominican people 23
Dommage 167
Dondon 80, 150
Don García (leader of Spanish troops) 117
Dorsainville, Roger 168
Duclos, Jean-Jacques 80
Duménil 80
Dupuy, Alex (historian) xxxi
Duvalier dictatorship ix, xiv, xvii, xxii, xxxi, 181, 187
  propaganda of 181
  Trouillot family resistance to ix, 19n6
Duvalier, François x, xviii, 187
Duvalier, Jean-Claude x, xiv, xviii, xxii
  jean-claudisme ix–x, xvii
East, eastern (side of Hispaniola) 11n3, 23n10, 116–17
  see also Dominican Republic, Spanish

economic dominance 136
education in Haiti
  as a litany of lies 22
education (of elites)
  Bauvais, Louis-Jacques (in France) 83n45
  Biassou, Jean-François (school of the Brothers in Cape Haitian) 125
  child of Henri Christophe (in France) 165
  child of Toussaint Louverture (in France) 160
émigrés 99–100
  returning to Saint-Domingue with money to invest 100
England xxx, 70, 72, 95, 99, 103, 104, 128, 130
English 10, 82, 94, 99, 104, 128–29, 150, 160
  as hawks 105
  boats 11, 92, 95
  Christophe assuming aristocratic affectations of 164
  colonialism in Hindu regions 55
  defeat of by Toussaint Louverture and André Rigaud 96–97, 117, 147, 169
  mulatto plantation owners siding with 100
  relations with Toussaint Louverture 103, 107
  seizing opportunity to attack in South 70, 72
  support of commodity crops 131
  Third Civil Commission's order to crush 93
  war against 106, 158
equality 79, 106, 115, 125, 162
  linguistic xxxi
  political 164, 165
Éstimé, President Léon Dumarsais 155
exploiter class 19

family disguise
  Dessalines' use of 157
  race as an entire family 164
  to conceal conflicts between *nouveaux libres*, sometimes *anciens libres* 157
  Toussaint Louverture's use of 157
  see also Louverture's Ideology
Farmers *see* fieldworkers
Fatton, Robert (historian) xxxi, xxxvi
Faubaix 91
Faubert, Jean-Pierre 110
feudal ideology 164
field 25, 52, 54
  freedom equated with 133
  right to plant one's own 54
Flaville (plantation) 40
Florida 104
Fonds-des-Nègres 112
food crops 127
  versus big plantations 127
food plots
  as interest of masses 132
  versus big plantations 123, 125, 133, 137
foreign aid workers xxxi
Fort-Liberté 129, 150
France *see* French
Frankétienne (Franketyèn, Franck Étienne) xiii, xxi, 175–77, 180
freebooters (pirates) 11
freedmen *see anciens libres*
Freedom for All 71
  as political position 78, 90, 146–47, 107, 116, 130
  as rallying cry 50, 58, 60, 132, 137, 140, 142
  as unifying principle 157, 166, 168
  central demand/interest of slave masses 79–80, 114, 122
  emancipation throughout the island 117
  inscribed within Constitution of 1801 137, 139
  resistance of Spanish (Dominican) landowners to 116
  triumph of *nouveaux libres* 99
Freedom, freedom 93, 109
  army 82–83

black freedom fighters xxix
camp 83, 125, 154
Civil Commission's offer of (1793) 71–73, 79, 82, 84, 98–99
curtailment of within 1801 Constitution 139–40
demand of Toussaint Louverture, Biassou, Jean-François 54–55
Drums of Freedom (*Tanbou Libète* theater group) xxxiii
economic goal of Saint-Domingue
equivalence with land 54, 133
equivalence with thought 16
fighting to obtain (*koupé tèt boulé kay*) 58–59, 78
French dismissal of concept 52
guaranteed within Constitution of 1801 137
Louverture recruitment strategy 79
Louverture's bait and switch tactics 117, 122, 126, 132–33, 143, 161–62
Louverture's failure to secure via political independence 168–69
political position of slave masses 67–68, 80, 90, 127, 136
risks of losing 99–100, 124, 126
slave agency in seizing it 80, 98, 115, 123, 133, 136
urban slaves' greater enjoyment of 29–30, 125
versus slavery (conflict) 37, 123–24, 133
see also *anciens libres, nouveaux libres,* rallying cry
French, France
1625 French assault on Saint-Domingue 11
1802 invasion of Cape Haitian *see* Leclerc
1825 recognition of Haitian independence 7
anciens libres joining army 167
as colonists xxx, 22–23, 47, 152
as early settlers in Saint-Domingue 11, 23n8
as language xxviii, xxxi-xxxiii, 10, 57, 79, 89, 122, 137–38, 175n1, 178, 186
bourgeoisie 17–18, 26, 44–45, 47, 49–52, 62–63, 106, 161–62, 168
camp (or army) involving formerly enslaved soldiers 82, 91n51, 100–103, 107, 114, 133, 146
capture of Toussaint Louverture 122, 168
colonial army xxvii, 81
colonial possession of Saint-Domingue 14, 28n13, 55, 68, 72–73, 77, 92, 97, 116, 120–22, 162
commissioners in Saint-Domingue 38, 42–49, 62–64, 68, 70–73, 81–83, 86–87, 89, 92–94, 98–99, 123–24, 131, 166
economic interests in Saint-Domingue 34, 94, 104–105, 124n67, 128–29, 162, 166n90
government officials in Saint-Domingue 10, 62–67, 70, 85
ideas of freedom picked up by the enslaved 125
internal conflicts within French government 63–64
laws and regulations xxviii
legal rights guaranteed citizens 62, 73, 106
loss of Cape Haitian 144
loss of power in Saint-Domingue 90–96, 99, 117
Louverture's role in army 152, 161
manners and affectations 165
military presence in Saint-Domingue 13n4, 81–82, 86–87, 92–93, 112, 117–18, 126–28, 148–49
participation in American Revolution 47n23
participation in slave trade 24, 55
political discourse 162, 167
rebel slave leaders' support of King 67–68
Revolution 47, 70, 100–101, 146n81, 162n89, 163

214   *Stirring the Pot of Haitian History*

spelling within text xxviii-xxix
stance towards Louverture's
    organization 116

Galbaud Affair 77, 124, 125
    colonists leave afterwards 86, 88, 92, 124
    consequences of 127
Galbaud, François-Thomas 70, 71
    conflict with Sonthonax 71
Gallifèt (plantation) 40
Gaulard 107
general dominance 136-37
generations, habits of past 4
    burdens of past generations 8
    transmission of eye disease
        (metaphor for suppression) 15
Georgia 103
German musicians 130, 160, 165
ginger 135
God
    Catholic position bestowed upon
        Toussaint Louverture 158-59
    gives freedom 133
    laughing 103
    prayer to at Bwa Kayiman 56
    use of for political power 158, 160
Goman (rebel leader) 7, 54
Gonaïves 80
Gordian knot 134, 141
    Gordian knot function of State 138-39
Grand-Goâve 109, 112
Grande Anse, La (Grand'Anse) 8, 71
Grande Rivière 47
grands blancs (wealthy whites) colonists 18, 34, 48-49, 70
    Rigaud's clash with 100
Grinn Prominnin ('Walking Seed') xxviii, 6, 7, 82, 170, 176
Gros Morne 80
Guadeloupe 155
guerrilla, guerrillas 54, 56, 167
Guinea 24, 39
Gwayamouk River 63, 72, 73

Haiti
    as original name of Hispaniola 22
Haitian Creole *see* Creole
Hardy, Jean (French general) 120
Hédouville, Gabriel-Marie-Theodore-Joseph 96-97, 151
    chased by Moïse's wife's regiment 149
    cornered by Moïse 102
    defender of French interests 99, 100-101
    distrust of Moïse 150
    opponent of Freedom for All 169
    ouster by Toussaint Louverture 102, 116, 124
    underhanded dealings 103
    weakness of prejudice 105
    working with Rigaud to defeat Louverture 99, 106, 109
Hinche 153
Hindu regions 55
Hispaniola 22
History (of Haiti) xvii, xx-xxi, xxiii, xxvi, xxviii-xxix, xxxiii, 10, 13, 23, 29-30, 50, 52-53, 58, 63, 71, 80, 86, 93, 106, 108-109, 114-15, 123, 125, 148, 154, 156, 163, 176-79, 185-88
Hueda (site of Igelefe slave fort) 52
hurricane Hazel 19

ideological dominance 136
ideology *see* Louverture's Ideology
Idlinger 147
Igelefe slave fort 52, 56
illness
    hereditary 25
importers (living in France)
    investing in sugar 24
indentured workers 11, 24
    indentured workers versus slaves 11
independence (Haitian) 68, 115
    1825 recognition of by France 7, 128
    African movements 181
    dependence of freedom on 169
    quarrel between Christophe and Pétion after 114

Index 215

Toussaint Louverture giving up on 168
versus dependence 36, 38, 123–25, 138
war of independence 31, 142
indigenist, indigenists
  as political ploy 164
  posturing as aristocrats under Toussaint Louverture 165
  posturing as great intellectuals in twentieth century 165
  race as an entire family 164
indigenous culture *see* native-born culture
indigo 24
industries 22

Jacmel 69, 76, 110–13, 115–16, 129–30
Jakomèl 21
Jamaica 29, 69, 103–104
Jean-François (rebel leader) 72, 169
  involvement in slave trade 126
Jean, Padre 13, 58
Jérémie (town) 7–8, 76, 106, 167
Jews 129
joker (card game) 25
Jonassaint, Jean xxvi, xxviii, xxx, xxxv, 175, 189
justice 21

Kabayo 59
kawo (1.3 hectares) 133
king (French) 44, 46, 47, 64, 68, 70, 95
  as puppet king 64
  d'Esparbès' support for 70
  Spanish King 67, 68
  supporters of in Saint-Domingue 66, 67
kòd (legal code, cord) 10, 14
  as a weapon of those in power 18
  covering up exploitation of slaves 17
  enflaming tempers 17
  Kòd Noua (1685) 10, 14–19
  legal status of freedmen versus whites 18
  preventing assembly 17
  preventing cooperation with slaves 18
  preventing freedmen from benefiting slaves 17
  preventing revolt 18
  tool of upper classes 18
Kouidor (theater group) xi, xix, 178, 179n13
Koukourouj *see* 'lightning bug'
koupé tèt boulé kay xxix, 58
krik~krak (invitation to a story~accepting) 31

La Colline 59
Lacombe 166
L'Acul 80, 144, 152
Lafrance, Paul 146
La Hotte 59
Lakansièl (Haitian diaspora journal) vii, x–xiv, xvii–xviii, xx–xxii, xxvi, 170, 176–78, Appendix (extracts from *Lakansièl*), 191–202
laloua (laws) *see kòd*
Lamartinière, Louis Daure 148–49
  joining the *nouveaux libres* 149
Lamartinière, Marie-Jeanne 149
Lamèsi, Sister Lamèsi 6, 8, 11, 12, 19, 54, 84, 96, 117, 129, 145, 170
  assembly of intelligent people 168
  assessing Toussaint Louverture's wealth 130
  bean pot heating up 13, 18
  big reputation kills little dogs 102
  good enemy better than bad friend 99
  questioning Louverture 125
  throw it away to forget, but pick up it to remember 132
land
  feature of native-born culture 53
  service to African spirits lies within 54
  see also field
La Plaine du Nord 59, 117
laplas (chief assistant to priest) 141
Laplume, Jean-Joseph 91, 110, 120, 167

La Rochelle 34–35, 38
La Romana 117
La Selle 59
Lavaud, Étienne 82–83, 88–90, 116, 146
   bestowal of power upon Toussaint Louverture 125
   imprisonment of 85–86
   leader in 1794 87
   Louverture's assurances to 162
   wanted to divide up plantations for workers 133
laws *see kòd*
Lear, Tobias 130, 166
Leclerc, Victor Emmanuel 115
   1802 arrival in Saint-Domingue 120, 130, 144n76, 145n78, 147n83, 149–50, 153, 166n91
Lecun, Father 158, 166
   1802 invasion of Cape Haitian 122, 127, 167
   brother-in-law to Napoleon Bonaparte 120
   inability to re-enslave people 166
   Louverture's surrender to 167–69
   planning the 1802 invasion of Saint-Domingue 150
left (-wing politics) xx, 8, 12, 53, 148, 176, 177
   banner of the left within army 153
Le Havre 35
Lenormand de Mézy plantation 56, 58
   location of Bwa Kayiman 56
Léogâne 48, 57n30, 91n50, 110
Les Cayes 47–48, 76, 91n51, 112, 120, 129, 143, 167
Léveillé, Baptiste 146
Liberal Party (in Haiti) 163
lightning bugs (*koukourouj*, metaphor for people denouncing abuses within Haiti's government) 6, 7, 170
Limbé 80, 97, 120, 144, 152
Lire Haïti xv, xvii-xviii, xxii, ix-x
loua
   in a ceremony 137
   inscribed within *vèvè* 137
   Louis XIV

   wild loua 141
   see also spirits
loua ('law') 10, 14–15, 18
Louis Thomas, Comte de Villaret de Joyeuse 166
Louverture, Paul 80
Louverture's Ideology 161
   aristocratic aspects 161, 164–65
   bourgeois aspects 161, 164
   disguising political power as magical power 160
   entrusting capable people 163
   family disguise 156–57
   freedom for all as central, unifying principle 168–69
   indigenist ploy of race as family 164
   loyalty to France as weakness 167
   propped up on Christian and Vodou religion 158–60
   respecting property 161–62
   satisfaction of work 161
Louverture, Toussaint 72
   as Alexander the Great 157
   as black Spartacus 159, 165
   as Bonaparte of Saint-Domingue 157
   as Hercules 157
   as *makandal* (spirit) 158
   as standard bearer 29
   attempts to entrap and crush 96–99
   authoritarian agrarian system (*caporalisme agraire*) 142–43
   betrayal of 166
   collecting white women and German musicians 165
   commissioners deal with in 1794 82
   condemnation of Moïse 153
   conflict with Moïse 144–45, 148–52
   courtyard watchman and coach driver 30
   crossing to revolutionary camp 125
   demands made to colonists 55
   differences with Civil Commission 79
   dissatisfaction inside of Louverture's army 117
   exploitation of Corail Affair 106

extent of his army's control in 1794 80
forced labor on plantations 133
general staff abandons masses 154
giving up on independence, not freedom 168
impact of policies on *nouveaux libres* 132
importance of commodity crops 131–32
injustice of 163
leaning on Vodou 159
legacies 169
let the poison of color prejudice take root 108–109
massacre of Vodou initiates 160
mistakes of 163
mulatto support 108
observing Leclerc's forty-seven ships (in 1802) 120
ouster of Sonthonax 95, 99, 142
preferences for Catholic religion 158–59
preserving plantations 133–34
pressure of traders in 1802 129
prohibition of Vodou dances 159–60
re-enslavement 67, 152
relationship to France and Hédouville 100–101, 109
relationship with Sonthonax 94–95
re-submission to France in 1802 120–21
role in Lavaud's imprisonment 85–86
seeking Roume's approval to invade Spanish side of the island (1795) 116–17
surrender in Cape Haitian (1802) 122, 167
takeover of Saint-Domingue's political apparatus 128
taking Les Cayes in 1800 112
tariffs and taxes 128–29
threatened by Vodou 159
use of color prejudice against Rigaud 107–108
War of the South against Rigaud 92, 103–105, 110–13
Louverture's organization and government
    acquisition of weapons, training, and status 82
    amassing wealth 86, 88
    American influence and trade 104, 128, 130
    as a political and military coalition 81, 90, 126, 142
    central demand of freedom and equality 79–80, 123–24
    ensuring Toussaint Louverture's power 76
    land seized and controlled by 84
    recruitment of *anciens libres* 87, 146
    relationship to Vodou organizations 159
    social classes 31
    supremacy by 1799 114
lower class 14, 15
    ignoring laws 19
    misleading of 19

Macaya (mountain) 59
Magny, Étienne 147, 149, 166
Maine 130
Makandal, François 58, 159
    as Vodou priest 158
    setting out to exterminate whites 58
    skilled poison-maker 158
makandal (magician) 158, 159
Makaya (rebel leader) 81, 167
Makenzie, Charles 143
Malfèt (rebel leader) 7
Malfou (rebel leader) 7
manbo (Vodou priestess)
    sacrifice of pig at Bwa Kayiman 57
    Toussaint Louverture's beating of 160
Manigat 103
maps
    Dominican Republic 121
    Northern region of Saint-Domingue-Haiti 41

218   *Stirring the Pot of Haitian History*

Southern region of Saint-Domingue-Haiti 111
marble game (metaphor for social struggle) 31–33
Marmelade 80, 152
maroon, maroons 7, 29, 58
   agreement with Louverture and Dessalines 110
   bands of 7
   fighting against Rigaud 113
   former 125
   maroonage 59
   of La Grand'Anse
   situation in North versus South 59–60
   soldiers 149, 153, 167, 169
   workers 167, 169
Marseilles 35, 38
Martinique 155, 167, 179
Massachusetts 130
masses see *slave masses*
Maurepas 80
Mazaka Lakoua 138
mazon (song to reject a wild *loua*) 141
Ménard, Nadève xxxv
Ménestrels, Les ("The Minstrels," performance group) xi, xix
Meunier, Christophe 80
Michel, Pierre 81, 88, 146
   former slave in Lavaud's army 146
   leader of *nouveaux libres* 90
   Toussaint Louverture's personal enemy 90
middle class xviii, 67
   hidden contradictions within 31–34, 38
   ideology 164
   part of the free people's coalition 42–43, 48
Miragoâne 112
Moïse (Gilles Bréda)
   appointment by Sonthonax 93
   arrests Roume 117
   as black member of general staff 106
   as Louverture's adopted 'nephew' 148, 156
   attacked by Rigaud 110
   attacked Santo-Domingo 117
   attitude of American consul Edward Stevens towards 151
   backed by fieldworkers 117, 144
   conflict with Louverture 144–45, 148–52
   disobeyed military commanders 149
   execution of 144–45, 153, 156, 162
   General 117
   military commission that pronounced judgment on 152
   opposition to Constitution of 1801 152
   problems with American consul 151
   properties under his control 127
   rejected color prejudice 148–49
   squabble with Hédouville 150
   standard-bearer of the left's position 148, 152
   taking the lead in Santo-Domingo 150
   wife of 149
Moïse Affair 144–45, 154
   impact on Toussaint Louverture's reputation 158
Môle Saint-Nicolas 107, 117, 129
money (paper) in circulation 89
Monpoint 147
Montreal xx, xxxii, 34, 176, 182
Montrouis 120
Morin 146
Morisset 84, 147
Morisset, Jean-Edouard, xi, xxiii, xv, xix, xxiii
Morne Beaubrun 59
Morne Bijou 59
Morne Rouge 30, 40, 56, 59
Mount Marinette 65
mulatto, mulattos 91, 110
   as a racial and social category 22, 28, 32–33, 143, 146–47
   as a racist racial category xxix
   as *anciens libres* ('freedmen') 17–18, 22, 84, 86–89, 113, 117, 147, 150, 152, 156, 167

Index 219

as merchants 156
as part of 'capable people' ideology 163
as part of color problem 43, 47, 105–108
as part of Family Ideology 156, 187
as part of middle class 42–43, 46, 49, 67
as plantation owners 27–28, 42–43, 46–49, 51, 62, 66–67, 71–73, 92–93, 98, 100–101
defeat by Toussaint Louverture 117
fleeing enslaved troops 51
impact of War of the South on 108
Moïse as 'too soft' on 149–50
pitted against blacks 17–18, 32–33, 43, 106, 115, 137, 143
recruitment of by French commissioners 46–48
rights of 47, 49, 62, 106–107, 156
social advantages of 32–33, 47, 73
support for Toussaint Louverture 107–108

Native Americans 55
Cacique Henri, Taíno chief 59
Caonabo, Taíno chief of Maguana nation 23
loss of land to Spanish 22
native-born culture
as main ingredient of uprising 52
giving conviction to fight 53
Nérette 167
New England (role in trade with Saint-Domingue) 104
New Hampshire 130
New York 170, 176–77, 188
critique of repressive laws within 19
Trouillot family experience in x–xii, xiv, xx, xxii, xviii, xxxii–iii
North (of Haiti) 41 (map), 51, 70, 82, 106, 127, 150
arrival of Leclerc 167
birthplace of Vincent Ogé 46
declining wealth 89
origin of Haitian Revolution (August 1791) 40, 58–60, 148
rebellion against Toussaint Louverture 107, 110, 144
responses to 1791 uprising 48, 66
site of defeat of *petits blancs* (1793) 69
site of Sonthonax's decree of freedom (1793) 73
split with South (of Haiti) during civil war 23n10, 110n62
struggle between Louverture and Hédouville 102
takeover by Louverture 76, 84, 90, 106
Vilatte conspiracy 92
North America (Haitian migration to) xviii, 178
Northwest 72, 76, 107, 114
controlled by *anciens libres* 86–88
heritage of black *anciens libres* 107–108
nouveau libre, nouveaux libres 117, 167
collaboration with *anciens libres* 110
conflict between leaders and masses 83
conflicts among *nouveaux libres* 154
conflicts with *anciens libres* 84, 96
Constitution of 1801, impact of 139
control of Saint-Domingue with commissioners 94
controlling Catholic organizations 159
differences with *anciens libres* 87
family disguise to placate masses 165
fighting the *anciens libres* 89, 93
freedom for all as main interest of 142
general dominance of 137
ideology of 155, 161
lack of control over Vodou organizations 159
land seizures of 84
leaders as soldiers 114
leaders controlling the land 86

220   *Stirring the Pot of Haitian History*

leaders of 86, 90
leaders securing freedom 98–99
leaders' dependency on Americans and English 128
majority of Toussaint Louverture's officers 147
military successes of masses 146
Moïse's politics toward 150
political agenda of 90
political and military power of 86
political dominance of 136
problems of leaders 127
relationship to France 100
relationship to the Villatte Affair 90
role of military organization in securing freedom 122, 137
role of War in the South in preparing 115
setting fire to Cape Haitian 120
significance of Moïse Affair 153
Sonthonax's support of 93
threats from commissioners 116
transfer in social class 133
two social forces within 126
unskilled 163
victory in revolution 114
nouveaux riches
controlling Catholic organizations 159
Noyé (plantation) 40

Ogé, Vincent 46–48
attacking Ogé with 3,000 slaves 51
invited white plantation owners to join forces with mulattos 46, 71
prediction of the War 52
racism of 109
O'Gorman, Comte Arnold-Victoire-Martin 148
orange tree (little)
metaphor for Haiti's potential 76, 86
oungan (Vodou priests) 56, 160
as guerrilla leaders 56
Padre Jean 13, 58
'papas of the spirits' 57
Toussaint Louverture attacking 160

paddy wagon 135
Padre Jean, *oungan* 13, 58
Pageot, François Marie Sébastien 152
Pandou 153
Papillon, Jean-François 54
Paris xxxii, 188
1792 overthrow of King 64
central role in Saint-Domingue's economic activity 34
death of Pinchinat 89
Prussian (German) siege of Paris 34
Pascal 147
Paternalism 157
peasants 44, 95
1801 peasant revolt in North 144
abandoning plantations (after 1798) 133, 141
forced to work by *nouveaux libres* leaders 86
impact of 1801 Constitution on 140
joining army 113
killing peasants as deterrence 153
Louverture controlling peasants 142
Louverture forcing peasants to work on plantations 133
Louverture opposing land redistribution for 162
Moïse's support for 145
political awareness of 122
relationship to authority 125
versus commodity crops 131
Péralte, Charlemage 54
Pérou 89
Peru 55
Petit-Goâve 91, 109–10, 112
Petite-Rivière 153
Pétion, Alexandre xxvi, 110, 114, 152, 155, 169, 188
as first president of Haitian Republic 110n62, 138n74
coalition with André Rigaud 107
confrontation with Jean-Jacques Dessalines at Jacmel 110–12, 115
fighting *nouveaux libres* 112
petits blancs (poor whites) 33, 72
against commissioners 45, 69

Index 221

attacking mulatto landowners 66
coalition against blacks and
  mulattos 43, 67
coalition with plantation owners 48
color prejudice as ideological
  interest of 98
commissioners' recruitment of 46
conflicts in 1792–1793 69–70
defeat in 1793 by commissioners 73,
  92
limited embrace of bourgeois
  revolutionary ideology 47, 51
skepticism of *grands blancs* 49
Philadelphia 128
Pickering, Timothy 104
Pierre-Paul 107
Pierrot (rebel leader) 81
Pinchinat 89
pirates 11, 23, 26
Plaine du Nord 59, 117
Plaisance 80, 120
plantation, plantations 22–28, 30, 160
  abandoned by colonists and seized
    by army 86
  army forced peasants to stay on
    plantations 139, 142, 143
  as feature of primary industry 123
  big plantations replacing small ones
    24, 25, 26
  controlled by André Rigaud and
    Toussaint Louverture 127
  dividing under General Moïse 117
  fieldworkers demanding plantations
    151
  fieldworkers refusing to toil on 155
  fleeing plantations 141
  Lavaud's 1794 division of plantations
    for workers 133
  Louverture forced peasants to work
    on plantations 133
  Louverture's policy of preserving
    133
  owned by Louverture and leaders of
    his army 83, 99, 126
  plantation owners 22
  population density of in North 60

rebuilt by *anciens libres* 88
relation to Dependence and
  Commodity crops 134, 154
revolts on 58, 144
role in supporting maroons 59
Sonthonax and the 94
sugar plantation system 22
thriving plantations in 1801 134
versus food plots 125, 127, 132, 133,
  137
wealth of Saint-Domingue in 53
where the offensive against colonists
  began 40
white owners after 1796 86
whites who returned to reclaim 100
Plidò's group 58
political dominance 136
potomitan (centerpost) 166, 169
Polverel, Étienne 62, 69, 70, 73, 77
Ponpon Blan 46, 48–49
Ponpon Rouj 46
Port-au-Prince x, xviii, xxxi, xxxii, 27,
  35n17, 48, 51, 69, 106–107, 120, 129,
  130, 149, 166
Port-de-Paix 76, 88, 120, 144
Port Margot 144, 152
pot (bean pot, cooking pot, soup pot)
  as metaphor for simmering social
    conflicts 13, 18, 94, 164
Praloto (Prélot), Jacques 13
predatory countries (hawks as
  metaphor for) 10, 17, 43, 93, 105,
  128, 130
President Tibab 6
primary conflict, conflicts 2, 30, 32, 38,
  40, 44, 58
  as rooted in primary industry 26
  classes contesting the 27
  features of 27
  going beyond entangled stage 50
  keeping it out of sight 42
  reaching unbound stage 53
primary industry 54, 124
  as sugarcane 26
  classes bound up with 161
  features of 123

four features being slavery,
  dependence, commodity crops,
  large plantations 123
 middle class and 32
proletariat 14
proverbs 12

Raboteau 69
race 22, 181
 as family 164
 avenging 165
 mixed-race xxix
 people who denigrate the race 164
 political equality of 164
 race prejudice 47
Raimond, Julien 46
rebel slaves
 in Spain's camp 87
 leaders as overseers, house slaves or slaves from towns 125
regiment, regiments 115, 158
 Christophe's betrayal by Tobias Lear, 167
 defeat of *anciens libres* by Dessalines 114–15
 Dessalines commanding those of Louverture 110
 execution of Moïse 144
 Moïse's regiment 102, 110, 148–51
 position of *anciens libres* 101
 preference of Bauvais 110
 republican requirement that soldiers not depart without permission 142
revolution, revolutions (Haitian)
 1789–1820: only slave revolution in human memory 8
 1804 25
 acceleration of revolution 44
 as Louverture's debt 168
 Bourgeois Revolution in France 44–45, 52
 causes of the Haitian Revolution 40–43
 colonists unwittingly help revolution 72
 condition necessary for a revolution 49
 contribution of Louverture's ideology to 166
 definition 25
 field slaves and skilled slaves as engine of revolution 30
 French camp as revolution's enemy 114
 French Revolution (1789) 25, 94, 126, 161
 Haitian Creole text about the Haitian Revolution xxvi
 history of revolutionary thought in Haiti xxiii
 ideas of Haitians as revolutionary catalysts xxvi
 impact of French Revolution in Saint-Domingue 51, 95, 100–101
 impact of Louverture's 1800 victory on 113
 impact of *nouveaux libres* on 114
 impact of War on the South 114–15
 impact on social classes 126
 impact on South Carolina and Georgia 104
 importance of multi-class support for 145
 Kòd Noua ('Black Code/Cord') to prevent revolution 15
 left wing of revolution 149–55
 Louverture's claim that mulattos betrayed 106
 Louverture's crossing over to revolutionary camp 125
 mulattos who experienced the start of French bourgeois 73
 Ogé's strategy to prevent 47
 origin of the leaders 29
 plantation owners who refused 147
 political Freedom as 166
 pretending to support revolution in France 46, 67

Index 223

problem of balance during 140
raised with revolution 148
reappearance of classes with masks on faces during 31
revolution (twentieth century) xix
revolutionary organization (*Tanbou Libète*) xx
Sonthonax as bourgeois revolutionary 62
Sugarcane Revolution 24
versus reactionary camp 30
Rhode Island 130
Rigaud, Bénoit Joseph André 71, 82, 85, 91, 147, 150
    as King in the South 82, 95–96
    coalition with Hédouville 99–103, 124
    color prejudice and manipulation 106–109, 169
    conflict between leaders of *anciens libres* and *nouveaux libres* 86
    defeat by Louverture and Dessalines 114–15, 124n67
    English and American isolation of 103–104
    Hédouville's preference for (over Louverture) 97, 99, 105–106
    role in Corail Affair 106
    role in Vilatte Affair 127
    role in War of the South 91–93, 109–14
ritual words 6, 7
Rodriguez 146
Rogers, Captain 166
Romaine-la-Prophétesse 159
    guerrilla leader 57
    Vodou priest 57
Roume, Philippe-Rose Saint-Laurent (special commissioner with France's First Civil Commission) 109–10
    arrival in Saint-Domingue 116
    Louverture's challenge of 117
    Moïse's arrest of 117, 150–51
royal palm
    symbol of Haiti's maturity 76

Saint-Domingue
    1625 French occupation of 22
    Peace of Ryswick (1697) 22–23
    slave labor as basis of 25
Saint Jacques 59
Saint-James 146–47
Saint-Louis 112, 129
Saint-Malo 34–35
Saint-Marc 45–46, 48, 69
Saint Michel 112
Saint Paul 105
Saint Peter 105
Saint Raphaël 153
Salnave, President Sylvain 7
Salomon, President Lysius 155
Samba poet-priests 55
Sam, President Tirésias Augustin Simon 65
Sansousi (rebel leader) 167
Santa Maria 159
Santo-Domingo 7, 117, 120, 150
Savary, Cézaire 146
Sédènié 6, 7
sharecroppers 131
    see also tenant-farmers
Sila (rebel leader) 167
silver 89
slave, slaves (enslaved people) 7, 11, 12, 22, 33, 133
    arming slaves in 1789 51
    army of former slaves 80, 82, 146
    as furniture 15
    as problematic category xxix
    condition of slaves before the revolution 163
    difference between those in North and elsewhere 59
    domestic slaves 28–31
    economic condition interconnected to subsistence crops 53–54
    establishing a native-born culture 50, 52
    field slave 30
    first mission of rebels was setting fire to 50, 161

freedom as primary interest 122, 131, 145
freeing the slaves on August 29, 1793 62, 71, 73, 77, 79, 81, 84
growth in slave population 24
keeping divided 52
Louverture's organization's relationship with 113
outlawing assembly of 15
overseer slaves 28
preventing from arming 17
rebel slaves 56, 72, 78
revolting 140, 148
skilled slave 30
slave revolution 8
slaves and suicide 59
slaves who killed their children 59
slaves' trust in Louverture 109
suppressing intellect 17
urban slaves 29–31
urban versus field slaves 33
working harder 24
Slave Masses 33
   agency of 72–73, 143
   as group applying pressure to society 66–67
   as social force blocking French commissioners 67–68
   becoming empowered (with weapons) 67–68
   break from Louverture's coalition 76
   developing a political position 67, 72
   holding perspective different from that of rebel leaders 125–26
   military advantages and disadvantages 78
   obtaining freedom via Sonthonax's decree 72–73
   social class with greatest stakes for overthrowing society 79–80
slavery 11, 106, 148
   abolition of slavery in Constitution of 1801 137
   American support for 107
   anti-slavery Society of the Friends of the Blacks 46n21
   as a Brazilian system 25
   basis of Saint-Domingue's society 42
   ending slavery on August 22, 1791
   feature of primary industry 26, 123
   Kòd Noua's legal support of 17
   maroons who took flight from 58
   slavery in disguise under Louverture 139
   slavery's impact on Haitian history 29
   Toussaint Louverture born into 100
   versus freedom as banner conflict 38, 79, 123
Sonthonax, Léger Félicité 65
   1794 departure of 87
   1795 assessment of prejudice in South 106
   1796 return 92
   arming *nouveaux libres* 93
   attacking *petits blancs* 69
   attitudes about *petits blancs* 67
   colonists helped crush colonial system 71
   consequences of 1797 ouster 95, 99, 142
   consequences of order to free slaves 82
   declaration of Rigaud as outlaw 93
   expulsion back to France by Louverture 93–94, 116, 124, 128
   French political commissioner 92
   landowners' opposition to 70–71
   leader of Third Civil Commission 116
   Major General of Saint-Domingue 85
   order to free slaves in 1793 62, 79, 81, 84
   rallying slave masses with freedom 73, 77
   relationship with Toussaint Louverture 93–94
   seeking to keep Saint-Domingue under French control 73
Soulouque
   killing Dominicans 23

South (of Haiti) 23n10, 46, 69, 111
	(map), 120, 138n73, 147, 156, 167
	color aristocracy of André Rigaud
		within 169
	conflict with government in North
		89–90
	control of lands within by *anciens
		libres* 83, 87–88
	English plans to attack 72
	French commissioners in 62n33
	Louverture's takeover of 76
	maroon presence in 59–60
	peasant revolt by Goman 54n27
South Carolina 103
South, War of 91–96, 100–08, 110,
	113–17, 124, 128, 140, 148, 150, 157
	see also Rigaud, André, South (of
		Haiti)
Spain, Spanish
	1697 Treaty of Ryswick, ceding
		France western part of island 22
	1793 attack (with the English) on
		Saint-Domingue 70
	1794 surrounding (with the English)
		of Saint-Domingue 82
	abandonment of ally Papillon
		(Jean-François) 55
	army not dependent on formerly
		enslaved people 82
	army's distribution of land to rebel
		slave leaders 72
	arrival to Hispaniola and
		destruction of native culture 55
	Biassou fights on their side against
		France 29
	boats pirated by Frenchmen 11
	Cacique Henri's stance towards 59
	Clervaux and Paul Louverture's
		defeat by the French 120
	colonists on eastern side of the
		island 11
	commanders relinquish Ogé and
		Chavannes to French colonists
		48
	invasion and defeat by Louverture
		117, 128, 150

Louverture and Vernet's
	participation in army 107
Louverture's takeover of the island's
	eastern half 76, 116
Moïse's participation in army 149
mulatto plantation owners' interest
	in joining army 72–73
part of island where Louverture's
	organization developed 100
power of the King 67–68
reaction to Haitian Revolution 169
rebel slave leaders' loyalty to army
	81
regulations imposed by Louverture
	on commodities and sale of
	animals 129, 132
resistance shown by Anacaona (wife
	of Caonabo) 23
stealing land 22
spirit, spirits 16, 137
	arbor of the spirits 56
	bad spirit xxvi, 6, 179
	belief in the power of 56
	diversity of 52
	granny's 52
	loua (Vodou *lwa*) 16
	Louverture's Ideology and spirits
		160
	priests as 'papas of the spirits' 57
	relationship to land 53
	relationship to *vèvè* 137
	returning the dead to Igelefe fort 56
	wild *loua* 141
State, the (Haitian)
	abuses committed by 54n27
	as a biased referee 136
	as a catalog of conflicts within the
		society 137–38
	as *chwal* 141
	as creditor, issuer of money 89, 129
	as repressive towards Haitian people
		134, 151–52
	authority of 21, 135
	birth of xxi, 147n84
	confiscation of property of *anciens
		libres* 88

226   *Stirring the Pot of Haitian History*

conflict with fieldworkers 153
control of by bureaucrats and
    military 36, 42
control of by colonists (*Kòd Noua*,
    'Black Code/Cord') 10
desire of mulatto plantation owners
    for voice within 98
distribution of land to Louverture's
    army leaders 83
employees as social class 32
function of the counterweight 134,
    140–41
function of the Gordian knot
    138–41
function of the *vèvè* 137–41
Louverture's government 142–43,
    166, 169
marginalization of *Kreyòl* (Creole)
    xxxi
political apparatus of (radio
    metaphor) 65, 185
regulations and laws of 10
Stevens, Edward 104, 129, 150–51
sugarcane 24–27
    as primary industry 26
    in Brazil 24
    mills 24
    size of plantations 24
    Sugarcane Revolution 24
Swedes 129
Switzerland 116

Tanbou Libète ('Drums of Freedom'
    cultural performance group in
    NYC) x-xii, xiv-xv, xviii-xx, xxiii,
    177
tea
    cinnamon 135
    cotton 8, 19
Tel Aviv 34
Télémaque, César 167
tenant-farmers 135
    see also sharecroppers
Thibaut, Archbishop 69
Ti Nouèl Priyè (rebel leader) 167
Tipine (plantation) 40

Tokyo 34
Tourelle (Camp) 79
Trou Bordette 40
Trou d'Eau 59
Trouillot, Ernst xiii, xxi, 182, 183n21,
    185
Trouillot, Evelyne xi, xviii, xx, xxii,
    xxix, xxxv, 3, 182, 189n33
Trouillot, Hénock xiii, xxi, 182, 185
Trouillot, Jocelyne xiv
Trouillot, Lyonel ix, xvi, xxiii, xxxv,
    xxvi, xxviii, xxxiii, xxxv, 3, 176–77,
    182, 189n33
Trujillo, Rafael Leónidas
    massacre of Haitian laborers 23
twin conflict (*marasa*)
    definition 37–38

United States xvi, xviii, xxxi, xxxii,
    53n26, 54n28, 85, 94, 99, 103–104,
    129–30, 135
    see also America, Americans
upper class, upper classes 14–19, 24, 40,
    48, 63, 124
    becoming richer 24–25, 32
    coalition to exploit the people 42
    collapse of in Saint-Domingue 49
    escaping and fighting against 59
    struggle with lowest class 53
    Vodou and Creole struggling against
        56

vegetables 24
    in opposition to commodity crops
        25
Venais, André 80–81
Vernet, André 107, 147, 152, 156
vèvè (ritual drawing in Vodou
    ceremony)
    course of the *vèvè* 141
    definition 138
    loua and ritual stations inscribed
        within it 137
    relationship to Gordian knot
        function 139
    vèvè function of the State 137, 141

Index 227

Vieux Bourg d'Aquin 112
Villatte Affair 86, 90, 124, 125, 127, 149
   Moïse during 150
Villatte, Jean-Louis 83, 85–86, 87–88, 127
   conspiracy 92
Vincent, Charles-Humbert-Marie 107, 146
Vodou 16
   as Toussaint Louverture's disguise 158
   calinda dance 57
   ceremonies 141
   choir leaders 160
   Constitution of 1801 disadvantaging Vodou initiates 140
   creation of 16
   dances as causing laziness according to Toussaint Louverture 160
   feature of native-born culture 53
   folding of Catholicism into Vodou 16
   gave rebels conviction for fighting 55
   initiates 140
   Louverture's massacre of initiates 160
   Louverture's refusal to recognize 159
   Marasa (lwa) 36n18
   Mazaka Lakoua 138n74
   opposition to Catholicism organizations 57
   political aspect of oath ceremonies 57
   reasons for hatred of Vodou 16
   ritual language (*langaj*) 141
   ritual stations of ceremony 137
   role in the Ceremony of Bwa Kayiman 57
   singer 135
   source of conviction for fighting 58
   source of organization for slaves 58
   surpassing Vodou 159
   tool of resistance 56
   Vodou priests 26
Vodou priest *see oungan, manbo*
Vodou Temple of Freedom 60

warehouses 114, 129
War of the South
   learning how to fight during 115
   managers of 34
   of the bourgeoisie 131
   reasons Toussaint Louverture won 113–14
Washington, D.C. 34
Washington, President George 103, 130
West (western side of Hispaniola) 59–60, 62, 66, 69–70, 73, 82, 87, 106, 110, 116, 120
whirlwind (metaphor for Haitian Revolution) 19, 40, 43, 55–56
whites
   coalition of 43–44
   split of coalition 48–49
   whites from France 22
   see also grands blancs, petits blancs
wives
   of Moïse, Belair, and Lamartinière 148
worker, workers 14, 16
   1801 Constitution's limitation of freedom 139, 142
   1801 Constitution's support for Catholic church at expense of 158
   6,000 fieldworkers fighting with Moïse 117, 144, 149–50
   abuse and beating of by Louverture's officers 141, 143
   beasts of burden for big American bourgeois 130
   becoming plantation owners 126
   bourgeois treatment of workers after French Revolution 45, 95
   coalition that allowed success for 169
   coalition with bourgeoisie and peasants in French Revolution 44
   cooperation with *nouveaux libres* leaders 136
   deceiving fieldworkers with disguises 154–55, 157, 159
   dependence as Louverture's fundamental problem 127

domestic workers as source of
  leadership 30
factory workers in France 64
farm workers in France 64
fieldworkers 12, 116
fieldworkers fighting with
  Christophe 120
fieldworkers joining army 113
fieldworkers marching behind
  Rigaud 107
fieldworkers taking up arms 51
ideology of 164
importance of food crops for 131
influence of Vodou organizations
  on 160
Lavaud's idea of dividing plantations
  for 133
Louverture demanding more
  productivity from 161
Louverture's disdain for 125
mistreating fieldworkers 143
Moïse's pro-worker position 151
organizing fieldworkers like a
  military organization 142–43
political agenda of 134, 142
skilled 42, 43
support for Louverture's freedom
  agenda 122, 166
tensions with Louverture's State
  153
treating workers like a caste 163

Yasint (Vodou priest and guerrilla
  leader) 56

Zaka (Vodou lwa Azaka Mede) 21
Zemi spirit sculptures 55
zombie, zombies 29, 79, 134